DICTIONARY OF BRITISH EDUCATIONISTS

By Richard Aldrich

Sir John Pakington and National Education (1979)
An Introduction to the History of Education (1982)
Education: Time for a New Act? (1985) with P. Leighton

By Peter Gordon

The Victorian School Manager (1974)
Philosophers as Educational Reformers (1979) with J. White
Selection For Secondary Education (1980)
The Study of Education: Inaugural Lectures 3 vols. (1980–8)
The Red Earl. The Papers of the Fifth Earl Spencer 1835–1911 2 vols.
(1981, 1986)
HMI (1987) with D. Lawton

DICTIONARY
OF
BRITISH
EDUCATIONISTS

RICHARD ALDRICH and PETER GORDON
University of London Institute of Education

WOBURN PRESS

First published 1989 in Great Britain by
THE WOBURN PRESS
Gainsborough House, Gainsborough Road
London E11 1RS, England

and in the United States of America by
THE WOBURN PRESS
c/o Biblio Distribution Centre
81 Adams Drive, P.O. Box 327, Totowa, N.J. 07512

British Library Cataloguing in Publication Data

Aldrich, Richard
 Dictionary of British educationists
 1. Great Britain. Education. Biographies.
 Collections
 I. Title   II. Gordon, Peter, *1927–*

 ISBN 0-7130-0177-1
 ISBN 0-7130-4011-4 Pbk

Library of Congress Cataloging-in-Publication Data

Aldrich, Richard.
 Dictionary of British educationists / Richard Aldrich and Peter
 Gordon
  p. cm.
 ISBN 0-7130-0177-1. ISBN 0-7130-4011-4 (pbk.)
 1. Educators—Great Britain—Biography—Dictionaries.   I. Gordon,
 Peter, 1927– . II. Title.
 LA2375.G7A53 1989
 370'.941—dc19
 [B]   88-12114
                                                         CIP

Printed in Great Britain by BPCC Wheatons Ltd, Exeter

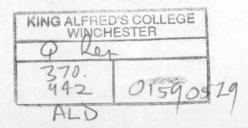

INTRODUCTION

This Dictionary has a simple purpose: to provide the reader with an easily accessible guide to the biographies of approximately 450 educationists. At present there is no one place where such information can be found, and it is hoped that this Dictionary will go some way towards filling the gap.

Three criteria were used in choosing entries. First, entries were almost entirely restricted to those men and women whose main careers were from 1800 onwards; second, none of the subjects is still alive; finally, all were British, or, if born abroad, made a direct contribution to education in Britain. Full details of some candidates whom we would have wished to include were not available. Further research will be necessary in these areas. Nevertheless, although this is not a comprehensive Dictionary, it is representative of many of the different categories which can be subsumed under the term 'educationists'. Those who chaired influential committees on education, for example Burnham and Taunton, have been included, even though their contributions to education may otherwise have been modest. On the same principle, politicians and administrators who at some time in their careers contributed to educational policy-making also appear.

Each entry is self-contained and in most cases concludes with a select bibliography and, where appropriate, a brief list of the subject's own writings. Names in the text which are printed in bold type indicate that separate entries will be found elsewhere. At the end of the Dictionary there is a guide to further reading which will be of help in tracing information about educationists.

In compiling this Dictionary we have drawn upon the knowledge, advice and suggestions of several colleagues and friends too numerous to mention individually. We thank them all. We are particularly grateful to Sue Bailey, Lesley Cornish and Sybil Spence for their help in preparing the manuscript for publication.

Obviously, in a work such as this it is inevitable that errors and omissions will occur. We should be grateful if readers would contact us on either matter for correction in possible future editions.

R.A.
P.G.

Aberdare, Henry Austin Bruce, 1st Baron (1815–95). Statesman. Born Duffryn, Aberdare, Wales

to which the family of Scottish origin had moved in the eighteenth century. Educated at Swansea Grammar School. Called to the bar from Lincoln's Inn, 1837, but ceased practice after 1843. MP for Merthyr Tydfil from 1852. Succeeded **Robert Lowe** as Vice-President of the Committee of Council on Education in 1864 and became a member of the Privy Council and a Charity Commissioner. Though defeated at Merthyr Tydfil in 1868 found a new seat in Renfrewshire, Scotland and became Home Secretary in **Gladstone**'s first government. Responsible for the unpopular Licensing Law of 1872, and in 1873 on assuming the office of Lord President of the Council was raised to the peerage. After the Liberal defeat of 1874 the rest of his life was devoted to a variety of educational, economic and social questions. Elected FRS in 1876 he also became president of both the Royal Historical Society and the Royal Geographical Society. In 1882 he chaired a commission on reformatory and industrial schools. In 1880 he was appointed chairman of the departmental committee appointed to inquire into intermediate and higher education in Wales and Monmouth which led to the Welsh Intermediate Education Act of 1889. President of University College, Cardiff from its foundation in 1883, and Chancellor of the new University of Wales in 1895. See his *National Education* (1866); *Lectures and Addresses* (1900); *Letters of the Rt. Hon. H.A. Bruce* (2 vols., 1902), and Evans, W.G., 'The Aberdare Report and Education in Wales', *Welsh History Review*, 11 (2), 1982.

Acland, Sir Arthur Herbert Dyke, 13th Bt. (1847–1926). Politician and educationist. The first Cabinet minister to be appointed with responsibility for education only. Son of **Sir Thomas Dyke Acland**

1

the educational reformer. Educated Rugby and Christ Church, Oxford. Tutor, Keble College, Oxford, 1872–5, Principal, Oxford Military College at Cowley, 1875–7. Served as treasurer of Somerville, bursar at Balliol and steward at Christ Church, Oxford, 1880–83, senior student, 1884. Strongly interested in improving the working classes through education and the Co-operative movement. Undertook lectures in 1882–3, later became involved in university extension work. Served as Liberal MP for Rotherham, 1885–99. Advocated technical education and served with **Sir Henry Roscoe** as first secretary of the National Association for the Promotion of Technical Education from 1888. Played leading part in the introduction of the Welsh Intermediate Schools Bill 1889, which provided for the establishment of secondary schools based on county authorities. Acland became Vice-President of the Committee of Council on Education in **Gladstone**'s 1892 government, making several important changes, including the raising of the school-leaving age to 11 and bringing about the ending of 'payment by results'. Left office in 1895. Chairman, Consultative Committee of the Board of Education, 1900–16. See his *The Education of Citizens* (1883); *A Handbook of the Political History of England*, with Ransome, C. (1882); *Studies in Secondary Education*, with Llewellyn Smith, H. (1892), and Armytage, W.H.G., 'A.H.D. Acland, 1847–1926', *Journal of Education*, 79, Oct. 1947; Holmes, G.M., 'The Parliamentary and Ministerial Career of A.H.D. Acland', *Durham Research Review*, 15, 1964; Acland, Lady, *A Devon Family* (1981).

Acland, Sir Thomas Dyke, 11th Bt. (1809–98). Politician and educational reformer. Born at Killerton, Devon. Educated at Harrow and Christ Church, Oxford, 1827–31, gaining a double first in classics and mathematics. Fellow, All Souls, Oxford, 1831–9. A college contemporary of **Gladstone**, Acland remained a lifelong friend. MP, West Somerset, 1837–47. Unsuccessfully contested Birmingham as a moderate Liberal against John Bright, 1859, but sat for North Devon, 1865–85 and the Wellington division of Somerset, 1885–6, when defeated because of his support for Irish home rule. His earliest educational interests were in establishing diocesan theological colleges and in defending church schools. Of greater importance was the leading part he played, together with **Frederick Temple**, in helping to establish the Oxford Local Examinations system for schools in 1858 and the promotion of technical and agricultural education through his work with the

Bath and West of England Agricultural Society. Member, Schools Inquiry Commission under **Lord Taunton**, 1864–8. Took an active part in the debates on the committee stage of **W.E. Forster's** Education Bill, 1870. See his *Some Account of the Origins and Objects of the new Oxford Examinations* (1858); *An Introduction to the Chemistry of Farming for Practical Farmers* (1891), and Acland, A.H.D., *Memoirs and Letters of the Right Hon. Sir Thomas Dyke Acland* (1902).

Adam, Alexander (1741–1809). Teacher and scholar. Born Laurieston in Moray, the son of a farmer. Educated at dame and parish schools. Taught locally and from 1757 worked as a tutor whilst studying in Edinburgh. Master of the George Watson's Hospital from 1760 and from 1765 taught at the Edinburgh High School where he became Joint Rector in 1768. Adam's famous pupils at Edinburgh included **Brougham**, who considered him the best teacher he had ever known, and Sir Walter Scott. His publications included a *Latin Grammar* (1762) which went through several editions and achieved an international reputation, *Roman Antiquities* (1791), *Classical Biography* (1800) and a *Latin Dictionary* (1805). In 1780 awarded the degree of LL.D by the University of Edinburgh. See Henderson, A., *An Account of the Life and Character of Alexander Adam* (1810); Steven, W., *History of the High School of Edinburgh* (1849).

Adams, Sir John (1857–1934). Educationist. Born Glasgow, educated at St David's School, Jordanhill Training College, and Glasgow University where he gained first class honours in mental and moral science. Headmaster of Jean Street School, Glasgow, and rector of Campbeltown Grammar School. Lecturer, and from 1890 principal, of Aberdeen Free Church Training College; from 1898 principal of Glasgow Free Church Training College which he combined with a lectureship in Education at the University of Glasgow. President of the Educational Institute of Scotland, 1896–7. In 1902 visited Canada, published an account of the Protestant schools in Quebec, and was appointed principal of the London Day Training College and first professor of Education in the University of London. After his retirement in 1922 Adams' international reputation was enhanced by his lecture tours in the Commonwealth and the USA, where he died in Los Angeles. An impressive lecturer and prolific writer, in 1925 he was knighted and received an honorary LL.D from the University of St Andrews in Scotland. See

THE EVOLUTION

OF

EDUCATIONAL THEORY

BY

JOHN ADAMS, M.A., B.Sc., LL.D.

PROFESSOR OF EDUCATION IN THE UNIVERSITY OF LONDON

MACMILLAN AND CO., LIMITED
ST. MARTIN'S STREET, LONDON
1912

his *Herbartian Psychology applied to Education* (1897); *Exposition and Illustration in Teaching* (1909); *The Evolution of Educational Theory* (1912); *The Student's Guide* (1917); *Modern Developments in Educational Practice* (1922); *Everyman's Psychology* (1929), and Sadler, M., *John Adams* (1935), Rusk, R., 'Sir John Adams 1857–1934', *British Journal of Educational Studies*, 10 (1), 1961.

Adamson, John William (1857–1947). Educationist. A pupil teacher at a Church school in Marylebone. Educated at Cheltenham Training College, and King's College, London. Taught in London and became second master of the Great College Street Board School. Head of the Training Department and Master of Method at King's College, London, 1890–1924. Lecturer in Education, 1901, and professor, 1903; president of the Teachers' Training Association, 1909–10; lecturer in History of Education to the Teachers' Training Syndicate, University of Cambridge, 1919–35; chairman of the Military Education Committee, University of London, 1926–37. Adamson was the most distinguished historian of education of his day. See his *Our Defective System of Training Teachers* (1904); *Pioneers of Modern Education 1600–1700* (1905); *English Education 1789–1902* (1930); *The Illiterate Anglo-Saxon* (1946), and Barnard, H.C., 'John William Adamson, 1857–1947', *British Journal of Educational Studies*, 10 (1), 1961; Thomas J.B., 'The Curriculum of a Day Training College. The logbooks of J.W. Adamson', *Journal of Educational Administration and History*, 11 (2), 1979.

Adderley, Sir Charles Bowyer, 1st Baron Norton (1814–1905). Statesman. Born at Knighton House, Leicestershire. Educated by private tutor, at a school near Bristol and at Christ Church, Oxford. Pass degree, 1835. Inherited from his uncle large family estates around Birmingham. Conservative MP for North Staffordshire, 1841–78. Vice-President of the Education Committee of the Privy Council, 1858–9, Under-Secretary for the Colonies, 1866–8. KCMG, 1869. President of the Board of Trade, 1874–8, when he took the title Baron Norton and retired from office. Adderley's main interests were in colonial development – he was secretary of the Colonial Reform Society – and in education, particularly the education of juvenile offenders. From 1847 he promoted the Saltley Training College, and in 1852 founded the Saltley Reformatory. In 1852 he introduced a Reformatory Schools Bill and in 1854 was responsible for the Young Offenders Act. Spoke regularly in Parliament on educational issues and was a member of the Reformatory and Industrial Schools Commission of 1883, and of the Cross Commission on the Elementary Education Acts which reported in 1888. See his *Punishment is not Education* (1856); *A Few Thoughts on National Education and Punishment* (1874), and Pemberton, W.S.C., *Life of Lord Norton 1814–1905* (1909).

Alderson, Sir Charles Henry (1831–1913). Civil servant. Educated at Eton and Trinity College, Oxford, first class moderations and second class *literae humaniores*, 1851–4. Called to the Bar, 1855. Fellow, All Souls. HMI, 1857–72. Chief Inspector, 1882–5. Member, Cross Commission on Elementary Education, 1886–8. Second Charity Commissioner, 1885–1900, Chief Charity Commissioner, England and Wales, 1900–3. Knight, 1903. Editor, *Memoir of Baron Alderson* (1858).

Allen, John (1810–86). School inspector and clergyman. Born at Pembroke, Wales, son of a clergyman. Educated privately, at Westminster School and Trinity College, Cambridge, a contemporary and friend of Hallam, Tennyson and Thackeray. BA, 1832, Taught at St Peter's School, Pimlico, 1832. Chaplain, 1833–46, and lecturer in Mathematics, 1833–9, at King's College, London. The first of Her Majesty's Inspectors, 1839–46. Vicar of Prees, Shropshire, 1846–83, and Archdeacon of Salop, 1847–86. Master of St John's Hospital, Lichfield, 1883–6. Sunday school teacher, a supporter of the Woodard schools, particularly St Chad's College, Denstone. Supporter of the temperance movement and vice-president of the United Kingdom Alliance. See Grier, R.M., *John Allen: A Memoir* (1889).

Allen, William (1770–1843). A Quaker, scientist and philanthropist. Born Spitalfields, London, educated at boarding school, Rochester. Conducted chemical experiments at Plaistow. Fellow of Linnean Society, 1801, of Royal Society, 1807. Lectured at Royal Society, and at Guy's Hospital, 1802–26. Opposed slave trade and slavery. Many international contacts including Alexander I of Russia. Member of the Committee formed to support **Lancaster**, 1808, subsequently treasurer of the British and Foreign School Society. In 1814 with **Bentham, Robert Owen** and others bought the New Lanark Mills in Scotland. Allen insisted on some Bible instruction. In later years promoted the agricultural colony with industrial schools at Lindfield, Sussex. See *Life of William Allen compiled* *from his Diary and Correspondence* (3 vols., 1846–7), and Sherman, J., *Memoir of William Allen* (1851); Doncaster, L.H., *Friends of Humanity with special reference to the Quaker William Allen* (1965); Muckle, J., 'Alexander I and William Allen: A tour of Russian schools in 1819 and some missing reports', *History of Education*, 15 (3), 1986.

Allies, Thomas William (1813–1903). Pioneer of Catholic education. Born Midsomer Norton, Somerset, son of an Anglican priest. Educated Bristol Grammar School, Eton and Wadham College, Oxford, 1828–32, studying classics. Fellow, Wadham College, 1833. Took orders, 1838 and examining chaplain, Bishop of London, 1840–2. Vicar, Launton, Oxfordshire, 1842–50, where he became acquainted with **John Henry Newman**. Joined the Catholic Church, 1850 and moved to London. First secretary, Catholic Poor School Committee, 1853–90. Allies successfully promoted the cause of Catholic elementary education. He pressed for ecclesiastical inspection of religious instruction: such a system was established in 1875. In 1870, there were 666 Catholic schools under inspection; by 1882 there were 1562. Allies also saw the need for training facilities for Catholic teachers. A women's college, Notre Dame, Liverpool, was opened in 1874 and was followed by another, the Sacred Heart at Wandsworth and one for men, St Mary's Training College, Hammersmith. The number of teachers rose from 799 in 1870 to 2943 in 1883. Briefly professor of Modern History, Catholic University of Ireland, 1855. See his *The Formation of Christendom*, an 8-volume work on the philosophy of history (1865–96), and Allies, M.H., *Thomas William Allies* (1907).

Althans, Henry (1783–1855). Educationist and part-time inspector. A corn factor in London, 1818–55 and secretary of a Sunday School Union. Published descripton of Borough Road monitorial school and then appointed half-time agent to British and Foreign School Society for the Metropolitan area, 1831. His task was to make surprise visits to British schools within a radius of 12 miles of London. The salary was £80 per annum. Reports on the schools were published in the Society's journal. Althans continued with the work until 1854. Witness, Select Committees on the State of Education, 1834 and on the Education of the Poorer Classes, 1835. See Bartle, G.F., 'The Agents and Inspectors of the British and Foreign School Society 1826–84', *History of Education Society Bulletin*, 34, 1984.

7

Althorp

Althorp, Viscount, John Charles, 3rd Earl Spencer (1782–1845). Politician. Born London, educated Harrow and Trinity College, Cambridge. MP for St Albans from 1804 and for Northamptonshire, 1806–34. Appointed Chancellor of the Exchequer and Leader of the Commons in 1830. In 1833 introduced the proposed grant of £20,000 'in aid of Private Subscriptions for the erection of School Houses for the Education of the Children of the Poorer Classes in Great Britain'. Succeeded to the earldom in the next year and thereafter devoted much time to trying to restore the family finances. Althorp took little delight in public affairs and was principally interested in country life and sport. He was a founder of the Yorkshire Agricultural Society, first president of the English Agricultural Society formed in 1838 and later the Royal Agricultural Society of England, and one of the founders of the Royal Agricultural College at Cirencester in 1844. See Le Marchant, D., *Memoir of Lord Althorp* (1876); Myers, E., *Lord Althorp* (1890).

Anderson, Elizabeth Garrett (1836–1917). Pioneer of medical education for women. Born Whitechapel, London, but moved to Aldeburgh, Suffolk in 1841. Educated privately, but association with **Emily Davies** and others aroused her interest in the women's cause. In 1860 student hostility defeated her first attempt to gain medical training at Middlesex Hospital. After four years of private tuition in 1865 she passed the Apothecaries' Hall examination and began to practise in London. In 1870 she became visiting physician to the East London Hospital, and was awarded an MD by the University of Paris. In 1871 she was elected to the first London School Board but neither her marriage to the ship-owner James Anderson in the same year nor the subsequent birth of three children interrupted her medical work. In 1872 she opened the New Hospital for Women, and five years later was elected to the British Medical Association. Dean of the London School of Medicine for Women, 1883–1903. Supported the constitutional suffrage movement for women as expressed by her sister Millicent Fawcett, and in 1908 followed her father and husband as mayor of Aldeburgh, the first woman in Britain to hold the office of mayor. See Anderson, L., *Elizabeth Garrett Anderson* (1939); Manton, J., *Elizabeth Garrett Anderson* (1965).

Anson, Sir William Reynell, 3rd Bt. (1843–1914). Academic and politician. Eldest son of Sir J.W.H. Anson, 2nd Bt. Born Walberton, Sussex, succeeding to the title in 1873. Educated Eton and Balliol College, Oxford, 1862–6, obtaining a first in classical moderations and in *literae humaniores*. Barrister, Inner Temple, 1869 and Bencher, 1900. Vinerian Reader in English Law, Oxford, 1874–81. Warden, All Souls, Oxford, 1881–1914, and Vice-Chancellor, Oxford, 1898–9. Elected unopposed, MP, Oxford University, 1899–1914. Became first Parliamentary Secretary to the Board of Education, 1902, though without a seat in the Cabinet. A firm supporter of the 1902 Education Bill, he assisted in its passage through the Commons. In the following year, he helped to steer successfully the London Education Bill through its stages. His best-known publications are *Principles of the English Law of Contract* (1879) and *Law and Custom of the Constitution* (1886 Part I, 1892 Part II), but he also edited *The Autobiography and Political Correspondence of Augustus Henry, 3rd Duke of Grafton* (1893). See Henson, H.H., *A Memoir of the Rt. Hon. Sir William Anson* (1920).

Applegarth, Robert (1834–1924). Trade unionist. Born at Hull, Yorkshire, son of a fisherman, Applegarth spent some time in a dame school but started work at the age of ten. He visited the USA, 1854–7, and subsequently was employed as a carpenter in Sheffield, becoming president of his trade union branch. General Secretary of the Amalgamated Society of Carpenters and Joiners, 1862–71. Chairman of the International Working Men's Association, 1868. Secretary of the five man 'Junta' which dominated the trade union movement of the 1860s and 1870s. He was also a founder member and member of the executive of the National Education League from 1869, and a powerful advocate, in speeches and newspaper articles, of state-provided, compulsory, unsectarian, free education. Visited educational establishments in Europe, 1869–70, and was consulted by **W.E. Forster** over the 1870 Education Bill. Applegarth narrowly failed to be elected to the first London School Board. Pioneered the development of electric light in Britain, elected a member of the Institute of Electrical Engineers, 1886. Founder and first secretary of the short-lived National Industrial League, established in 1911, which advocated state-provided, free post-school industrial, professional and commercial training. See Humphrey, A.W., *Robert Applegarth: Trade Unionist, Educationist, Reformer* (1913); Griggs, C., *The Trades Union Congress and the Struggle for Education, 1868–1925* (1983).

9

Armstrong, Henry Edward (1848–1937). Science educator. Born in Lewisham, South London. Educated at Colfe's Grammar School, Lewisham, Royal College of Chemistry, 1865–7 and Leipzig University, 1867–70 where he gained a doctorate in chemistry. Appointed to the London Institution, Finsbury Circus, to give evening lectures in analytical chemistry in 1870, and nine years later lecturer in chemistry at the newly-opened City and Guilds Institute of London. Armstrong became well known when in 1884, as the professor of Chemistry at the Technical College of the Institute, he propounded the principles underlying the heuristic method in science in a lecture given as part of the International Health Exhibition in London. He encouraged this new approach to the teaching of science, where the pupil 'not only may but must be absolutely in the position of an original discoverer'. He was responsible for the setting up of a special committee of the British Association to consider the teaching of science in schools and acted as secretary. Armstrong was a strong believer in making scientific knowledge better known to the public, mainly through lectures and writings. He retired as professor in 1911. FRS, 1876. Numerous publications, including 'The Heuristic Method of Teaching, or the Art of Making Children Discover Things for Themselves', Board of Education Special Reports on Educational Subjects, ii (1898), *Essays in the Teaching of Scientific Methods* (2nd edn. 1925); *The Art and Principles of Chemistry* (1927). See also Van Praagh, G. (ed.), *H.E. Armstrong and Science Education* (1973).

Arnold, Edward Penrose (1828–78). School inspector. Third son of **Dr Thomas Arnold**. Educated at Rugby and Balliol College, Oxford, 1845–8. Fellow, All Souls, Oxford, 1851. Curate, Charlton, Wiltshire, 1852. Appointed Assistant Inspector, south-west England, HMI, 1864–77. See Hopkinson, D., *Edward Penrose Arnold* (1981).

Arnold, Matthew (1822–88). School inspector and poet. Born Laleham, Middlesex, eldest son of **Dr Thomas Arnold**, who became headmaster of Rugby School. Educated at Winchester, 1836–7, Rugby, 1837–41 and Balliol College, Oxford, 1841–4, gaining second class honours in *literae humaniores*. Fellow, Oriel College, Oxford, 1845, followed briefly by teaching at Rugby. Private secretary to **Marquess of Lansdowne**, Lord President of the Council, 1847–51, who obtained an inspectorship for Arnold in 1851. From this time, he developed as a poet, publishing a number of volumes

which included the poems 'The Scholar Gypsy' and 'Sohrab and Rustum'. Professor of Poetry, Oxford University, 1857–67, which led to two volumes of literary criticism on the translation of Homer in 1861 and 1862. His accounts of inspection of elementary schools in 1852, 1869 and 1880 are contained in an edition published by **F.S. Marvin** in 1908. He opposed the imposition of 'payment by results' and published an important pamphlet, *The Twice Revised Code*, on the matter in 1862. Arnold travelled to France, Holland and Switzerland in 1859 to report on popular education in these countries for the Newcastle Commission on elementary education. His visit resulted in a wider consideration of the nature of popular education: 'A French Eton or Middle-Class Education and the State' appeared in *Macmillan's Magazine* in 1863–4. His final Oxford lecture in 1867, entitled 'Culture and its enemies' was published, together with others on the same theme, as *Culture and Anarchy* (1869). Arnold had lived and inspected in London, but later moved to Harrow and then to Cobham, Surrey in 1878. Five years later, in 1883, he received a Civil List pension of £250 and was thus able to retire from the Inspectorate and devote himself to his writings. See Trilling, L., *Matthew Arnold* (1963 edn.); Connell, W.F., *The Educational Thought and Influence of Matthew Arnold* (1950); Honan, P., *Matthew Arnold* (1981).

Arnold, Dr Thomas (1795–1842). Scholar and headmaster. Born at East Cowes, Isle of Wight, educated at Winchester and Corpus Christi College, Oxford, where his contemporaries included J.T. Coleridge and John Keble. In 1814 he achieved a first in classics, and a fellowship at Oriel in the following year. In 1818 he became a deacon and in 1819 established a school at Laleham near Staines in Middlesex to prepare pupils for university. Awarded BD and DD degrees in 1828, the year in which he became headmaster of Rugby School. This post and the chaplaincy of the school he held until his death. His four sons, **Matthew**, Thomas, **Edward** and William all

attended the school. Arnold's reputation as the man who reformed the public schools of England by his moral and religious example and teaching to produce truth-telling Christian gentlemen was fostered by **Thomas Hughes** in *Tom Brown's Schooldays* (1857). In 1841 Arnold was appointed regius professor of Modern History at Oxford. See his *History of Rome* (3 vols., 1838–43); *Lectures on Modern History* (1842); *Sermons* (6 vols., 1878 edition), and Stanley, A.P., *Life and Correspondence of Dr Arnold* (2 vols., 1844); Wymer, N., *Dr Arnold of Rugby* (1953); Bamford, T.W., *Thomas Arnold* (1960).

Asquith, Herbert Henry (1852–1928). Statesman. Born Morley, Yorkshire, educated at the City of London School and Balliol College, Oxford, gaining a first in classics, 1875. Called to the bar, Lincoln's Inn, 1876, QC, 1890, Bencher 1894. Liberal MP, East Fife, 1886–1918 and Paisley, 1920–4. Home Secretary, 1892–5, Chancellor of the Exchequer, 1905–8, Secretary of State for War, 1914 and Prime Minister, 1908–16. Strongly opposed the 1902 Education Bill during its passage through the Commons, deploring the abolition of School Boards and the boost given to denominational schools. The Liberal government's 1906 Education Bill was intended to remedy the main defects of the earlier legislation but came to grief through Conservative and Church opposition. In the deadlock reached between the Commons and the Lords, King George V called a conference between the two sides, consisting of three representatives of government headed by Asquith and three of the Opposition, led by the Archbishop of Canterbury, but no compromise was reached and the bill failed. Early in 1916 Asquith presided over a Reconstruction Committee consisting of seven cabinet colleagues which later decided to investigate questions of public interest, among them education. The accession of Lloyd George in place of Asquith as Prime Minister in December 1916 led to the removal of responsibility from the Reconstruction Committee to *ad hoc* bodies, thus lessening the impact of their recommendations. Nevertheless the four reports issued between 1918 and 1921 are impressive documents: on natural science (1918), modern languages (1918), English (1921) and classics (1921). Asquith was leader of the Liberal party, 1908–26. Created Earl of Oxford and Asquith, 1925. See his *Fifty Years of Parliament* (2 vols., 1926); *Memories and Reflections* (2 vols., 1928); and Spender, J.A., and Asquith, C., *Life of Herbert Henry Asquith, Lord Oxford and Asquith* (2 vols., 1932); Jenkins, R., *Asquith* (1964); Lloyd, J.M., 'The Asquith Reconstruction Committee and Educational Reform', *Journal of Educational Administration and History*, 8 (2), 1976.

Atholl, Katherine Marjorie Stewart-Murray, Duchess of (1874–1960). Politician and reformer. Born Edinburgh, daughter of Sir James Ramsay and educated at Wimbledon High School and the Royal College of Music where she studied the piano. In 1899, married John George Stewart-Murray, who succeeded as 8th Duke of Atholl in 1917. She took a keen interest in Scottish local government and social service matters and was a firm Conservative supporter. MP, Kinross and Western division of Perth and Kinross, 1923–38. The Duchess was the first woman Scottish MP and, on her appointment as parliamentary secretary to the Board of Education in 1924, the first Conservative woman to hold ministerial office. During her five years in office, 1924–9, she carried out her duties with great thoroughness and efficiency. However, she opposed a Woman's party in Parliament in her book *Women and Politics* (1931). She publicly deplored the growth of totalitarianism in Europe, attacking Russian oppression, and later condemned Chamberlain for his policy of appeasement towards Germany. Resigned the Whip in 1938, sitting as an Independent. In a by-election that same year, at which she supported Churchill's call for re-armament, she was defeated by the Conservative candidate and withdrew from politics. Member of numerous official committees and commissions including the Royal Commission on the Civil Service, 1929–31. DBE, 1918. See her autobiography, *Working Partnership* (1958).

Baden-Powell, Robert Stephenson Smyth, 1st Baron (1857–1941). Soldier and founder of the Boy Scouts and Girl Guides. Born in London, sixth son of Revd Baden-Powell, Savilian professor of Geometry, Oxford University. Educated at Charterhouse, 1870–6, and then enlisted in the Army. served in many parts of the world,

but it was in India that he first developed scouting as a part of the training of soldiers. Badges were awarded for efficiency and the men were encouraged to develop initiative. Baden-Powell's schemes were set out in his book *Aids to Scouting* (1899). He became a national hero for his part in withstanding the siege of Mafeking during the Boer War; after its relief in May 1900, Baden-Powell was promoted to major-general at the age of 43, and to lieutenant-general in 1907. He retired from the Army in 1910.

Many teachers were using his *Aids to Scouting* and Baden-Powell held a trial camp, for boys from different social classes, at Brownsea Island, Poole in 1907. The success of the experiment, which encouraged boys to work in small units and to high standards of accomplishment and behaviour, led to the publication of *Scouting for Boys* (1908) and the setting up of Boy Scout troops throughout the country. Baden-Powell became Chief Scout. A parallel organization, the Girl Guides, also came into being. This was followed in 1916 by Wolf Cubs, for younger children, based on Kipling's Mowgli stories in the *Jungle Books*; after the war, for older youths, the Rover Scouts. Although the Scout movement spread to many parts of the world it was open to the criticism that it prepared youths for military training. Created 1st Baron Baden-Powell of Gilwell in 1929, on the occasion of the Scout Jamboree held at Gilwell, Essex, that year. See also his *Quick Training for War* (1914); *My Adventures As A Spy* (1915), and Carter, M.E., *Life of Baden-Powell* (1956); Rosenthal, M., *The Character Factory* (1986).

Badley, John Haden (1865–1967). Headmaster and scholar. Born Dudley, Worcestershire, educated at Rugby and Trinity College, Cambridge. Classical tripos, 1887. Taught for one term at Bedford Grammar School, and two and a half years at Abbotsholme, 1889–92. In January 1893 he founded Bedales School where he was headmaster (and known as 'The Chief'), 1893–1935. After his wife's death in 1956 returned to live his last years within the school grounds. At Bedales Badley's ideals of coeducation, international understanding (there was a high proportion of children from over-seas), co-operation for common ends, and a broad curriculum including the arts and manual training, received full expression. See his *Bedales, a pioneer school* (1923); *A Schoolmaster's Testament* (1937), and Brandreth, G., and Henry, S., (eds.), *John Haden Badley, 1865–1967* (1967); Henderson, J.L., *Irregularly Bold: a story of Bedales School* (1978).

Bain, Alexander (1818–1903). Psychologist and writer on education. Born Aberdeen, one of eight children of a farmer, who was a strict Calvinist. Left school at eleven, continued with evening classes. 1836, entered Marischal College, Aberdeen, and studied 'mental science', and became assistant to the professor of Moral Philosophy, 1841. Bain visited London the following year and became acquainted with **J.S. Mill, Grote,** Carlyle and **Edwin Chadwick**. Assistant secretary, Metropolitan Sanitary Commission, 1848–50. Lecturer, Bedford College for Women, 1850–5, professor of Logic and English Literature, St Andrews University, 1860–80, Lord Rector, Aberdeen University, 1881–7. Bain's writings were extensive and display his range of interests. Besides his works on psychology, philosophy and English, Bain wrote on educational and public issues. *The Senses and the Intellect* was published in 1856, *The Emotions and the Will* three years later. *The Study of Character* (1861) contained an estimate of phrenology. Bain wrote a number of books on grammar and literature, including *On Teaching English* (1887). An important book, *Mental and Moral Science*, appeared in 1868 and *Education As A Science* in 1879. A biography of John Stuart Mill with personal reminiscences was published in 1882. See also Bain's *Autobiography* (1904), ed. Davison, W.L.

Baines, Sir Edward (1800–90). Politician and newspaper owner. Born Leeds, educated at the Protestant Dissenters' Grammar School, Manchester. In 1815 began work on the *Leeds Mercury* which he subsequently inherited from his father. His interest in education was aroused by hearing **Joseph Lancaster** speaking in Leeds. Visited infant schools in New Lanark and Westminster. One of the founders of the Leeds Literary and Philosophical Society, 1818, of the Leeds Mechanics' Institute 1824, and of the Yorkshire Village Circulating Library, 1853. A Sunday school teacher for more than 40 years; a lifelong supporter of the temperance movement; a leader of the Voluntaryist movement in education, 1843–67; president of the Yorkshire Union of Mechanics' Institutes,

1837–81; chairman of the Council of the Yorkshire College of Science, 1881–6; a member of the Taunton Commission; Liberal MP for Leeds, 1859–74. Knighted on his 80th birthday, when the £3,000 subscribed to him was devoted to the Yorkshire College of Science. In 1843 Baines led the opposition to the education clauses of Graham's Factory Bill, and subsequently championed voluntary education promoted without any assistance or interference from government. Appointed, however, to the Taunton Commission in 1864 as a representative of voluntaryism, in 1868 he signed its report as an advocate of state aid. See his *Strictures on the New Government Measure of Education* (1853); *Education best promoted by Perfect Freedom, not by State Endowments* (1854); *National Education* (1856); *Memorial to Edward Baines* (1880).

Balfour, Arthur James, first Earl of Balfour (1848–1930). Statesman and philosopher. Born at Whittingehame, East Lothian, Scotland, brother of **Eleanor** (see **Sidgwick**), later principal of Newnham College, Cambridge, and nephew of Lord Salisbury, the Prime Minister. Educated at Eton, and Trinity College, Cambridge. Second class in moral science tripos. Conservative MP for Hertford, 1874–85, East Manchester, 1885–1906, City of London, 1906–22. President of the Local Government Board, 1885–6; Secretary for Scotland, 1886; Vice-President of the Committee of Council on Education for Scotland, 1886–7; Chief Secretary for Ireland, 1887–91; First Lord of the Treasury and Leader of the House of Commons, 1891–2, 1895–1906; Prime Minister, 1902–5; Foreign Secretary, 1916–19, responsible for the Balfour Declaration which promised a national home for the Jews in Palestine; Lord President of the Council, 1919–21, 1925–9. In 1922 received KG and an earldom. The Education Act of 1902, usually referred to as the Balfour Act, ended the School Boards, transferred local authority for education to county and borough councils, and provided rate aid for voluntary schools. President of the British Association, 1904, and of the British Academy, 1921–8. OM, 1916. Rector of the Universities of St Andrews, 1886, and Glasgow, 1890; and Chancellor of Edinburgh, 1891 and Cambridge, 1919. Honorary degrees from 16 universities in England, Greece, Ireland, Poland, Scotland, Wales and the USA. See his *A Defence of Philosophic Doubt* (1879); *Foundations of Belief* (1895); *Essays Speculative and Political* (1920), and Dugdale, B.E.C., *A.J. Balfour* (2 vols., 1936); Egremont, M., *Balfour* (1980).

Balfour, Sir Graham (1858–1929). Educational administrator. Son of Surgeon-General T. Graham Balfour, President, Royal Statistical Society. Educated at Marlborough and Worcester College, Oxford, first class honours classical moderations and *literae humaniores*, 1882. Barrister, Inner Temple, 1885. Travelled widely for over a decade, residing for a time in Samoa. Assistant Secretary, Delegacy, Oxford Local Examinations, 1897–1902. He was Director of Education, Staffordshire, 1902–26, and introduced a number of innovations. Balfour was the first Director to organize school gardens on a large scale (1904), and also rural libraries (1916). Member, Committee on the Position of Science in Education, 1916–17, the Reconstruction Committee on Adult Education, 1917–19, and the Consultative Committee, Board of Education, 1926–9. Knight, 1917. He wrote two authoritative works, *The Educational Systems of Great Britain and Ireland* (1903) and *Educational Administration* (1921).

Ball, Sidney (1857–1918). Academic and social reformer. Born at Pershore, Worcestershire, son of a solicitor. Educated at Wellington and Oriel College, Oxford, 1875–9, gaining a first in classical moderations and a second in *literae humaniores*. Spent three years in Germany and attended lectures by Lotze at Göttingen University. In 1882, Ball was appointed lecturer in philosophy at St John's College, Oxford and became a fellow of the College. A Liberal influenced by the teachings of **T.H. Green** and **Arnold Toynbee**, Ball developed his ideas of reconciling an organic state with individualist economics. He was active in the 1880s in the Oxford Economic Society, which studied the economics of welfare and whose membership included **Michael Sadler**, D.G. Ritchie, W.J. Ashley and **W.A.S. Hewins**. It was in his rooms at St John's that his friend **Samuel Barnett** delivered a Toynbee lecture on 17 November 1883 entitled 'Settlements of University Men in Great Towns': this led to the establishment of Toynbee Hall in the East End of London two years later. He was also active in encouraging

17

Albert Mansbridge to promote the Workers' Educational Association. At a conference at an Extension meeting at Oxford in August 1907, Ball introduced a paper for discussion entitled 'What Oxford Can Do for Working People'. This provided the inspiration for a report in the following year, *Oxford and Working-Class Education*, which recommended a broadening of educational opportunities to all classes at the university. Ball joined the Fabian Society in 1886 and was attracted to Socialism, becoming President of Oxford University Fabian Society in 1895. His views are expressed in Fabian Tract No. 72 *Moral Aspects of Socialism* (1896). See Ball, D.H. (ed.), *Sidney Ball. Memories and Impressions of An Ideal Don* (1923).

Ballard, Philip Boswood (1865–1950). Educationist. Born Maesteg, Glamorgan, educated there and at Borough Road College, London. Taught in London schools, 1886–98, but returned to Glamorgan as headmaster of the Pupil Teachers' School at Tondu, 1898–1903. Inspector of Schools in Glamorgan, 1903–5, and subsequently in London, 1906–30. Ballard was not merely a leading teacher and inspector, who twice presided over the Association of Inspectors and Educational Organizers, he also achieved MA and D.Litt. degrees from the University of London, winning a gold medal and the Carpenter medal. His interests in mathematics, English, handiwork, intelligence and testing were reflected in his many publications. See for example *Group Tests of Intelligence* (1920); *Teaching the Essentials of Arithmetic* (1928); *Teaching and Testing English* (1939), and *Things I Cannot Forget* (1937).

Barker, Sir Ernest (1874–1960). Political philosopher. Attended Manchester Grammar and Balliol, Oxford, 1893–8, first class in classical moderations and modern history. Fellow, Merton College; lecturer, modern history, Wadham College; fellow and lecturer, St John's College; and fellow and tutor, New College, Oxford, between 1898 and 1920. Principal, King's College, London, 1920–8, first professor of Political Science at Cambridge, fellow of Peterhouse, 1928–39. A Liberal in politics and advocate of the welfare state, he was active both in the co-operative movement and the Workers' Educational Association. Member, Consultative Committee, Board of Education and chairman of the drafting committee of the Hadow Report on *The Education of the Adolescent* (1926). Knight, 1944. See his *Political Thought in England from Herbert Spencer to Today* (1915, revised edn., 1947); *Age and Youth* (1953), an autobiography, and Catlin, G.E.G., 'Sir Ernest Barker', *Proceedings of the British Academy*, 46, 1960.

Barlow, Sir (James) Alan (Noel), 2nd Bt. (1881–1968). Public servant. Born London, eldest child of Sir Thomas Barlow, physician to three monarchs and president of the Royal College of Physicians. Educated at Marlborough College and Corpus Christi College, Oxford. In 1907 chosen by **Sir Robert Morant** to be a junior examiner in the Board of Education. Private secretary to the Parliamentary Secretary, 1914. At the Ministry of Munitions, 1915–18, and then transferred to the Ministry of Labour as principal assistant secretary in charge of the Training Department. Principal private secretary to Ramsay MacDonald, 1933–4, Under-Secretary and Second Secretary at the Treasury, 1934–48. Chairman of the Barlow Committee on Scientific Manpower which reported in 1946, and recommended that the universities should double their output of scientists. The university population of 50,000 in 1938–9 doubled to 100,000 in 1958–9. Served for several years on the Advisory Council on Scientific Policy, as a trustee of the National Gallery, and on the court of the University of London. Barlow's important oriental ceramics collection was bequeathed to the Victoria and Albert and British Museums, and to the University of Sussex for teaching purposes. See the Report of 1946, and Sharp, E.A., *Sir Alan Barlow 1881–1968. An Address* (1968).

Barnardo, Dr Thomas John (1845–1905). Philanthropist. Born Dublin, son of furrier formerly from Germany. Barnardo's strong religious convictions were due to his mother's influence. Educated Dublin private schools, leaving at 14 to work as a wine merchant's clerk. After his 'conversion' at a revivalist meeting in May 1862, Barnardo determined to become a missionary. Qualified in medicine at London Hospital, LRCS, 1876, FRCS, 1879. During this time, he taught and became superintendent of an East End ragged school, visited the slums and began preaching there. Abandoning his plans to go to China, Barnardo decided to devote his time to helping destitute children. Opened boys' home in Stepney, 1870, which became the basis for the 'Dr Barnardo's Homes'. A similar venture was started for girls in 1874, developed two years later into a village home at Barkingside, Essex, with its own church and schools. Later, he sent boys and girls to Canada, where a settlement was established. Over a quarter of a million children in need had been helped during his lifetime. After Barnardo's management of the homes had been investigated in 1877, they were incorporated under the Companies Act, but still retained Barnardo's name. See his *My First Arab; or How I began my life work* (1888), and Wagner, G., *Barnardo* (1979).

Barnes, Revd William (1801–86). Schoolteacher and poet. Born Rushhay, Bagber, Dorset, son of a farmer. Educated at elementary school, leaving at the age of 13, becoming solicitor's clerk, Dorchester. In 1823, opened boys' boarding school at Mere, Wiltshire, moving on his marriage in 1827 to larger premises, Chantrey House Academy, in the same village, where a wide and liberal curriculum was offered. In 1834, Barnes wrote his first poems of rural life in the Dorset dialect. He also began to publish pamphlets on mathematics and later, on many different subjects. Opened schools at Dorchester in 1837 and 1838, where he attracted a middle-class clientele. Barnes's educational principles were put into practice; language teaching was revolutionized and practical science was introduced. Moved premises 1847 and studied at St John's College, Cambridge; Bachelor of Divinity, 1850. On closure of his school in 1862, took living of Came, Dorset, where his fame as philologist and poet was acknowledged. See his *Poems of Rural Life in the Dorset Dialect* (collected edn., 1879), and Hearl, T.W., *William Barnes* (1966); Chedzoy, A., *William Barnes, A Life of the Dorset Poet* (1986).

Barnett, Dame Henrietta Octavia Weston (1851–1936). Social reformer. Born Clapham, London. From an early age, displayed concern for the poor, working with **Octavia Hill**. In 1873, married **Samuel Barnett**, then a young curate and thenceforth worked together to ameliorate social conditions in the East End. The first woman guardian and manager, Forest Gate district school, 1875–97. From 1877, arranged country holidays for sick children. Co-founder 1884, Children's Country Holidays Fund. Established London Pupil Teachers' Association, 1884. President, 1891–1907. With her husband, helped to found Toynbee Hall in Whitechapel where education classes for adult poor were held. In 1903, formed Hampstead Garden Suburb Trust to raise funds for providing rented houses for all classes. This was one of the earliest examples of town planning. Provision of churches, schools and recreational facilities were important features of the scheme. She was a promoter of the Dame Henrietta Barnett school in Hampstead as well as

Barnett House, Oxford. CBE, 1917. Dame, 1924. Author of *Canon Barnett* (2 vols., 1918), and *Matters that Matter* (1930).

Barnett, Percy Arthur (1858–1941). Educationist and school inspector. Born London. Educated City of London School and Trinity College, Oxford. Professor of English, Firth College, Sheffield, 1882–8, Principal, Borough Road Training College, Isleworth, 1889–93. HMI, 1893–1918. Assistant Inspector, Training Colleges, 1894. Seconded for imperial service as Superintendent of Education, Natal, 1902–4. Chief Inspector, Teacher Training, Board of Education, 1905–12. Civil adviser, War Office, on Army education, 1919–21. His best known works are *Teaching and Organisation*, editor and contributor (1897), and *Common Sense in Education* (1899, 5th edn., 1906); also *The Story of Robinson Crusoe in Latin* (1906); *Common Sense Grammar* (1923).

Barnett, Samuel Augustus (1844–1913). Clergyman and social reformer. Born Bristol. Educated at home and at Wadham College, Oxford. Second class degree in law and history, 1865. From 1867 curate at St Mary's, Bryanston Square, London, in 1873 went to St Jude's Whitechapel where he became immersed in the problems of the London poor. Canon of Bristol from 1894 and canon of Westminster from 1906. Barnett used unorthodox methods to bring people to church, with secular music and non-biblical readings. His art exhibitions from 1881 led to the building of the Whitechapel art gallery, and his parish library became the Whitechapel public library. His education reform league founded in 1884 promoted art and handwork in schools, and pupil-teacher centres. He contributed to the Oxford Day Training College, and began a 'children's country holiday' fund. His major innovation, however, was the university settlement movement. Toynbee Hall was founded in 1884 to bring university men into deprived city areas, and Barnett was its first warden, 1884–96. See his *Practicable Socialism* (1888); *The Ideal City* (1894), and Barnett, H.O.W., *Canon Barnett* (2 vols., 1918).

Beale, Dorothea (1831–1906). Pioneer of education for girls and women. Born Bishopsgate, London. Her strong personal commitment to learning was complemented by a varied education; governesses, private coaching with her brothers, boarding schools in England and France, lectures at Gresham College and Crosby Hall Literary Institution. Student at Queen's College, London, and subsequently for seven years tutor in mathematics and Latin, and headteacher of the attached school. Headteacher of the Clergy Daughters' School at Casterton, 1856–7. From 1858 until her death principal of Cheltenham Ladies' College, and teacher of scripture and other subjects. In 1866 gave evidence to the Taunton Commission and in 1894 to the Bryce Commission. Advocated higher education for women and sponsored St Hilda's Hall, Oxford. Honorary LL.D, Edinburgh, 1902. A vice-president of the Central Society for Women's Suffrage. See her *History of the Ladies College, 1853–1904* (1905); Beale, D., Soulsby, L., and Dove, J., *Work and Play in Girls' Schools* (1898), and Raikes, E., *Dorothea Beale of Cheltenham* (1908); Shillito, E., *Dorothea Beale* (1920); Kamm, J., *How Different from Us* (1958).

Bell, Andrew (1753–1832). Educationist. Born and educated at St Andrews in Scotland where he attended the university and from

which he later received the degrees of DD and LL.D. After a short spell as a tutor in Virginia, Bell took Episcopal orders and sailed to India in 1787. In 1789 he became superintendent of the Madras Male Orphan Asylum where he introduced the system of mutual instruction by the pupils themselves, later known as the monitorial system. In 1796 Bell returned to England with a considerable fortune and East India Company pension, and in the following year published *An Experiment in Education, made at the Male Asylum of Madras* (1797). Rector at Swanage, Dorset, 1801–9. With the establishment of the National Society in 1811 Bell became superintendent of an organization which boasted some 12,000 schools during his lifetime. In 1819 he became a prebendary of Westminster Abbey where he was buried. He left £120,000 for educational purposes, mainly in Scotland, half of which was given to St Andrews, and the remainder to educational institutions in Aberdeen, Edinburgh, Glasgow, Inverness, Leith and the Royal Naval School in London. In 1872 £18,000 of his capital was used to found chairs of Education at

Edinburgh and St Andrews. See Southey, R., and Southey, C.C., *Life of the Rev Andrew Bell* (3 vols., 1844); Meiklejohn, J.M.D., *An Old Educational Reformer, Andrew Bell* (1881).

Bellairs, Henry Walford (1812–1900). School inspector. Born Hunsingore, Yorkshire, son of a vicar. Educated Shrewsbury and New Inn Hall, Oxford, BA, 1835. Ordained priest, 1836, and curate at Hunsingore, Chester and Stockport, 1835–44 and served until 1872. Actively supported the founding of Cheltenham Ladies' College. Vicar of Nuneaton, 1872–91, canon, Worcester Cathedral, 1880–1900. Wrote religious novels, published as *Tales of the Town* (1843), *Work, the Law of God, the Lot of Man* (1852) and *The Teacher's Mission and Reward* (1855). See also his *The Church and the School: or Hints on Clerical Life* (1868).

Beloe, Robert (1905–84). Educational administrator. Son of head-master, Bradfield College, Berkshire. Educated at Winchester and Hertford College, Oxford, 1924–7, second class honours in history. Taught at Bradfield, Eton and a Reading elementary school, 1927–31. Assistant, Kent Education Office, 1931–4, Assistant Education Officer, Surrey, 1934–9, and Chief Education Officer, 1940–59. Chairman, Secondary School Examinations Council, 1947–64. Beloe was chairman of a committee appointed by the Council in 1958 to review the examination arrangements for secondary school pupils who were not capable of taking the General Certificate of Education (GCE) examinations. The Report, published in 1960, recommended a new examination, the Certificate of Secondary Education (CSE) for those in the 40 per cent ability band below GCE entry standard. Lay Secretary, Archbishop of Canterbury, 1959–69.

Bentham, Jeremy (1748–1832). Writer on law and ethics. Born in London, son of an attorney and uncle of the botanist George Bentham who acted as his secretary, 1826–32. Educated West-minster School and Queen's College, Oxford. Studied law at Lincoln's Inn, London, called to the bar in 1772 but never practised. In *A Fragment on Government* (1776) Bentham argued that laws and institutions, including educational institutions, should be sub-jected to the test of utility and should promote 'the greatest happi-ness of the greatest number'. In 1808 he met **James Mill** and the radical Benthamite group was formed. Bentham was a founder of the *Westminster Review* and of University College, London, where his fully-clothed and mummified body and papers are kept. See his *Chrestomathia* (1815); *Church of Englandism* (1818); various editions of his collected works, the first by Bowring, J., (1838–43); the most recent under the editorship of Burns, J.H. (1968–83), and Everett, C.W., *Jeremy Bentham* (1966); Harrison, R., *Bentham* (1983).

Bergman-Österberg, Martina Sofia Helena (1849–1915). Educationist. Born in Skäne, Sweden, daughter of a farmer. Nothing is known about her education, but she became a governess, 1870, and a librarian, 1874–7. Entered Royal Central Gymnastic Institute, Stockholm, 1879, and pursued a two-year course in pedagogical and medical gymnastics. Trained in the Swedish System of Gymnastics, an approach devised by Per Henrik Ling (1776–1839) which was concerned with the 'harmonious development of the body', taking into account individual differences. On graduating in 1881, she was appointed by the London School Board as Lady Superintendent of Physical Exercises in Girls' and Infants' schools. Miss Bergman organized courses for teachers involving Swedish gymnastics, theory of movement, anatomy and physiology. The Swedish system was thus introduced into London girls' schools and her displays were attended by royalty and leading educationists. On her marriage to Per Österberg in 1886, she became known as Madame Österberg. An enthusiastic feminist, she gave evidence before the Cross Commission on Elementary Education in 1887 on the training of teachers of gymnastics. In the previous year, she opened her own teacher-training establishment in Hampstead as well as introducing her work to students at Whitelands, Maria Grey and Cambridge training colleges. After leaving the London School Board post in 1888, Madame Österberg devoted her energies to expanding the Hampstead College. The success of the enterprise led to the need for larger premises: these were secured at Dartford, Kent and the new building was ready in Sept. 1895. As the reputation of the College increased teacher-training establishments were keen to appoint Dartford students to their staffs. In 1908, the British Army officially adopted the Swedish system in its *Manual of Physical Training*. Shortly before her death in 1915, the Kingsfield Physical Training College, Dartford, was accepted by the Board of Education for the nation. See May, J., *Madame Bergman-Österberg Pioneer of Physical Education for Girls and Women* (1969); Fletcher, S., *Women First: The Female Tradition in English Physical Education, 1880–1980* (1984).

Beveridge, William Henry, 1st Baron of Tuggal (1879–1963). Academic, civil servant and social reformer. Born Rangpur, Bengal, son of an Indian civil servant. Educated Charterhouse and Balliol College, Oxford, gaining a first in classical moderations and *literae humaniores*, 1897–1902. BCL, 1902. Stowell Civil Law Fellow, University College, Oxford, 1902–9. Sub-Warden, Toynbee Hall, 1903–9, qualifying as a barrister, Inner Temple, 1904. Leader writer for *Morning Post* on social questions, 1906–8. Assistant Secretary, Board of Trade, Labour Exchanges and Unemployment Insurance, 1909–14. Assistant Secretary, Ministry of Munitions, 1915–16. Second Secretary, Ministry of Food, 1916–18, launching national rationing scheme in 1918, Permanent Secretary, 1919. Director, London School of Economics, 1919–37, successfully building up its international reputation. Master, University College, Oxford, 1937–45. Liberal MP, Berwick-upon-Tweed, 1944–5. Chairman, Interdepartmental Committee on Social Insurance and Allied Services, 1941–2. This resulted in the famous Beveridge Report published December 1942 on social security which dealt with the fundamentals of social policy and started the debate on the Welfare State. A Government White Paper in 1944 accepted many of the Report's recommendations. Knight, 1919, Baron, 1946. Many publications, including *Unemployment. A Problem of Industry* (1909, revised 1930); *Full Employment in a Free Society* (1944); *Voluntary Action* (1948); *A Defence of Free Learning* (1959) and an autobiography, *Power and Influence* (1953), and Beveridge, J., *Beveridge and his Plan* (1954); Harris, J., *William Beveridge* (1977).

Birkbeck, George (1776–1841). Founder of Mechanics' Institutes. Born at Settle, Yorkshire, studied medicine in London and Edinburgh where in 1799 he took the degree of MD. In the same year appointed professor of Natural Philosophy at Anderson's College, Glasgow. In 1800 he began a course of lectures on Saturday evenings on Science which soon attracted an audience of 500 working men. In 1823 this mechanics' class became the Glasgow Mechanics' Institute. In 1804 Birkbeck had moved to London where he practised as a physician, and in 1824 took the leading part in forming the London Mechanics' Institute and became its first president. As Birkbeck College it is now part of the University of London. A founder and member of the first council of University College, London and prominent in campaigns to repeal newspaper taxes and reform patent laws. See Godard, J., *George Birkbeck, the Pioneer of*

Birley

Popular Education (1884); Burns, C.D., *A Short History of Birkbeck College* (1924); Kelly, T., *George Birkbeck* (1957).

Birley, Sir Robert (1903–82). Schoolmaster and academic. Born Midnapore, India, son of Chief Secretary, Government of Bengal. Educated at Rugby, 1917–22 and Balliol College, Oxford, 1922–5, obtaining a first in history. Assistant master, Eton, 1926–35 and headmaster, Charterhouse, 1935–47, where he introduced a number of enlightened reforms. Member, Fleming Committee on Public Schools, 1942–4, and an active participant in the small drafting committee. Educational adviser to the Military Governor of the British Zone, Germany, 1947–9. Headmaster, Eton, 1949–62; Birley set about modernizing the curriculum whilst encouraging scholarship. Visiting professor of Education, Witwatersrand University, South Africa, 1964–7, where he identified himself with the liberal white community opposed to apartheid. Knight, 1967. Professor of Social Sciences and Humanities, City University, 1969–70; Visiting professor, 1970–1. See his *The School, Society and the Delinquent* (1951); *Sunk Without Trace* (1962), and Teague, S. John, *The City University: A History* (1980); Hearnden, A., *Red Robert: A Life of Robert Birley* (1984).

Birrell, Augustine (1850–1933). Statesman and author. Born Wavertree, Liverpool where his father was a Baptist minister. Educated at Amersham Hall School, near Reading and Trinity Hall, Cambridge, graduating 1872. Called to the bar, Inner Temple, 1875, QC, 1895, Bencher, 1903. Quain Professor of Law, University College, London, 1896–9. Liberal MP, West Fife, 1889–1900 and North Bristol, 1906–18. In Campbell-Bannerman's Liberal administration, Birrell became President of the Board of Education. He was in charge of the 1906 Education Bill, which was designed to redress the religious grievances of Nonconformists caused by the 1902 Education Act. After a long battle in the Commons, the Bill received a third reading but was turned down by a large majority in the Lords. After only 13 months in office, Birrell became Chief Secretary for Ireland, serving from 1907 to 1916, though without Cabinet rank. His literary reputation rested mainly on two volumes of essays entitled *Obiter Dicta*, published in 1884 and 1887, though he continued to write after giving up politics, including an autobiography, *Things Past Redress*, which appeared posthumously in 1937.

26

Blackie, John Stuart (1809–95). Scholar and university reformer. Born Glasgow. Educated at Marischal College, Aberdeen, and at the Universities of Edinburgh, Göttingen and Berlin. In 1834 called to the Scottish bar and published a translation of *Faust*. Regius professor of Humanity at Marischal College, 1841–52. Professor of Greek at Edinburgh, 1852–82. Campaigned for a reformed secondary education, and for an entrance test for every university class. A keen advocate of Scottish national culture, Blackie secured the endowment of a chair of Celtic Studies at Edinburgh in 1882. An inveterate traveller, eccentric and entertaining lecturer and prolific writer in a variety of fields including philosophy, history, classics and the law. See his *University Reform* (1848); *Political Tracts* (1868); *On Self Culture* (1874), and Kennedy, H.A., *Professor Blackie* (1895); Stoddart, A.M., *John Stuart Blackie* (2 vols., 1895).

Blair, Sir Robert (1858–1935). Educational administrator. Born Wigtown, Scotland, son of a cobbler, eldest of ten children. Educated at Wigtown Free Kirk School, Garlieston Endowed School where he became pupil teacher in 1873, and Edinburgh University, 1876–80, graduating with MA. Assistant master, Kelso High School, 1880–1, and then at Haberdashers' Aske's School, Hatcham, South London, 1881–93, where he also undertook part-time study for a London University B.Sc. degree in science. Headmaster, School of Science and Technical School, Cheltenham, 1893–4, inspector, North Scotland, for Science and Art Department, 1894–8, and then for the Scottish Education Department, 1898–1900; inspector, Science and Art, Ireland, 1900–1 and Assistant Secretary for Technical Instruction, Ireland, 1901–4. Blair became Education Officer for the London County Council in June 1904 responsible for the entire education service, a post which he held until his retirement in 1924. One of his many important tasks was to fuse the work of the London School Board and the Technical Education Board and also to develop the notion of a partnership between the local authorities, the Board of Education and the teachers. One of Blair's lasting achievements was the reorganization of evening work in 1913 which resulted in raising the status of technical education. After the 1918 Education Act he saw the day continuation school as the best way of improving the lot of the less able child, but the scheme was abandoned later because of opposition in 1922. As the head of the largest education service in the United Kingdom, Blair set an example in administration and policy-making for other authorities to emulate. Knight, 1914. See Thoms,

27

Blake

D.W., *Policy Making in Education: Robert Blair and the London County Council 1904–1924* (1980).

Blake, William (1757–1827). Poet, painter, engraver and mystic. Born in London, son of a hosier. Apprenticed to an engraver. In addition to his major paintings, for example *Jacob's Dream* and *The Last Judgement*, Blake illustrated many of his own writings, whilst the *21 illustrations to the book of Job* (1826) represented a unique religious visionary power. Blake's poems included *Songs of Innocence* (1789) which celebrated the joys of children, particularly in natural surroundings. In contrast the *Songs of Experience* (1794) denounced those forces in society (particularly urban society) which denied the true natures of children and adults. Thus the child is the central subject of all bar one of the poems of the *Innocence* collection, but of only half of those in *Experience*. Blake distrusted formal schooling, however, once stating: 'There is no use in education. Thank God I was never sent to school.' See Coveney, P., *The Image of Childhood* (1957); Bentley, G.E. (ed.), *William Blake's writings* (2 vols., 1978); Lindsay, J., *William Blake: his life and work* (1978).

Bodichon, Barbara (1827–91). Campaigner for women's rights. Born at Watlington, Sussex, daughter of Benjamin Leigh Smith, MP for Norwich. Educated at Westminster Infants' School, and Bedford College, London, where she concentrated on art and became a skilled water colour painter who subsequently contributed regularly to the Society of Female Artists. On coming of age was presented by her father with an annual income of £300. Married Dr Eugene Bodichon in 1857. Bodichon was a tireless advocate of women's rights in such areas as employment, married women's property and the suffrage. In 1858 helped to found and finance *The Englishwoman's Journal* which became the major voice of nineteenth-century feminism. In 1852 established the non-denominational, coeducational Portman Hall School in Paddington, London, which she ran for ten years with her friend Elizabeth Whitehead. Helped **Emily Davies** to found and endow Girton College, Cambridge where some of her paintings may be seen. See her *A Brief Summary in Plain Language of the Most Important Laws concerning Women* (1854); *Women and Work* (1857), and Burton, H., *Barbara Bodichon, 1827–91* (1949); Herstein, S.R., *A Mid-Victorian Feminist, Barbara Leigh Smith Bodichon* (1986).

Bosanquet, Bernard (1848–1923). Philosopher. Educated Harrow and Balliol College, Oxford, 1867–70, gaining first class in classical moderations and *literae humaniores*. Fellow, lecturer and tutor, University College, Oxford, 1871–81. On the death of his father in 1880, came into possession of an independent income which enabled him to follow his interests. An idealist philosopher with great interest in social problems. Chairman, Administration Committee, Charity Organisation Society, President, London Ethical Society, 1880–97 and of Aristotelian Society. Professor, Moral Philosophy, St Andrews, 1903–8. See his *Knowledge and Reality* (1885); *Logic* (2 vols., 1888); *History of Aesthetic* (1892); *The Education of the Young in 'The Republic' of Plato* (1902), and Bosanquet, H., *Memoirs* (1924); Bradley, A.C., 'Bernard Bosanquet', *Proceedings of the British Academy*, 11, 1924.

Bowen, Edward Ernest (1836–1901). Schoolteacher. Born Co. Wicklow, Ireland, a vicar's son. Educated at a private school in Blackheath, King's College, London, 1852–4 and Trinity College, Cambridge, 1854–8, classical tripos, fellow, 1859. Assistant master at Marlborough for one term 1859 and then to Harrow, where he remained for 42 years. Contributed to **F.W. Farrar**'s *Essays on a Liberal Education* (1867), criticizing the method then in vogue of teaching Greek and Latin grammar. In 1869, Bowen became master of the modern side at Harrow 'teaching no Greek, but lots of history, modern languages, science etc.'. An early and enthusiastic advocate of this approach, he claimed that, as compared with the classical side, it overcame 'the traditional repugnance of the school boy to sit down to his lesson'. Bowen resigned the mastership in 1892 on the principle 'that the Modern Side was not a harbour of refuge for less able and satisfactory pupils'. He is best remembered as the author of a series of verses for school songs, the first volume of which appeared in 1869, idealizing Harrow. Bowen's most famous words were those for 'Forty Years On' published in 1872. He stood as Liberal candidate in the 1880 general election at Hertford against **A.J. Balfour** but was beaten: became a Liberal Unionist in 1886. Bowen gave evidence to the Bryce Commission in 1894 on the supervision of secondary schools by an external authority and on the topic of the training of teachers. See Bowen, W.E., *Edward Bowen. A Memoir* (1902).

Boyle, Sir Edward Charles Gurney, Lord Boyle of Handsworth (1923–81). Politician. Educated at Eton and Christ Church,

Oxford. President of the Union, 1948. Conservative MP for Handsworth, Birmingham, 1950–70, when he moved to the Lords. Held junior government posts at Supply and the Treasury, 1954–6, but he resigned over Suez. Parliamentary Secretary to the Ministry of Education, 1957–9, Financial Secretary to the Treasury, 1959–62, Minister of Education, 1962–4, Minister of State, Department of Education and Science, 1964. Responsible for the establishment of the Schools Council. Boyle did not oppose the move towards comprehensive secondary schooling, and this led to several attacks from the Conservative rank and file. Pro-Chancellor of Sussex University, 1965–70. In 1970 he left the political arena to become Vice-Chancellor of Leeds University. Chairman from 1971 of the Top Salaries Review Body. See his *The Politics of Education* (with Crosland and Kogan) (1971); 'The politics of secondary school reorganization: some reflections', *Journal of Educational Administration and History*, 4 (2), 1972.

Bradley, George Granville (1821–1903). Cleric and schoolmaster. Born High Wycombe, half brother of the idealist philosopher Francis Herbert Bradley, and father of the poet and novelist Margaret Louisa Woods. Educated at Rugby School and University College, Oxford. In 1844 achieved a first class in classics and elected fellow of his college. Master at Rugby, 1845–58, headmaster of Marlborough, 1858–70, where he enlarged the buildings, increased the numbers of pupils, restored the finances and established the school's academic standing. Bradley himself did much of the sixth form teaching and Marlborough won more scholarships to Oxford than any other school at this time. Between 1870 and 1881 as master of University College, Oxford, Bradley effected similar reforms. All commoners were required to read for an honours school. In 1880 appointed a member of the Oxford University Commission, and canon of Worcester. Dean of Westminster, 1881–1902. Bradley was a close friend of Tennyson, and of **A.P. Stanley** whom he succeeded as Dean of Westminster. He published several sermons and schoolbooks including the widely-used *Latin Prose Composition* (1881). See also How, F.D., *Six Great Schoolmasters* (1904).

Brereton, Joseph Lloyd (1822–1901). Educational reformer. Born King's Lynn, Norfolk. Educated at an Islington proprietary school, Rugby and University College, Oxford. Graduated BA, 1846, MA, 1857. Curate in Norwich and London, rector of West Buckland, North Devon, 1852–67, and of Little Massingham, Norfolk in succession to his father, 1867–1901. Seriously injured in 1882 in a railway accident. Brereton advocated national education organized on a county basis, with particular reference to the needs of the agricultural and middle classes. He founded 'county' schools at West Buckland, Devon in 1858 and at Little Massingham, Norfolk in 1871. In 1873 a 'county' college was founded at Cambridge, named Cavendish College after the Chancellor the **7th Duke of Devonshire**. Financial difficulties led to its closure in 1892, though the buildings were subsequently used by Homerton College for women teachers. In 1881 Brereton formed the Graduated County Schools Association with the aim of establishing self-supporting schools and colleges for girls and women. See his *County Education: a Contribution of Experiments, Estimates and Suggestions* (1874), and Searby, P., 'Joseph Lloyd Brereton and the Education of the Victorian Middle Class', *Journal of Educational Administration and History*, 11 (1), 1979.

Brockington, Sir William Allport (1871–1959). Educational administrator. Born Birmingham and educated at King Edward's Grammar School, Aston and Mason University College, Birmingham, gaining an external BA first class honours in English, 1890. MA in Modern Languages, London University, 1893. He was a lecturer in English language and literature, Mason University College, Birmingham, 1893–8, then Principal, Victoria Institute, Worcester, 1898–1903. Director of Education, Leicestershire, 1903–47, creating an efficient and cohesive system of education in the county. His personal interest in schools extended, before the First World War, to carrying out the inspection of the 266 public elementary schools. Member, Consultative Committee Board of Education, 1903–47. Knight, 1946. Author of *Elements of Prose Language* (1899); *Elements of Military Education* (1916); *A Secondary School Entrance Test* (1934), and Seaborne, M., 'William Brockington, Director of Education for Leicestershire 1903–1947', in Simon, B. (ed.), *Education in Leicestershire 1540–1940* (1968).

Brookfield, William Henry (1809–74), School inspector. Educated Leeds Grammar School and Trinity College, Cambridge, 1830–3. Ordained priest, 1836 and curate in Southampton and London, 1836–48. HMI, 1848–65. Well known for his humorous yet biting reports on schools. Married to niece of Henry Hallam, the historian, and friend of, amongst others, Carlyle, Millais and Thackeray.

31

Brougham

Rector, Somerby, Lincolnshire, 1865–74. Prebendary, St Paul's, 1868–74. See Brookfield, J.C. (ed.), *Sermons* (1875) with biographical note by Lord Lyttelton, and Brookfield, C. and F., *Mrs. Brookfield and Her Circle* (2 vols., 1905).

Brougham, Henry, 1st Baron Brougham and Vaux (1778–1868). Legal reformer and political orator. Born Edinburgh, educated  there at the High School and University. Admitted to the Scottish and English bar. Co-founder and major contributor to the *Edinburgh Review*. First entered Parliament 1810. Between 1816 and 1818 brought the cause of popular education before Parliament by means of Select Committees. Secured important legal reforms particularly in libel and evidence. Defended Queen Caroline in 1820. Promoter of infant schools, mechanics' institutes, the Society for the Diffusion of Useful Knowledge and London University. Lord Chancellor 1830–4, and assisted passage of the Reform Bill. Self-confident, eccentric and prone to excessive invective, he was a difficult colleague and never again held office. Probably the real father of the Education grant of 1833, but his Education bills of 1820, 1835, 1837, 1838 and 1839 all failed. Founded the National Association for the Promotion of Social Science in 1857. Died at Cannes where he had lived for many years. See his posthumously published *Life and Times of Henry Brougham* (3 vols., 1871), and Aspinall, A., *Lord Brougham and the Whig Party* (1927); Hawes, F., *Henry Brougham* (1957); New, C., *Life of Lord Brougham to 1830* (1961); Stewart, R., *Henry Brougham 1778–1868: His Public Career* (1986).

Browning, Oscar (1837–1923). Historian and educationist. Born in London. Educated at Eton and King's College, Cambridge where he was President of the Union and placed fourth in the classical tripos, 1860. Fellow of King's College, 1859–1923. Master at Eton, 1860–75. Presented evidence to the Clarendon Commission.

32

Lecturer in History at King's from 1880 and university lecturer from 1883. A founder of the Cambridge University Day Training College for elementary teachers, and principal, 1891–1909. A bachelor, his wide-ranging interests included music, drama, swimming, hockey and cycling, he once crossed the Alps on a tricycle. His keen interest in pupils and students and his reforming energy and radicalism – he made three unsuccessful attempts to enter Parliament – made his life a controversial one. The last years were spent in Rome where he died. See his *History of Educational Theories* (1881); *Aspects of Education* (1888); *A History of the Modern World, 1815–1910* (2 vols., 1912), and Wortham, H.E., *Oscar Browning* (1927); Anstruther, I., *Oscar Browning: a biography* (1983).

Bruce *see* **Aberdare.**

Bruce, Hon. William Napier (1858–1936). Civil servant. Son of **1st Lord Aberdare**. Educated at Harrow, 1870–6, and Balliol College, Oxford, 1876–80. Barrister, 1883. Assistant Commissioner, Charity Commission, under Endowed Schools Acts, 1886–1900. Secretary, Royal Commission on Education, 1894–5. Assistant Secretary, Board of Education, 1900–3. Principal Assistant Secretary, Secondary Schools Branch, 1903, Second Secretary, 1919. Member, Royal Commission on University Education, Wales, 1916–18. Chairman, Departmental Committee on the organization of secondary education in Wales, 1919–20. CB, 1905. Author of *Life of General Sir Charles Napier* (1885); and edited *Autobiography and letters of Sir A.H. Layard* (1903).

Bryant, Sophie (1850–1922). Educationist and campaigner for women's rights. Born Dublin, and educated principally by her father, a clergyman, mathematician and campaigner for national education. In 1866 won an Arnott scholarship to Bedford College, London. Married Dr William Bryant, a physician, 1869, but widowed, 1870. Resumed studies, taught at Highgate, teacher of mathematics and German at the North London Collegiate School from 1875. BA in mental and moral science and mathematics, 1881, first woman D.Sc., in physiology, logic and ethics, 1884. Succeeded **Frances Buss** as headmistress of North London Collegiate School, 1895–1918. Appointed to Bryce Commission on Secondary Education, 1894; member of Consultative Committee of the Board of Education, 1900–11; president of the Association of Headmistresses, 1903–5; member of the Senate of the University of

London, 1900–7; and of the London Education Committee, 1908–14. Also prominent in the causes of Irish home rule and women's suffrage. Her several writings recognized by an honorary D.Litt. from Dublin University, 1904. An enthusiastic mountaineer, she died climbing Mont Blanc. See her *Short Studies in Character* (1894); *Moral and Religious Education* (1920), and Scrimgeour, R.M. (ed.), *The North London Collegiate School 1850–1950* (1950).

Bryce, James, Viscount (1838–1922). Historian and politician. Born Belfast, son of a schoolmaster. Moved to Glasgow and

attended the High School, 1846–54, and Glasgow University, 1854–7, studying Greek and Latin. Entered Trinity College, Oxford, 1857, first class honours in *literae humaniores*, BA, 1862. Bryce was a member of the Old Mortality Society, a discussion club, which included **T.H. Green**, Algernon Swinburne, **Edward Caird** and **A.V. Dicey**. Fellow, Oriel College, Oxford, 1862. DCL, 1870. Entered Lincoln's Inn, 1862 and barrister, 1867. Between these dates, Bryce studied law at Heidelberg, and in 1865–6 was an Assistant Commissioner for the Schools Inquiry Commission, making reports on schools in Lancashire, Shropshire, Worcestershire, Monmouthshire and eight Welsh counties. In his reports, Bryce urged that a comprehensive scheme of education should be formulated, by which elementary and secondary schools and universities should be co-ordinated. An advocate of women's education, Bryce was a friend of **Emily Davies**. Lecturer in law, Owens College, Manchester, 1868 and then professor of Law until 1874. Regius professor of Civil Law, Oxford University, 1870–93, during which time he revived the study of Roman law. Elected Liberal MP, Tower Hamlets, 1880–5, South Aberdeen, 1885–1906. Chancellor of Duchy of Lancaster, 1892–4 and President of the Board of Trade, 1894–5. In this latter post, Bryce became chairman of the Royal Commission on Secondary Education, whose report in 1895 bears his name. It recommended three major reforms: the establishment of a central authority for secondary education: the extension to local authorities of responsibility for secondary as well as elementary education; and the provision of scholarships for elementary school pupils. The report also noted the meagre supply of secondary school places for girls. Chief Secretary, Ireland, 1905–7, ambassador to Washington, 1907–13, Viscount, 1914. See his *Studies in Contemporary Biography* (1903); *Modern Democracies* (1921), and Fisher, H.A.L., *James Bryce* (2 vols., 1927).

Buchanan, James (1784–1857). Teacher. Born in Edinburgh, worked as a weaver, served as a Primitive Methodist lay preacher, and in the militia. In 1814 moved to New Lanark where he was chosen by **Robert Owen** to help conduct the infant school. In 1819 Buchanan became master of a new infant school in Westminster sponsored by, among others, **Henry Brougham** and **Lord Lansdowne**. Buchanan taught at this school, which moved from Brewer's Green to Vincent Square, for some 20 years. In 1839 he set sail for New Zealand, intending to start infant schools there, but stopped and settled instead at Cape Town and died at Pietermaritzburg. Buchanan was much criticized by Owen, and was probably not a good manager, but his delight in young children, music, movement, rhymes, pictures and objects reflected the basic spirit of the progressive infant school. See Buchanan, B.I., *Buchanan Family Records: James Buchanan and his Descendants* (1923); Rusk, R.R., *A History of Infant Education* (1933).

Burdett-Coutts, Angela Georgina, Baroness (1814-1906). Philanthropist. Born in London the daughter of Sir Francis Burdett, the popular Radical MP, and his wife Sophia Coutts of the great banking family. Educated by a succession of tutors and governesses including the Evangelical Hannah Meredith. In 1837 became the wealthiest woman in England upon the death of her step-grandmother. Mixed with crowned heads, the great political figures of her day, Peel, Disraeli, **Gladstone**, and the Duke of Wellington who rejected her proposal of marriage, and literary men including **Dickens**. In 1871 became the first woman to be raised to the peerage in her own right, and in the following year received the freedom of the City of London. In 1881 married William Ashmead Bartlett, some 40 years her junior, who assumed her name. Her charity was dispensed to a vast range of concerns; Anglican churches, housing schemes, food markets, animal welfare, colonial bishoprics and exploration. Children and education benefited in several ways.

Generous support was given to the Ragged School Union. In her father's former constituency she built the church of St Stephen's, Westminster, to which schools were added in 1849, and established the Westminster Technical Institute in 1893. She supported the introduction of sewing and cooking into elementary schools, and endowed two geological scholarships at Oxford University. In 1874 she subsidized training ships for poor boys and helped to found the National Society for the Prevention of Cruelty to Children in 1883. See her *Woman's Mission* (1893), and Healey, E., *Lady Unknown: The Life of Angela Burdett-Coutts* (1978); Orton, D., *Made of Gold: A Biography of Angela Burdett-Coutts* (1980).

Burgess, Richard (1796–1881). Scholar and cleric. Educated at St John's College, Cambridge, ordained a priest in 1823. Rector of Upper Chelsea, 1836–69, and of Horningsheath, Suffolk, 1869–81. Prebend of St Paul's Cathedral, 1851–81. Wide-ranging interests. Honorary member of the Royal Institute of British Architects, lectured at their early meetings in Covent Garden and Grosvenor Street, London. Corresponding member of the Pontifical Archaeological Academy at Rome. His writings included works on Roman archaeology, Greece and the Levant, Greek Christianity, and collections of sermons and lectures. Secretary for eight years of the London Diocesan Board of Education. Wrote educational pamphlets and public letters to prominent politicians and churchmen. See his *Educational Statistics* (1838); *Metropolis Schools for the Poor* (1846); *National Schools and National School Teachers* (1848), and Aldrich, R., 'National Education, by Rates or Taxes . . .', *Journal of Educational Administration and History*, 12 (1), 1980.

Burnham, Harry Lawson Webster, 1st Viscount (1862–1933). Politician and newspaper proprietor. Born in London, elder son of 1st Baron Burnham. Educated at Eton and Balliol College, Oxford, 1881–4. Awarded first class in modern history. Barrister, Inner Temple, 1889. Represented St Pancras, 1889–92, Whitechapel, 1897–1904 on the London County Council. Mayor of Stepney, 1907. Liberal MP, St Pancras West, 1885–92, Cirencester division of Gloucestershire, 1893–5, Tower Hamlets, London, 1905–6 and 1910–16, when he succeeded his father as Baron Burnham. Managing proprietor, *Daily Telegraph*, 1902–28. Companion of Honour, 1917. Created Viscount Burnham, 1919. Much sought after as an excellent chairman of public committees. Member,

Royal Comission on Civil Establishments (1889–94), the Speaker's conference on electoral reform (1916) and joint conference on the reform of the House of Lords under **Lord Bryce** (1918). However, he is best remembered for his work as chairman of the Standing Joint Committee, consisting of teachers and local education authority representatives, set up in 1919 to formulate new pay scales for teachers in State schools. Burnham acted as arbitrator in disputes between the two sides and was responsible for the establishment of the Burnham scales which henceforth formed the basis for teachers' salaries.

Burt, Sir Cyril Lodowic (1883–1976). Psychologist. Born London, son of a doctor. Educated at London elementary school, King's School, Warwick, 1892–5, Christ's Hospital, 1895–1902, and Jesus College, Oxford, 1902, obtaining second class honours in classical moderations and *literae humaniores*. Teachers' Diploma, Oxford University, 1907–8. Lecturer, experimental psychology and assistant lecturer in physiology, Liverpool University, 1908–13 and assistant lecturer, Psychological Laboratory, Cambridge University, 1912–13. Focused on problem of finding suitable tests for assessing intelligence in the study of mental differences. As a follower of **Galton**, Burt was also interested in the question of inheritance and concluded that individual mental capacities are inherited. He was appointed as the first psychologist (part-time) to the London County Council in 1913, holding that post until 1932, dealing with testing of subnormal and delinquent elementary school children. His publications from this time included *The Distribution and Relations of Educational Abilities* (1915), *Mental and Scholastic Tests* (1921), *The Young Delinquent* (1925), and *The Measurement of Mental Capacities* (1927). In 1927, Burt was appointed director of the first child guidance clinic in London. Part-time professor of Education, London Day Training College, 1924–32; professor of Psychology, University College, London, 1931–50. Knight, 1946. Burt provided chapters for the Hadow Report on the Primary School (1931) and for the Report on the Infant and Nursery School (1933) relating to mental development, and the Spens Report on Secondary Education (1938) contains an appendix on faculty psychology and the curriculum. Other works during this period include *The Backward Child* (1937), *The Causes and Treatment of Backwardness* (1952) and *The Gifted Child* (1975) which was posthumously published. Burt's views on intelligence, that IQ remains constant, have been challenged. In 1972 L.J. Kamin in his book *The Science and Politics of IQ* questioned the validity of Burt's studies of monozygotic twins and Professor L.S. Hearnshaw, Burt's biographer, has shown that from 1943, Burt's research reports must be regarded as suspect, with faked evidence having come to light. However, Hearnshaw states that Burt's individual psychology 'represents an important phase in the development of the subject, incorporates many advances in techniques and contains many elements of value'. See Hearnshaw, L.S., *Cyril Burt, Psychologist* (1979).

Buss, Frances Mary (1827–94). Pioneer of education for girls and women. Born Mornington Crescent, London, educated in small private schools. Started teaching at 14 and four years later opened her first school in Kentish Town. Met Revd David Laing and attended evening classes at Queen's College, London. In 1850 with the support of her family, and herself as headmistress, opened the North London Collegiate School for Ladies in Camden Town. In 1870 this became a public school and the model for the Girls' Public Day School Company. Inexpensive secondary education was provided without distinction as to class or creed, although daughters of the middle classes predominated. In 1865 Buss gave evidence to the Taunton Commission. She was president of the Association of Head Mistresses, 1874–94, a member of the Councils of the College of Preceptors, Maria Grey and Hughes Hall Training Colleges, and governor of University College, London, and of the London School of Medicine. See *Leaves from the Note-Books of Frances Mary Buss* (1896), and Ridley, A., *Frances Mary Buss* (1895); Burstall, S., *Frances Mary Buss* (1938); Kamm, J., *How Different From Us* (1958).

Butler, George (1819–90). Scholar and teacher. Born Harrow, eldest son of George Butler the headmaster of Harrow School, 1805–29, and brother of **Henry** who was headmaster, 1859–85. Educated at Harrow and Trinity College, Cambridge but transferred to Exeter College, Oxford and graduated BA with a first class in classics, 1845. MA, 1846. Winner of the Hertford scholarship, and Petrean fellow, 1842–52. Tutor at Durham University, 1849–51. In 1852 he married **Josephine** and subsequently supported her campaign for the abolition of the state regulation of prostitutes. Ordained priest in 1855. Butler was curate of St Giles, Oxford from 1854, and principal of Butler's Hall, a private college at Oxford, 1855–8. He acted as a public examiner for the University, and also for entrants to the War Office, and to the East India Company's civil service. Vice-principal of Cheltenham College, 1857–65 and principal of Liverpool College, 1866–82. Canon of Winchester, 1882 until his death. In 1882 the University of Durham awarded him the honorary degree of DD. See his *Principles of Imitative Art* (1852); *Sermons preached in Cheltenham College* (1862); *The Higher Education of Women* (1867); *The Public Schools Atlas of Modern Geography* (1872); *The Public Schools Atlas of Ancient Geography* (1877), and Butler, J.E., *Recollections of George Butler* (1892).

Butler, Revd Henry Montagu (1833–1918). Scholar and head-master. Born Gayton, Northamptonshire, fourth son of Dr George Butler, headmaster, Harrow. Educated at Harrow, 1846–51 and Trinity College, Cambridge, 1851–5, classical tripos and mathematics. Fellow of his college, 1855. Ordained as curate, St Mary's, Cambridge, 1858, but was appointed the following year to succeed **C.J. Vaughan** as headmaster at Harrow at the age of 26. During his long reign – he remained at the school until 1885 – Butler made a number of reforms in the curriculum. Butler recognized the 'modern' needs of society: as brother-in-law of **Galton**, he took an interest in science, introducing it into the school in 1866. Three years later, a 'modern' side was formed to complement the 'classical' side. In 1885, Butler left Harrow to take up the post of Dean of Gloucester. In the following year, he accepted the mastership of Trinity College, Cambridge, remaining there for the rest of his life. Vice-Chancellor, Cambridge University, 1899–1900. See his *Sermons Preached in the Chapel of Harrow School* (1861); *University and other Sermons, Historical and Biographical* (1899); *Some Leisure Hours of a Long Life* (1914), and Graham, E., *The Harrow Life of Henry Montagu Butler* (1920); Butler, J.R.M., *Henry Montagu Butler, Master of Trinity* (1925).

Butler, Josephine Elizabeth (1828–1906). Social reformer. Born Milfield on the Cheviot hills, a daughter of the agriculturalist, political reformer and Whig agent John Grey of Dilston. Received some schooling in Newcastle upon Tyne but mainly influenced by the political and religious climate of her parental home. Married **George Butler**, teacher, author of ecclesiastical works and canon of Winchester. President of the North of England Council for Promoting Higher Education of Women, 1867–70. Supported the causes of married women's property and female suffrage. Her main achievement was in mobilizing public and political opinion against the Contagious Diseases Acts of 1864, 1866 and 1869 which required the compulsory registration, medical inspection and licensing of prostitutes in designated garrison and dockyard towns. Finally repealed in 1886. Skilled parliamentary lobbyist. See her *Women's Work and Women's Culture* (1869); *Personal Reminiscences of a Great Crusade* (1896), and Johnson, G.W. and L.A., *Josephine Butler, an Autobiographical Memoir* (1909); Butler, A.S.G., *Portrait of Josephine Butler* (1954); Petrie, G., *A Singular Iniquity: The Campaigns of Josephine Butler* (1971).

Butler, Richard Austen (1902–82). Conservative politician. Born at Attock Serai, India, son of an administrator. Educated at Marlborough College and Pembroke College, Cambridge, President of the Union, double first class in history and modern languages, 1925; fellow of Corpus Christi College, 1925–9. MP Saffron Walden, Essex, 1929–65. Junior ministerial appointments at the India Office, Ministry of Labour and Foreign Office, 1932–41. President of the Board of Education and Minister of Education, 1941–45. Responsible for the Education Act of 1944, usually referred to as the Butler Act, which provided secondary schooling for all and eased the financial problems of the voluntary bodies. Minister of Labour, 1945; Chancellor of the Exchequer, 1951–5; Lord Privy Seal, 1955–9; Leader of the House of Commons, 1955–61; Home Secretary, 1957–62; Deputy Prime Minister, 1962–3; Foreign Secretary, 1963–4. Master of Trinity College, Cambridge, 1965, and in the same year made a life peer as Baron Butler of Saffron Walden. President of the Modern Languages Association, 1972. Holder of 13 honorary degrees, Rector of Glasgow University and Chancellor of the Universities of Sheffield and Essex. In 1957 and 1963 Butler was expected to become Prime Minister but lost out to Macmillan and Douglas-Home. See his *The Art of the Possible* (1971); *The Art of Memory* (1982), and Boyd, F., *R.A. Butler* (1956); Cosgrave, P., *R.A. Butler: An English Life* (1981); Howard, A., *RAB: The Life of R.A. Butler* (1987).

Butler, Samuel (1774–1839). Headmaster. Born Kenilworth. Educated at Rugby and St John's College, Cambridge. A brilliant scholar. Winner of three Browne's medals, two Chancellor's medals and the Craven scholarship. BA, 1796, senior optime in the mathematical tripos. Fellow of St John's, 1797; DD, 1811. In 1798

Butler became headmaster at Shrewsbury School, an appointment he held until 1836 when he was succeeded by **Benjamin Hall Kennedy**, one of his former pupils. Butler was both a leading scholar and an able organizer. His reform of classical teaching lessened the old grammar grind, and this was combined with a system of regular examinations and promotion by merit. The success of these reforms was shown when Kennedy won the Porson prize whilst still a pupil at the school. Butler also held a number of clerical appointments, vicar at Kenilworth from 1802, and archdeacon of Derby from 1821. In 1836 on leaving Shrewsbury he became Bishop of Lichfield and Coventry. Butler's writings included an edition of Aeschylus (4 vols., 1809–16); *A Sketch of Modern and Ancient Geography* (1813); *Thoughts on the Present System of Academic Education in the University of Cambridge* (1822), atlases and published sermons. See Butler, S., *The Life and Letters of Dr. Samuel Butler* (1896); Heitland, W., *Dr. Butler of Shrewsbury School* (1897); Colman, D.S., *Sabrinae corolla: the classics at Shrewsbury under Dr. Butler* (1950).

Caird, Edward (1835–1908). Philosopher. Born Greenock, Scotland, son of a shipbuilder and younger brother of **John Caird**. Educated Greenock Academy, Glasgow and St Andrews Universities, 1851–7, Balliol College, Oxford, first class in classical moderations, 1862 and first class in *literae humaniores*, 1863. Elected to the Old Mortality Society, an intellectually powerful group, whilst still an undergraduate. Among its members was **T.H. Green**; both Caird and Green were early disciples of Hegel, and radical in politics. Fellow and tutor, Merton College, Oxford, 1864–6. Professor of Moral Philosophy, Glasgow University, 1866–93. Caird and his brother John offered lecture courses there for women and attempted to persuade Senate in 1877 to admit them to the University. This was not achieved until 1892. Caird also supported the establishment at Oxford of Ruskin College for working people and the university settlement at Toynbee Hall in London's East End. Master of Balliol, 1893–1907. Amongst his many publications, see *A Critical Account of the Philosophy of Kant* (1877); *The Social Philosophy and Religion of Comte* (1885); *Essays on Literature and Philosophy* (1892); *Evolution of Religion* (1893); *Lay Sermons delivered at Balliol Hall* (1907), and Jones, H. and Muirhead, J.H., *The Life and Philosophy of Edward Caird* (1921); Gordon, P. and White, J., *Philosophers as Educational Reformers* (1979).

Caird, John (1820–98). Theologian and academic. Born Greenock, Scotland. Educated at Greenock Academy. Worked in the family marine engineering firm from the age of 15 but studied at Glasgow University, 1840–5. On graduating MA in 1845 Caird was ordained into the Church of Scotland and held pastorships in Edinburgh and in country parishes. At Errol in Perthshire where he was minister, 1849–57, he established an industrial school for girls. In 1857 he moved to Glasgow where his reputation as one of Scotland's greatest preachers was confirmed. Chaplain in ordinary to the Queen in Scotland, 1858–86, and awarded a DD by Glasgow University in 1860. Professor of Divinity at Glasgow, 1862, and Principal and Vice-Chancellor of the University from 1873. During his principalship which he held for the rest of his life, Caird promoted the higher education of women, university extension, and the broadening of the curriculum, all of which developments contributed to a rapid expansion of the University. As a theologian he pioneered the teaching of comparative religious history, and sought to reconcile Christianity with contemporary idealist philosophy. See his *Religion in Common Life* (1855); *The Fundamental Ideas of Christianity* (1900).

Carlingford, Chichester Fortescue, 1st Baron (1823–98). Politician. Born County Louth, Ireland. Educated privately and Christ Church, Oxford, 1841–5, gaining a first in *literae humaniores* and a Studentship, 1843–56. Married Lady Waldegrave, 1863. Liberal MP, Co. Louth, 1847–74, when defeated and created Baron Carlingford. Twice Chief Secretary, Ireland, 1865–6 and 1868–70; President, Board of Trade, 1870–4; Lord Privy Seal, 1881–4; and Lord President of the Council, 1883–5. Member of Cabinet in **Gladstone's** 1868 and 1880 ministries. Carried out work at the Education Office efficiently, with **A.J. Mundella** as his Vice-President. See Cooke, A.B., and Vincent, J.R. (eds.), *Lord Carlingford's Journal. Reflections of a Cabinet Minister 1885* (1971).

Carlisle, Nicholas (1771–1847). Writer. Born York. A purser in the East India Company service who in 1807 became secretary to the Society of Antiquaries. Assistant librarian to the Royal Library from 1812. Created DCL, Oxford in 1835. Carlisle compiled topographical dictionaries of the four Kingdoms, wrote an account of the foreign orders of knighthood and histories of the families of Bland and Carlisle. His *A Concise Description of the Endowed Grammar Schools in England and Wales* (1818) was dedicated to Queen

Charlotte. He circulated more than 1,400 requests for information under 14 headings and the two volumes contain information about 475 schools. See this work and Carlisle, N., *Collections for a History of the Ancient Family of Carlisle* (1822).

Carnegie, Andrew (1835–1919). Manufacturer and philanthropist. Born in Dunfermline, Scotland. Educated at a Lancasterian school. In 1848 the family emigrated to the USA. Joined a Scottish colony in Allegheny, Pennsylvania. Worked as a messenger boy in a Pittsburgh telegraph office. Voracious reader and prolific letter writer. Joined the Pennsylvanian railroad and introduced Pullman sleeping cars. In 1865 left the railroad to concentrate on iron production. From 1873 switched to steel and became a multi-millionaire. In 1901 he gave up his industrial career to concentrate upon disposing of his wealth. From 1887 he spent much of his time in Scotland, particularly at his favourite residence of Skibo Castle. Carnegie knew many British politicians, from **Gladstone** to Lloyd George and was friendly with such educationists as **Matthew Arnold** and **Herbert Spencer**. He gave $62 million to the British Empire including $10 million to the Scottish Universities Trust and $10 million to the United Kingdom Trust. Public libraries, education, both literary and technical, scientific research and the promotion of peace were among his favourite causes. Lord Rector of the Universities of Aberdeen and St Andrews. Declined a peerage as this would have meant surrendering his American citizenship. See his *Autobiography* (1920) edited by Van Dyke, J.C.; *A Manual of the Public Benefactions of Andrew Carnegie* (1919), and Hendrick, B.J., *The Life of Andrew Carnegie* (1932); Harlow, A.F., *Andrew Carnegie* (1963).

Carpenter, Mary (1807–1877). Educationist and penologist. Born in Exeter, eldest daughter of Lant Carpenter LL.D, Unitarian minister and educationist. Received a broad education including classics, mathematics and natural science. In 1829 kept a school at Bristol with her mother, and in 1835 founded a Working and Visiting Society in Bristol which she ran for 20 years. Opened the first ragged school in Bristol, 1846. Launched a reformatory school at Kingswood in 1852, and another at Park Row, Bristol in 1854 to which five years later a certified industrial school was also added. Played a major role in the Birmingham reformatory and school conferences of the 1850s. There and in papers to the National Association for the Promotion of Social Science she argued that children of the deserving poor merited aid and that juvenile offenders needed separate treatment from adults. Supporter of women's admission to university degrees. Between 1866 and 1876 paid four visits to India and one to Canada and the USA, to promote girls' education. See her *Reformatory Schools for the Children of the Perishing and Dangerous Classes, and for Juvenile Offenders* (1851, repr. Woburn 1969); *Juvenile Delinquents, their Condition and Treatment* (1853), and Carpenter, J.E., *The Life and Work of Mary Carpenter* (1879); Manton, J., *Mary Carpenter and the Children of the Streets* (1976); Selleck, R.J.W., 'Mary Carpenter: A confident and contradictory reformer', *History of Education*, 14 (2), 1985.

Cavendish, Lucy, Lady Frederick (1841–1926). Social reformer. Daughter of George William, **4th Baron Lyttelton,** himself a keen educationist and supporter of the Anglican Church. At the family home, Hagley Hall, Worcestershire, she received a cultured, intellectual and religious upbringing. As **Gladstone's** niece and the wife of the second son of the **7th Duke of Devonshire,** Lucy Cavendish had the highest political and social connections. After the murder of her husband by 'Irish Invincibles' in Phoenix Park, Dublin in 1882 she devoted her life to a variety of causes including peace in Ireland, the fate of Christian subjects under Turkish rule, and the education of girls and women. She was a very able public speaker. In 1894 her educational work received public recognition when she was appointed to the Bryce Commission on Secondary Education. Ten years later she received an honorary degree from the University of Leeds. In 1965 the Lucy Cavendish Hall for women graduate students was established at Cambridge University. See Bailey, J. (ed.), *The Diary of Lady Frederick Cavendish* (2 vols., 1927).

Cavendish, Spencer Compton, 8th Duke of Devonshire (1833–1908). Statesman. Born at Holker Hall, Lancashire. Son of **William Cavendish, 7th Duke.** Educated at home and Trinity College, Cambridge, 1851–4, mathematical tripos. Liberal MP, North Lancashire, 1857–68. On his father succeeding to the dukedom in 1858, became Marquess of Hartington. A Lord of the Admiralty, 1863, Under-Secretary, War, 1863–6, Secretary, War, 1866–7, Postmaster-General, 1868–71. Chief Secretary, Ireland, 1871–4. Secretary of State, India, 1880–2, Secretary of State, War, 1882–5. Liberal MP, Radnor district, 1869–80. Lancashire N.E., 1880–5. Rossendale division, Lancashire, 1885–91. Voted against Gladstone's home rule bill in May 1886 and joined the Liberal Unionists. Declined to be Prime Minister 1880, 1886 and 1887. In 1891 became 8th Duke, and played full part consequently in the Lords. 1895, Lord President of the Council and chairman, cabinet committee of defence. On Salisbury's retirement in 1902, Devonshire also became leader, House of Lords. Between 1895 and 1902, in charge of Education Department; during this time there was important legislation relating to education which came within his responsibilities, including the Voluntary Schools Act, 1897, the Board of Education Act, 1899 and the important Education Act, 1902. Resigned October 1902 on the question of tariff reform and the government's fiscal policy. Leader of the Opposition, House of Lords, 1905–7. See Holland, B., *Life of the Eighth Duke of Devonshire* (2 vols., 1911).

Cavendish, William, 7th Duke of Devonshire (1808–91). Scientist, industrialist and educationist. Born London, great-grandson of

4th Duke of Devonshire. Educated Eton and Trinity College, Cambridge, first class honours, classical tripos, 1829. A strong Whig, he was MP for Cambridge University, 1829–31, Malton Yorkshire, 1832 and Derbyshire, 1832–4. After succeeding to the dukedom in 1858, Cavendish gave up politics and devoted his time to science and industry. He was responsible for the development of Barrow-in-Furness, especially the iron mining and steel industry and the harbour facilities. First president, Iron and Steel Institute, 1868, and one of the founders of the Royal Agricultural Society, 1838 and its president, 1870. Cavendish had a wide interest in education. Chancellor, University of London, 1836–56, Chancellor, University of Cambridge, 1860–81 and Chancellor, Victoria University, 1881–91. Provided funds at Cambridge in 1870 to build a laboratory for experimental physics, called Cavendish Laboratory after its benefactor. Chairman, Royal Commission on Scientific Instruction and the Advancement of Science, 1870–5, known as the

Devonshire Commission. Its report recommended, amongst other changes, that six hours a week should be devoted to science in schools and that 'no-one should receive a degree who has not proved himself to be well-grounded in science as well as languages and mathematics'. To make these changes possible, an adequate number of professorships needed to be established and well-qualified science teachers needed to be trained for schools. Stewart, B., and Ward, A.W., *Essays and Addresses by Professors and Lecturers of the Owens College, Manchester* (1874), and 'The Seventh Duke of Devonshire' in Crowther, J.G., *Statesmen of Science* (1965).

Cecil, Hugh Richard Heathcote, Baron Quickswood (1869–1956). Politician and headmaster. Born at Hatfield, Hertfordshire, fifth and youngest son of 3rd Marquess of Salisbury. Educated at Eton and University College, Oxford, first class classical moderations, 1891 and fellow, Hertford College, Oxford, from 1891. Private secretary to Salisbury when Foreign Secretary, 1891–2. A firm supporter of the Church and the Conservative Party, he was active in Parliament after his election as MP for Greenwich (1895–1906) on a number of issues. He headed a group of young Unionists in the Commons, which included his lifelong friend Winston Churchill, which ridiculed the government on an unpopular measure of army reform and campaigned against free trade. Because of Cecil's prominent position, the group was known as the Hughligans. Cecil strongly supported the 1902 Education Bill, delivering some memorable speeches during its passage. MP, Oxford University, 1910–37. In this latter year, he was appointed Provost of Eton at the age of 68, remaining in the post until 1944. He was recommended for a peerage in 1941 by Churchill, when Prime Minister, and took the title Baron Quickswood. See his *Liberty and Authority* (1910); *Conservatism* (1912), and Rose, K., *The Later Cecils* (1975); Cecil, D., *The Cecils of Hatfield House* (1975).

Chadwick, Sir Edwin (1800–90). Social reformer. Born in Manchester and educated by private tutors. Law student at the Inner Temple, London, where he wrote for the *Westminster Review* and became a friend and follower of **Jeremy Bentham**. Poor Law Commissioner, 1833, and secretary to the new commission 1834–46; Commissioner at the Board of Health, 1848–54. Chadwick's extraordinary zeal for the collection of statistics and other information, and for devising remedies, covered a wide range of social problems. Those of particular relevance for education included the registration of births and deaths and their causes; the training of pauper children; the reduction in factory working hours for children and the introduction of the half-time system of education; the teaching of a trade to soldiers and sailors to ease their return to civilian life; competitive examinations for first appointments in the public service. Unsuccessfully stood for Parliament as candidate for the University of London, 1867. At times one of the most unpopular men in England, he was knighted belatedly in 1889. A voluminous writer. See Richardson, B.W., *The Health of Nations: a Review of the Works of Edwin Chadwick with a Biographical Introduction* (2 vols., 1889); Finer, S.E., *The Life and Times of Sir Edwin Chadwick* (1952).

Chalmers, Thomas (1780–1847). Theologian, preacher, philanthropist. Born Anstruther, Fife, Scotland. Educated at the parish school and the University of St Andrews. Minister at Kilmeney, Fife, 1803–14, but continued to teach mathematics and chemistry at St Andrews. In 1808 published *An Inquiry into the Extent and Stability of Natural Resources*. In 1815 moved to Glasgow as minister of the Tron parish where his oratory, partly published as *Astronomical Discourses* (1817) and *Commercial Discourses* (1820), took the city by storm. From 1820 as minister of the poverty-stricken St John's parish he established day and Sunday schools, and pauperism and crime diminished. DD of Glasgow, 1816, professor of Moral Philosophy at St Andrews, 1823–7, professor of Theology at Edinburgh, 1828–43, DCL of Oxford, 1835. In 1843 followed by 470 ministers he founded the Free Church of Scotland and became first moderator of its General Assembly. His last years were spent, as principal of the Free Church College, in completing his *Institutes of Theology* and in missionary work in Edinburgh. His published works in some 34 volumes are concerned principally with natural theology and social economy. See Hanna, W. (ed.), *Memoirs* (4 vols., 1849–52); *Correspondence* (1853); Brown, S.J., *Thomas Chalmers and the godly commonwealth in Scotland* (1982).

Chamberlain, Joseph (1836–1914). Statesman. Born London, son of a wholesale boot and shoe manufacturer. Educated at University College School, London, but entered his father's business at the age of 16. Two years later, went to Birmingham to work for his father's brother-in-law, Mr. Nettlefold, a screw manufacturer. Chamberlain was able to retire on his wealth after 20 years with the firm. A radical by temperament, he took a keen interest in education.

President of the National Education League of Birmingham, 1869; its aims were to ensure that the state education should be secular, free and compulsory. Chamberlain taught classes in connection with a Unitarian Sunday school. He became chairman of the National Education League in 1870 when the movement had reached national proportions. During the passage of **W.E. Forster**'s Education Bill in 1870, he denounced the Church's monopoly of education and welcomed the establishment of School Boards. Mayor of Birmingham, 1873–5, Liberal MP, Birmingham, 1876–85, and for Birmingham West, 1885–6, Liberal Unionist for the same constituency, 1886–1914. President of the Board of Trade, 1880–3, President of the Local Government Board, 1886 and Colonial Secretary, 1895–1903. During the passage of the 1902 Education Bill, Chamberlain, then a member of the Cabinet, proposed that all schools should have a secular majority of managers. See Garvin, J.L. and Amery, J., *The Life of Joseph Chamberlain* (6 vols., 1932–69); Jay, R., *Joseph Chamberlain* (1981).

Chambers, Sir Edmund Kerchever (1866–1954). Civil servant. Born West Ilsley, Berkshire, and educated at Marlborough and Corpus Christi College, Oxford, 1885–8, gaining first class in moderations and greats. His interest in English literature led him to become an expert in English stage history. A champion of women's education, Chambers lectured on Elizabethan literature for the Association for the Education of Women in Oxford, 1891–2 and took part in university extension teaching. Became Junior Examiner, Education Department, in 1892 and subsequently found time to contribute articles to a number of periodicals as well as produce an edition of Shakespeare's plays (1904–8) and edited English classics for schools. Senior Examiner, 1903, Assistant Secretary, 1910, Second Secretary, 1921 until his resignation in 1926. Chambers greatly admired **Robert Morant**, Permanent Secretary, Board of Education from 1903, and played a large part in devising a new administrative structure for elementary, secondary, technical and universities and teacher-training. He assisted in the promotion of adult education and also championed the day continuation school movement which, under the Fisher Education Act of 1918, envisaged part-time schooling for boys and girls between 14 and 18 years of age. Knight, 1925. See *The Medieval Stage* (1903); *The Elizabethan Stage* (4 vols., 1923); and Wilson, F.P., and Dover Wilson, J., 'Sir Edmund Kerchever Chambers', *Proceedings of the British Academy*, 42, 1956.

Chambers, William (1800–83). Publisher. Born Peebles and educated there. In 1814 apprenticed in the book trade in Edinburgh and with his brother Robert established a booksellers' business in 1819. The brothers later diversified into printing and publishing. Their main interests were in reference works, notably *Chambers' Encyclopaedia* (the first ten-volume edition was published, 1859–68), and periodical literature notably *Chambers' Edinburgh Journal* begun in 1832 which reached a circulation of 80,000. Chambers was Lord Provost of Edinburgh, 1865 and 1868, and initiated many improvements in the city. His private benefactions to Edinburgh and Peebles included a museum, library and art gallery. Chambers retained a lifelong interest in popular education and the first *Chambers' Educational Course* was produced in 1835. See Chambers, W., *Memoir of William and Robert Chambers* (1883), and Maggs, D. (ed.), *Memories of the Chambers Brothers* (1967).

Charles, Thomas (1755–1814). Promoter of schools and literacy. Born at Llanfihangelaber-cowin, Carmarthenshire. Educated at Llanddowror, at the dissenting academy at Carmarthen, and at Jesus College, Oxford. Ordained deacon, 1778, priest, 1780. In 1784 joined the Methodists. Settled at Bala in North Wales where his wife had a general store. Set up charity schools and trained and paid the masters himself. As with Griffith Jones' circulating schools, masters stayed in one place for about six months and then moved on to another. Permanent Sunday schools were established to continue the work. Sunday schools spread rapidly. These catered for all ages, and were democratically organized. In 1802 Charles secured the setting up of a Bible Society in London which produced a new edition of the Bible in Welsh. Charles devoted much of his time to the production of this and other volumes, including a four-volume Bible dictionary which he wrote himself. He also set up a printing press at Bala. Charles was the founding father of Welsh Calvinistic

Methodism and the chief promoter of Sunday schools and literacy in the principality. See Hughes, W. (ed.), *Life and Letters of the Rev. Thomas Charles* (1881); Jenkins, D.E., *Life of the Rev. Thomas Charles of Bala* (1908); Pritchard, R.A., *Thomas Charles* (1955); Gittins, C.E. (ed.), *Pioneers of Welsh Education* (1964).

Chester, Harry (1806–68). Civil servant. Born Ipswich, son of Sir Robert Chester, Master of Ceremonies to George III, George IV, William IV and Queen Victoria. Educated at Westminster and Trinity College, Cambridge but left without taking a degree. Clerk in the Privy Council Office, 1826–58. Assistant Secretary to the Committee of the Privy Council on Education, 1840–58. President and promoter of the Highgate Literary and Scientific Institution founded in 1839. Vice-President of the Society of Arts at whose instigation in 1854 a special loan exhibition of English and foreign educational aids was held in London. In the same year responsible for the first Society of Arts examinations. Gave evidence to the Newcastle Commission in 1859 and to the Select Committee on Civil Service Appointments in 1860. See his *Schools for Children and Institutes for Adults* (1860); *Education and Advancement for the Working Classes* (1863), and Hurt, J.S., 'Harry Chester, 1806–68', *Journal of the Royal Society of Arts*, 116, 1968.

Childers, Hugh Culling Eardley (1827–96). Politician. Born London, educated at **Dr Mayo**'s School, Cheam, 1836–43 and Trinity College, Cambridge, graduating in 1850. Emigrated to Australia the same year. Held post of inspector of schools briefly in 1851 and member of government of Victoria, 1851–7, with seat in Cabinet. Returned to England and elected Liberal MP, Pontefract in 1860, sitting for the borough till defeated in 1885. Served in a number of ministerial posts: First Lord of the Admiralty, 1868–71, Chancellor of the Duchy of Lancaster, 1872–3, Secretary of State, War, 1880–2 and twice Chancellor of the Exchequer, 1882–5 and 1885–6. Cabinet member in first three Gladstone governments. Chairman, Select Committee on Education, Science and Art (Administration) 1884 which recommended that elementary education should be placed under the supervision of one minister. The Committee also recommended that the 'Minister of Education' should be a member of the Cabinet. MP, Edinburgh South, 1886–92. See Childers, S., *Life and Correspondence of the Rt. Hon. Hugh C.E. Childers* (2 vols., 1901); Sweetman, E., *The Educational Activities in Victoria of the Rt. Hon. H.C.E. Childers* (1940).

Chuter-Ede *see* **Ede.**

Clarendon, George William Frederick Villiers, 4th Earl of Clarendon and 4th Baron Hyde (1800–70). Statesman. Born in London. Probably educated at Thomas Hill's school in Kensington, and at Christ's Hospital as a private pupil. Undergraduate at St John's College, Cambridge, 1816–20, and was admitted directly to the MA. Disliked logic and mathematics but excelled in modern languages and thus entered the diplomatic service. Attaché to the British embassy at St Petersburg in 1820, and thereafter served in Ireland, France and Spain. Succeeded to the earldom in 1838. Lord Privy Seal, 1839–41, President of the Board of Trade, 1846–7, Lord Lieutenant of Ireland, 1847–52, Foreign Secretary, 1853–8, 1865–6 and 1868–70. Chairman of the Royal Commission appointed to enquire into the revenues and management of certain colleges and schools, and the studies pursued and the instruction given therein. The report on these nine public schools, published in 1864, recommended revisions of school statutes and some broadening of the curriculum. Thus although classical languages and literature should continue to hold the principal place, these should be supplemented by mathematics, a modern language, natural science, history, geography and either drawing or music. Clarendon personally deplored 'the national loss that is sustained by forcing all minds into the same groove and compelling everybody to study classics'. See Maxwell, Sir H., *The Life and Letters of George William Frederick, fourth Earl of Clarendon* (2 vols., 1913).

Clarke, Sir Fred (1880–1952). Educationist. Born Witney, Oxfordshire. Educated at an elementary school – served as a pupil teacher,

Oxford Technical College, and St Catherine's, Oxford. BA first class in history, 1903. Senior master of Method at York Diocesan Training College, 1903–6; professor of Education, Hartley University College, Southampton, 1906–11; professor of Education, University of Cape Town, South Africa, 1911–29; professor of Education, McGill University, Montreal, Canada, 1929–34; professor of

EDUCATION AND SOCIAL CHANGE

AN ENGLISH INTERPRETATION

BY

F. CLARKE

LONDON
THE SHELDON PRESS
NORTHUMBERLAND AVENUE, W.C.2
NEW YORK: THE MACMILLAN COMPANY

Education and Director of the Institute of Education, University of London, 1936–45. Educational adviser to the National Union of Teachers. Knighted in 1943. First chairman of the Central Advisory Council for Education (England) established under the 1944 Act. Clarke's influence can be seen in the National Foundation for Educational Research, the report of the McNair Committee on the supply, recruitment and training of teachers and youth leaders, and in the disciplines of comparative education and sociology of education. See his *School History of Hampshire* (1909); *Foundations of History Teaching* (1929); *Education and Social Change* (1940); *Freedom in the Educative Society* (1948), and Mitchell, F.W., *Sir Fred Clarke, master teacher, 1880–1952* (1967).

Clegg, Sir Alec (1909–86). Educational administrator. Born Sawley, Derbyshire, son of a headteacher. Educated Long Eaton Grammar School, Bootham's School, York and Clare College, Cambridge, 1927–31, where he read modern languages, and London University, a teaching diploma. Assistant master, St Clement Dane's Grammar School, London, 1932–6, administrative assistant, Birmingham Education Office, 1936–9, Assistant Education Officer, Cheshire, 1939–42, Deputy Education Officer, Worcestershire, 1942–5, Deputy Education Officer, West Riding of Yorkshire, 1945 and in the same year, appointed County Education Officer, West Riding of Yorkshire, at the age of 35. Clegg remained in the post until his retirement in 1974. Many important innovations were introduced during his long span of office. He was a pioneer of the middle school; the 'Thorne scheme' of comprehensive schooling included a range of middle schools for the nine to 13 age group. He was a firm believer in the use of informal methods in the primary school as well as a supporter of the comprehensive principle. In-service training for teachers was another priority and a centre for courses and conferences was established at Woolley Hall. Clegg also built up a team of education officers who later became distinguished in their own right. Under his guidance, the West Riding became one of the leading local education authorities in the country. Member, Central Advisory Council on Education (England), 1956–67, taking a major part in the preparation of the Crowther Report, *15 to 18* (1959) and the Newsom Report, *Half our Future* (1967). Chairman, Centre for Information and Advice on Educational Disadvantage, 1976–9. Knight, 1965. See his *The Excitement of Writing* (1964); *Children in Distress* (with Megson,

B., 1968); *The Changing Primary School* (1972); *About Our Schools* (1981).

Clifford, Dr John (1836–1923). Theologian and educationist. Born Sawley, Derbyshire, son of a factory worker. Educated at elementary schools at Sawley and Beeston and Lenton, Nottinghamshire and went to work in a lace factory when 11 years of age. Clifford was baptized in 1851 and studied at Midland Baptist College, Leicester, 1855–8. Became pastor, Praed Street Baptist Church, Paddington, 1858, later moving to Westbourne Park Chapel, at the same time studying for degrees in arts, science and law at the University of London from 1861–6. A radical, Clifford's sympathies were with working people. He joined the Fabian Society and also supported the dock strike of 1890. He favoured the establishment of School Boards following the 1870 Education Act and promoted the notion of the 'conscience clause' in relation to biblical instruction in schools. The attempt by the London School Board, led by Athelstan Riley, to impose religious tests on teachers in its schools, was largely defeated through Clifford's campaign against the proposal. He vigorously opposed the 1902 Education Bill which sought to secure the cost of denominational schooling on the rates. Following the passing of the Bill, Clifford led the 'passive resistance' movement to the measure. He was an impressive public speaker and assisted in the defeat of the Conservatives in 1906. Companion of Honour, 1921. See Smith, I.G., *Dr Clifford on Education* (1903), and Marchant, Sir J., *Dr John Clifford* (1924).

Clough, Anne Jemima (1820–1892). Pioneer of education for girls and women. Born in Liverpool, sister of the poet **Arthur Hugh Clough**. Educated at home in Charleston, USA where she lived, 1822–36. Taught in a school for poor children and in Sunday schools, and also gained experience in London at Borough Road School and at the Home and Colonial School. In 1852 opened a school for the children of friends at Ambleside in Cumbria where Mary Arnold was one of the first pupils. Contacts with **Barbara Bodichon** and Millicent Fawcett aroused her interest in higher education. Clough was secretary of the North of England Council for Promoting the Higher Education of Women, 1867–70, and president, 1873–4. In 1871 she took charge of a residence for women who were attending lectures at Cambridge University, and by 1879 Newnham College was fully established with its own tutorial staff and with Anne Clough as principal. In 1885 she helped to promote the Cambridge

Training College for Women, and in 1887 the Women's University Settlement in Southwark, London. Thus her interest spanned the education and welfare of both working- and middle-class girls and women. See Clough, B.A., *Memoir of Anne Jemima Clough* (1903); Hamilton, M.A., *Newnham, an Informal Biography* (1936).

Clough, Arthur Hugh (1819–61). Poet. Born in Liverpool, brother of **Anne Jemima Clough**. Entered Rugby School in 1829 where he became the star pupil of **Thomas Arnold** and friend of **Matthew Arnold**. In 1837 won a scholarship to Balliol College, Oxford, though in 1841 he failed to secure the expected first class degree. Fellow of Oriel, 1842–8 and tutor from 1843. Clough knew many of his great Oxford contemporaries and was deeply influenced by the religious controversies aroused by Keble and **J.H. Newman**. Resigned his fellowship, 1848, disturbed by the political and religious establishment of the day. Principal of University Hall, London, 1849–51, and professor of English Literature at University College, London, 1850. In the USA 1852–3, where he took private pupils and began his revision of Dryden's translation of *Plutarch's Lives*. Examiner in the Education Department from 1853. In 1856 in the aftermath of the Crimean War toured military schools in Austria, France and Prussia. Private secretary to **Robert Lowe**, 1859. Died in Florence, Italy. See various editions of his poems including those by Palgrave, F.T., (1862); by his wife (2 vols., 1869), and Chorley, K., *Arthur Hugh Clough, The Uncommitted Mind* (1962); Biswas, R.K., *Arthur Hugh Clough* (1972).

Cobbett, William (1763–1835). Writer. Born Farnham, Surrey, son of a small farmer. Started work as a plough boy. In 1783 spent nine months in London, then enlisted in the 54th Foot Regiment. Largely self-taught (he was suspicious of schoolmasters, 'that new race of idlers') he studied French, fortification, geometry, logic and rhetoric. In America, 1792–1800, teaching English to French immigrants, publishing, bookselling and pamphleteering, especially against Tom Paine and **Joseph Priestley**. In 1802 began *Cobbett's Parliamentary Debates* later taken over by Luke Hansard. In the same year started his *Political Register* which continued until his death and, with a circulation of 60,000 copies, became the basic reading of the literate working class. Between 1821 and 1832 Cobbett undertook his 'Rural Rides' to see and record in notes published in the *Register* the true state of the country. Imprisoned for seditious libel, 1810–12. Stood for Coventry, 1821, and Preston, 1826, unsuccessfully, but returned as MP for Oldham in 1832. Prolific writer of more than 50 works. See his *English Grammar* (1818); *Advice to Young Men: and (incidentally) to Young Women* (1830); *Cottage Economy* (1831); *Rural Rides* (3 vols., 1930 complete edition by Cole, G.D.H. and M.,) and Spater, G., *Cobbett: The poor man's friend* (1982); Green, D., *Great Cobbett* (1983).

Cole, George Douglas Howard (1889–1959). Academic and authority on Socialism. Born Cambridge, son of a jeweller, later a surveyor, moving to London. Educated St Paul's School, 1902–8. Balliol College, Oxford, 1908–11, gaining a first in moderations and *literae humaniores*. Lecturer in philosophy, Armstrong College, Newcastle upon Tyne, 1911–13. Fellow, Magdalen College, Oxford, 1912–19. Joined the Fabian Research Committee (later, Department) 1913 and secretary, Research Committee for the reorganized Labour Party, 1919. Labour correspondent, *Manchester Guardian*, 1920. Director, tutorial classes, University of London, 1921. Robert Mynors Reader in Economics and fellow, University College, Oxford, 1925–44. Labour candidate, King's Norton, Birmingham, 1930–1. Chairman, Fabian Society, 1939–46 and 1948–50. President, 1952. Worked with **Beveridge** on the Manpower Survey, 1940. Regular contributor, *New Statesman* and chairman of the Board, 1957–9. Fellow, All Souls College, Oxford, 1944–57. Wrote extensively on economic, social, political and historical affairs; probably his best-known works are *The Common People 1746–1938* (1938) with Postgate, R., (2nd edn., 1956) and *A Short History of the British Working Class Movement 1789–1947* (3 vols., 1925–7, revised edn., 1948). He also wrote a number of crime novels with his wife, Margaret. See Cole, M., *The Life of G.D.H. Cole* (1971), and Carpenter, L.P., *G.D.H. Cole, an Intellectual Biography* (1973).

Cole, Sir Henry (1808–82). Official and writer. Born at Bath, educated at Christ's Hospital School. Clerk to Francis Palgrave of the Record Commission, 1824–9, one of the four senior assistant keepers of the Record Office, 1838–41. Studied painting and engraving and exhibited at the Royal Academy. Also published several children's books and guide books under the pseudonym of Felix Summerly. Designed the popular Summerly tea service for Minton, helped design the first postage stamps and originated the idea of Christmas cards. Edited the *Guide* (1837), *Post Circular*

(1838) and *Journal of Design* (1849–52). Member of Society of Arts, 1846, of the executive committee of the Great Exhibition, 1851, general adviser to the exhibition of 1862, secretary to the royal commission at the Paris exhibitions of 1855 and 1867, chief manager of exhibitions in London, 1871–4. Secretary to the School of Design, 1851, and to the Department of Practical Art, 1852. Secretary to the Department of Science and Art, 1853–73. CB, 1851, KCB, 1875. Cole organized the building of the South Kensington museums, and of the Royal Albert Hall opened in 1871. He also supported the School for Cookery, 1873–6, and the National Training School for Music, 1876, which became the basis for the Royal College of Music, 1882. See Cole, A.S., and H.L. (eds.), *Fifty years of public work of Sir Henry Cole* (2 vols., 1884), and Bonython, E., *King Cole* (1982).

Cole, Dame Margaret Isobel (1893–1980). Political writer and campaigner. Born Cambridge, daughter of J.P. Postgate, professor of Latin, University of Liverpool and educated Roedean and Girton College, Cambridge, first class honours, classical tripos, part one, second class, part two, 1911–14. Classics mistress, St Paul's Girls' School, 1914–16. She met her future husband, **G.D.H. Cole**, when assistant secretary, Labour Research Department, 1917–25, marrying in 1918. Lecturer, London University tutorial classes, 1925–49 and Cambridge, 1941–4. Honorary Secretary, New Fabian Research Bureau, 1935–9 and of Fabian Society, 1939–53. Chairman, 1955, President, 1963–80. Alderman, London County Council, 1952–65 and member of education committees under the Council and its successor, the Greater London Council, 1941–67. Dame, 1970. Publications include *The Diaries of Beatrice Webb* (1952); with Drake, B., *The Story of Fabian Socialism* (1961); *Life of G.D.H. Cole* (1971). Wrote several political works and detective works with her husband. See Vernon, B.D., *Margaret Cole* (1986).

Colenso, John William (1814–83). Divine, scholar and textbook author. Born at St Austell, Cornwall, educated at Devonport and St John's College, Cambridge. Second wrangler and Smith's prizeman, 1836. Fellow of St John's, 1837–46, mathematical tutor at Harrow School, 1839–42. Vicar of Forncett St Mary, Norfolk, a college living, 1846–53, BD and DD, 1853. Bishop of Natal, South Africa from 1853. Deposed by Bishop Gray of Cape Town in 1864 and excommunicated 1866, but these proceedings were declared invalid by the Judicial Committee of the Privy Council. Such difficulties arose particularly from Colenso's commentaries on the

Pentateuch. The first of his seven volumes sold 10,000 copies and provoked over 130 replies. Colenso's school books on *Algebra* (1841) and *Arithmetic* (1843) sold some half a million copies. He also supervised the production of a grammar and dictionary of the Zulu language, translated the Prayer Book and part of the Bible into the same tongue, and championed the native inhabitants of his diocese against unscrupulous British officials. Died in Durban, South Africa. See his *The Pentateuch and Book of Joshua critically examined* (7 vols., 1862–79), and Cox, G.W., *The Life of John William Colenso* (1888); Hinchliffe, P., *John William Colenso* (1964).

Coleridge, Derwent (1800–83). Author and educationist. Born Keswick in the Lake District, second son of the poet and philosopher Samuel Taylor Coleridge. Educated at a small school near Ambleside where he knew Southey and Wordsworth, and St John's College, Cambridge. BA, 1824, MA, 1829. Ordained, 1825 and became master of the grammar school at Helston, Cornwall, 1827–41, where **Charles Kingsley** was one of his pupils. First principal of St Mark's College, Chelsea, 1841–64, the premier training college of the National Society. Latin was included in the syllabus and choral services provided in the College chapel. This led to accusations that St Mark's students were better prepared for Anglo-Catholic holy orders than for teaching the humble poor. Prebendary of St Paul's Cathedral, 1846–83, and rector of Hanwell, 1864–80 where he organized the building of a new parish church. Coleridge was declared by **Dean Stanley** to be the most accomplished linguist of his day. In addition to his mastery of the classical and modern European languages Coleridge could read Arabic, Coptic, Hawaiian and Zulu. See his *The Scriptural Character of the English Church* (1839); *The Education of the People* (1861); *The Teachers of the People* (1862), and Bloomfield, B.C., 'Derwent Coleridge', *Education Libraries Bulletin*, 4, 1959.

Collings, Jesse (1831–1920). Politician. Born Littleham, Devon. Educated at a dame school and later, a private school for tradesmen's sons. Began work at age of 15 in ironmonger's warehouse in Birmingham retiring as head of the firm, Messrs Collings and Wallis, in 1879. Town councillor, Edgbaston, 1868, alderman, 1875 and Mayor of Birmingham, 1878–9. Close friend of **Joseph Chamberlain**, with whom he worked for municipal reform in Birmingham. Sat as a Radical MP for Ipswich, 1880–6 and as a Unionist for Bordesley, Birmingham, 1886–1920. Under-Secretary, Home Department, 1895–1902. In 1868, published pamphlet advocating free, non-sectarian education and active when the National Education League was established that year. Great interest in the condition of the rural labourer, working in Parliament for land reform movement and strong supporter of Joseph Arch and the formation of the National Agricultural Labourers Union. Collings' amendment on small holdings in January 1886 brought about the downfall of the Salisbury ministry. Spectacularly defended rural endowments against the operations of the Endowed Schools Commissioners after 1869, particularly at Scarning, Norfolk and West Lavington, Wiltshire. See his *Land Reform* (1906); *The Colonization of Rural Britain* (1914), and Collings, J. and Green, J.L., *Life of the Right Hon. Jesse Collings* (1920).

Combe, George (1788–1858). Phrenologist and educationist. Born Edinburgh, and educated there in private schools, the parish school of St Cuthbert's, the High School and the university. Apprenticed in the law office of Higgins and Dallas, 1803–10. Admitted Writer to the Signet, 1812; commissioned Notary Public, 1815. By 1816 Combe had embraced phrenology which he regarded as a combination of science and philosophy. He believed that moral and intellectual training developed the brain, just as physical exercise developed the muscles. For the next 20 years, in lectures and writings he advocated phrenology and practical education. In 1836 unsuccessful in his bid to become professor of Logic at Edinburgh University. Retired from the legal profession in 1837, and thereafter travelled widely, particularly in England, Ireland, Germany and North America. From 1845 until his death Combe led a movement for secular education, and worked with **William Ellis** and others to establish secular schools. Advocated rate-supported secular schools, although time should be set apart for religious instruction in accordance with parental wishes. See his *Essays on Phrenology* (1819); *The Constitution of Man* (1828); *Remarks on National Education* (1846); *What should Secular Education embrace?* (1848), and Gibbon, C., *The Life of George Combe* (2 vols., 1878); Jolly, W. (ed.), *Education its principles and practices as developed by George Combe* (1879).

Cook, Revd Frederick Charles (1810–89). School inspector. Born in Berkshire. Sizar, St John's College, Cambridge, 1824, BA, classics 1831. Studied at Bonn under Niebuhr. Ordained priest, 1839, and curate, Trinity Church, Gray's Inn Lane, 1839–41. Secretary and inspector of schools, London Diocesan Board, 1841–4. One of four Church of England appointments as HMI in 1844. Took keen interest in problem of how to introduce good literature into schools. In 1847, when women's training schools were to be inspected for the first time, Cook alone was given this task and in 1850 was invited by **Lingen** to submit a memorandum on the subject of 'the Inspection of Female Training Institutions'. As a result of this memorandum, he was appointed inspector of these institutions. Cook retired in 1865. Chaplain to the Queen, 1857, Canon, Exeter Cathedral, 1865 and Precentor, 1872–89. Author of *Poetry for Schools* (1849) and *The Origins of Religion and Language* (1884).

Cook, Henry Caldwell (1886–1939). Teacher. Born Liverpool. Educated at a preparatory school in St John's Wood, Highgate School, London, and at Lincoln College, Oxford. Second class honours school of English language and literature, 1909, Oxford Diploma in Education with distinction, 1911. English master at the Perse School, Cambridge, 1911–15 and 1919–33. Cook believed that the existing school system hampered true education. His major work *The Play Way, an Essay in Educational Method* (1917) became the centre of controversy for a generation. He argued that 'Proficiency and learning come not from reading and listening but from action, from doing and from experience. The natural means of study in youth is play.' Cook was a bachelor of independent nature and means. War service in the Artists' Rifles in France influenced him greatly. He became depressed and died in comparative obscurity. See his *Littleman's Book of Courtesy* (1914) and Beacock, D.A., *Play Way English for Today. The Methods and Influence of H. Caldwell Cook* (1943).

Courthope, William John (1842–1917). Civil servant. Born South Malling, Sussex, where his father was rector of the parish. Educated at Blackheath and Harrow. Exhibitioner, New College, Oxford, 1862, first class in classical moderations and *literae humaniores*, 1864. Examiner, Education Department, 1869. Civil Service Commissioner, 1887, Senior Commissioner, 1892–1907, humanizing the examinations for higher appointments. Courthope, like two other Examiners, **F.T. Palgrave** and **J.W. Mackail**, was elected to the Oxford professorship of Poetry, 1895–1900. Author of *Life of Pope* (1889), *A History of English Poetry* (6 vols., 1895–1910) and contributed to several literary journals, and Mackail,

J.W., 'W.J. Courthope', *Proceedings of the British Academy*, 9, 1917–18.

Cowper-Temple, William Francis, Baron Mount-Temple (1811–88). Statesman. Born at Brockett Hall, Hertfordshire. Educated at Eton, and in 1827 entered the army. Became private secretary to his uncle Lord Melbourne in 1835. Liberal MP for Hertford, 1835–68, and for South Hampshire, 1868–80. Created Baron Mount-Temple, 1880. Lord of the Admiralty, 1846–52, 1852–5. President of the Board of Health, 1855–7. First Vice-President of the Committee of Council on Education, 1857–8. Commissioner of Works, 1860–6. Chairman of the National Education Union, and as such a spokesman for denominational education. In 1870 tabled an amendment to the Elementary Education Bill to exclude from all rate-aided schools every catechism and formulary distinctive of denominational creed. This was accepted and became famous as the Cowper-Temple clause. His intention, however, was not to prevent teachers from explaining Christianity according to their own convictions but to forbid the use of certain books and prescribed forms of words. See Mount-Temple, Lady, *Memorials of W.F. Cowper-Temple* (1890); Bradley, J.L., *The Letters of John Ruskin to Lord and Lady Mount-Temple* (1964).

Craik, Sir Henry (1846–1927). Civil servant and politician. Born Glasgow, one of nine children and son of a Scottish minister. Educated Glasgow High School, Glasgow University, 1860–5, Balliol College, Oxford, 1865–9, first class in classical moderations and *literae humaniores*. Junior Examiner, Education Department, 1870, Senior Examiner, 1878–85. Then appointed to the secretaryship of the Scottish Education Department, Whitehall, a post which he filled with great distinction until his retirement in 1904. KCB, 1897, Baronet, 1926. Principal, Queen's College, Harley Street, London, 1911–14. Conservative MP, Glasgow and Aberdeen Universities, 1906–18 and one of the members for Scottish Universities, 1918–27. Author of *Life of Swift* (1882); *The State in its Relation to Education* (1884); *A Centenary of Scottish History* (2 vols., 1900).

Cranbrook *see* **Gathorne-Hardy.**

Crewe-Milnes, Robert Offley, 2nd Baron Houghton and Marquess of Crewe (1858–1945). Statesman. Born London, son of Richard Monckton Milnes, MP, Pontefract, 1837–62, a Liberal formerly ranked as a Conservative and 1st Baron Houghton, 1862. Educated at Harrow and Trinity College, Cambridge, BA, 1880. Succeeded to title, 1885. Marquess, 1911. Assistant private secretary to **Lord Granville**, 1883–5, Lord-in-Waiting, 1886 and in **Gladstone**'s last ministry, appointed Viceroy of Ireland in 1892, retaining the post until the fall of Rosebery's government in 1895. Lord President of the Council, 1905–8; Secretary of State, Colonial Office, 1908–10, Lord Privy Seal, 1908–11 and 1912–15, Secretary of State, India Office, 1910–15 and Lord President, 1915–16, leaving that office when Lloyd George succeeded **Asquith** as prime minister. Crewe was chairman of the committee appointed in November 1919 to inquire into the position of classics in the educational system of the United Kingdom. Its membership included **Sir Henry Hadow**, Gilbert Murray, **Cyril Norwood** and **A.N. Whitehead**. Its report, issued in 1921, recommended 'that the position of Latin needs strengthening and that steps should be taken to make the study of Greek accessible to every class of the community'. Ambassador to France, 1922–8, Secretary of State, War, 1931. Leader of the Independent Liberals, House of Lords, 1936–44. Crewe published a volume of poems, *Stray Verse 1889–90* (1891) and a biography of his father-in-law, *Lord Rosebery* (2 vols., 1931).

Crichton-Browne, Sir James (1840–1938). Physician and psychologist. Born Edinburgh, eldest son of William Browne, the first medical superintendent of the Crichton Royal Institute, Dumfries. Educated at Dumfries Academy, Trinity College, Glenalmond and Edinburgh University. Trained as a doctor, though early in his student days he had shown a marked interest in psychology. LRCS (Edinburgh), 1861. MD, 1862, with thesis on 'Hallucinations'. From 1865, assistant medical officer in several asylums and in 1866, appointed medical director, West Riding Lunatic Asylum, Wakefield. He lectured at Leeds School of Medicine on mental disease and was co-editor of *Brain*, 1878–85. Lord Chancellor's Visitor in Lunacy, 1875–1922. FRS, 1883, Knight, 1886. Crichton-Browne (he added one of his Christian names to his surname) was particularly concerned with public health and education. In 1884, **Mundella**, then Vice-President of the Committee of Council on Education, invited Crichton-Browne to investigate cases of alleged 'overpressure' in London schools caused by the demands of the Code. The dramatic picture presented by Crichton-Browne of its effects on the health and mental stability of school children was effectively countered in a memorandum written by **J.G. Fitch**,

HMI, who visited many of the schools with Crichton-Browne. Both documents were presented to Parliament. See Report of Dr Crichton-Browne upon the alleged Overpressure, P.P. 1884 1xi, ff. 259–311 and Memorandum relating to Dr Crichton-Browne's Report by Mr J.G. Fitch, ibid., ff. 311–37. See also his *Victorian Jottings* (1926), and *What the Doctor Thought* (1930).

Crosland, (Charles) Anthony (Raven) (1918–77). Politician. Born St Leonard's, Sussex. Educated Highgate School, London, and Trinity College, Oxford. First class in politics, philosophy and economics, President of the Union, 1946. Fellow and lecturer in Economics at Trinity, 1947–50. Entered Parliament in 1950 as Labour MP for South Gloucestershire, but sat for Grimsby from 1959. As Secretary of State for Education and Science, 1965–7 he issued Circular 10/65 requesting Local Education Authorities to submit plans for secondary school reorganization on comprehensive lines, and in his Woolwich speech of April 1965 outlined the binary policy which led to the creation of 30 polytechnics the following year. Ended the Central Advisory Councils which were not reappointed after 1966. President of the Board of Trade, 1967–9; Secretary of State for Local Government, 1969–70; for the Environment, 1974–6; for Foreign Affairs, 1976–7. See his *The Future of Socialism* (1964); *The Politics of Education* (1971) (with Boyle and Kogan), and Crosland, S., *Tony Crosland* (1982).

Cross, Richard Assheton, 1st Viscount Cross (1823–1914). Statesman. Born at Red Scar near Preston. Educated at Rugby under **Thomas Arnold**, and Trinity College, Cambridge. President of the Union. Called to the bar at the Inner Temple, 1849, practised in the Northern Circuit, Bencher of his Inn, 1876. Conservative MP for Preston, 1857–62; South West Lancashire, 1868–85; Lancashire (Newton), 1885–6. Created Viscount, 1886; GCB, 1880; GCSI, 1892. Home Secretary, 1874–80, 1885–6. As Home Secretary Cross was responsible for measures concerned with housing, health, factories, friendly societies, trade unions, and the preservation of open spaces. In 1886 he was appointed chairman of a Royal Commission to inquire into the working of the Elementary Education Acts in England and Wales. There was little agreement amongst its members, however, and in 1888 two reports were issued. The majority report proposed that voluntary schools should be given assistance from the rates and that school boards should be absorbed by the new county councils. The minority report, signed by eight of the 23 members, opposed rate aid for voluntary schools and also objected to the continuation of the pupil-teacher system. There was more agreement, however, on the need for university day training colleges and for the abolition of payment by results. Secretary of State for India, 1886–92; Lord Privy Seal, 1895–1900. See his *A Family History* (1903); *A Political History* (1903), and Smith, P., *Disraelian Conservatism and Social Reform* (1967); Roberts, J.T., 'The Genesis of the Cross Commission', *Journal of Educational Administration and History*, 17 (2), 1985.

Crosskey, Henry William (1826–93). Unitarian minister. Born Lewes, Sussex. Educated Manchester College, 1843–8. Minister at Friargate Chapel, Derby, 1848–52, St Vincent, Glasgow, 1852–69 and minister of the Church of the Messiah, Birmingham, 1869–93. Believed that every child should have the opportunity for realizing his/her educational potential. An original member of the National Education League which met at Birmingham, 1869. Crosskey favoured a more militant approach in opposing the 1870 Education Bill, especially the clauses relating to School Boards' power to determine the religious character of their schools. For this purpose, the Central Nonconformist Committee was founded with Crosskey and **R.W. Dale** as joint secretaries. Advocated the establishment of a university in Birmingham. He also was a firm supporter of the caucus organization in Birmingham, of which **Joseph Chamberlain** was the leader. Member, Birmingham School Board, 1876–93. See Armstrong, R.A., *H.W. Crosskey, His Life and Work* (1895), and Briggs, A., *History of Birmingham* (2 vols., 1952).

Crowther, Geoffrey, Baron (1907–72). Economist. Educated Leeds Grammar School, Oundle School, Clare College, Cambridge, and at the Universities of Columbia and Yale, USA. Joined *The Economist* 1932, deputy editor from 1935, editor, 1938–56. Deputy Head of Joint War Production Staff, 1942–5. Chairman of the Central Advisory Council for Education (England), 1956–60 which in 1959 produced the Crowther Report on the education of 15–18 year olds. This recommended compulsory full-time education to 16 and part-time education to 18. Chairman of the Commission on the Constitution, member of the governing body of the London School of Economics, Chancellor of the Open University, 1969. Knighted 1957, life peerage Baron Crowther of Headingley, 1968. See his *Economics for Democrats* (1939); *An Outline of Money* (1941).

Cullen, Paul (1803–78). Cleric. Born Prospect, County Kildare. Educated at Shackleton Quaker School, Ballitore, at Carlow College under Dr Doyle and from 1820 at the College of Propaganda in Rome. Ordained in 1829 and became rector of the Irish College in 1832. He urged Pope Gregory XVI to oppose the Queen's Colleges and the 'mixed' system of education in Ireland. Appointed Archbishop of Armagh in 1849 and translated to Dublin in 1852. Created a Cardinal in 1866. Cullen opposed the Young Ireland and Fenian movements and in 1850 presided over the national synod held at Thurles. He worked tirelessly for Catholic education, was the leading figure in the founding of the Catholic University in 1854 and in the appointment of **J.H. Newman** as its first rector. Established the Dublin diocesan seminary at Clonliffe College and was himself buried there. See Bowen, D., *Paul Cardinal Cullen and the shaping of modern Irish Catholicism* (1983).

Culverwell, Edward Parnall (1855–1931). Progressive educationist. Educated Trinity College, Dublin, 1875, senior moderator in Mathematics and Experimental Science at the college, 1877 and fellow from 1883. Although he published papers on calculus of variation and mathematics and physical theories of the Ice Age, he is best known for his advocacy of modern teaching methods, based on his admiration for Montessori, contained in his book *The Montessorian Principles and Practice* (1913).

Cumin, Patric (1823–90). Educated at Shrewsbury, Glasgow University and Balliol College, Oxford. BA, 1845, MA, 1850. Published a manual of civil law, 1854, called to the bar, at the Inner Temple, 1855. In 1859 appointed by the Newcastle Commission to inquire into educational charities in South West England. In 1862 became editor of *The London Review*. Private secretary to **W.E. Forster**, 1868–71. Secretary to the Scottish Education Commission, 1867. Assistant Secretary to the Education Department, 1870–84, in which capacity he favoured the Board Schools as opposed to private venture schools. Secretary of the Education Department, 1884–90. Exercised a tighter control over the inspectorate, and gave evidence to the Cross Commission on the need for day training colleges and for county authorities for educational purposes. See Anon, *Patric Cumin, Secretary of the Education Department. A Sketch* (1901); Armytage, W.H.G., 'Patric Cumin, 1823–1890', *Bulletin of the John Rylands Library*, 30, 1946–7.

Dale, Robert William (1829–95). Congregationalist divine. Born Newington Butts, Surrey. Attended three schools before in 1844

becoming an usher to Ebenezer White at Andover, Hampshire where he joined the Congregational church. Subsequently an usher at schools in Surrey and Warwickshire, and in 1847 became a theology student at Spring Hill College, Birmingham. MA, London University 1853, and winner of the gold medal in philosophy. Assistant minister, 1853, minister from 1859 at Carr's Lane Chapel, Birmingham. From 1858 lectured on literature, philosophy and homiletics at Spring Hill College. Chairman of the Congregational Union, 1869, editor of the *Congregationalist*, 1872–8, president of the international council of Congregational churches, 1891. Very prominent in the educational life of Birmingham, including its School Board and grammar schools, and of the Congregational church. Member of the Cross Commission on the Elementary Education Acts which reported in 1888. Supported the removal of Spring Hill College to Mansfield College, Oxford in 1889. Visited Germany, 1863, Egypt and Palestine, 1873, USA, 1877, Australia, 1887. DD Yale, 1877; LL.D Glasgow, 1883. See his *The Atonement* (1875); *Nine Lectures on Preaching* (1877); *A Manual of Congregational Principles* (1884), and Dale, A.W.W., *The Life of R.W. Dale* (1898); Shillito, E., *Three Great Congregationalists* (1935).

Darwin, Charles Robert (1809–82). Exponent of the theory of evolution. Born Shrewsbury, grandson of Erasmus Darwin, the doctor, poet, inventor and botanist. His father Robert, was also a doctor, his mother Susannah a daughter of Josiah Wedgwood the potter. Educated at a day school in Shrewsbury, at Shrewsbury School under **Samuel Butler** as a boarder, at Edinburgh University, 1825–7, where he studied medicine, and at Christ's College, Cambridge. BA, 1831, and in the same year recommended by **John Henslow** as the naturalist on HMS *Beagle*. During the voyage, 1831–6, Darwin visited South America, Tahiti, New Zealand and

Tasmania and gained a unique knowledge of the geology, flora and fauna of several countries. From 1842 until his death he lived as a country gentleman at Downe in Kent where he continued his researches into animal and plant life. He published many works but in 1859 achieved international fame, and notoriety, with his *The Origin of Species by Means of Natural Selection.* This book and *The Descent of Man* (1871) established Darwin as the world's leading authority on evolutionary biology, and called into question the account of the creation of the earth and of the human race as contained in the Christian Bible and in the sacred writings of other religions. See his several writings including *The Variation of Plants and Animals under Domestication* (1867); *Climbing Plants* (1875), and Darwin, F., *The Life and Letters of Charles Darwin* (3 vols., 1888); Darwin F., and Seward, A.C., *More Letters of Charles Darwin* (2 vols., 1903); Barlow, N., *The Autobiography of Charles Darwin* (1958); Vorzimmer, P.J., *Charles Darwin: The Years of Controversy* (1970); Allan, M., *Darwin and his Flowers* (1977).

Dasent, Sir John Roche (1847–1914). Educational administrator. Son of Sir G.W. Dasent, scholar and Civil Service Commissioner. Educated Westminster School and Christ Church, Oxford, 1866–9, second class honours, classical moderations and second class, *literae humaniores*. Nephew of J.T. Delane, editor of *The Times*, for whom he worked briefly, 1870. Junior Examiner, Education Department, 1876, private secretary to four Lords President of the Council between 1880 and 1895, i.e. **Spencer, Carlingford**, Kimberley and Rosebery. Assistant Secretary, Board of Education, 1900–8. Knight, 1908. Editor, *Accounts of the Privy Council* (new series) (32 volumes, 1890).

Davenport Hill *see* **Hill.**

Davies, (Sarah) Emily (1830–1921). Pioneer of women's education. Born Southampton, daughter of an evangelical clergyman, Revd John Davies, DD, rector of Gateshead. Educated at home and with her brothers. Took part in district visiting and Sunday school teaching. In 1862 after the death of her father she moved to London and met many feminist pioneers including **Elizabeth Garrett Anderson** and **Barbara Bodichon**, with whom she campaigned for the admission of women to the medical profession and to the degrees of London University. By 1865 she had secured permanent permission for girls to sit the Cambridge Local Examinations for schools and in that year she gave evidence to the Taunton Commission. In 1866 she helped to organize the first petition for female suffrage and in 1890 joined the Executive Committee of the London Society for Women's Suffrage, though she was later to oppose the militant suffragette methods. In 1866 she also formed the London Schoolmistresses' Association and acted as its secretary for more than 20 years. In 1871 she was elected to the first London School Board. In 1869 she established a women's college at Hitchin, Hertfordshire, which in 1873 moved to Cambridge as Girton College. Davies was mistress of Girton, 1873–5 and honorary secretary, 1873–1904. See her *The Higher Education of Women* (1866); *Thoughts on Some Questions relating to Women, 1860–1908* (1910), and Stephen, B., *Emily Davies and Girton College* (1927); Bradbrook, M.C., *'That Infidel Place': A Short History of Girton College, 1869–1969* (1969).

Dawes, Revd Richard (1793–1867). Clergyman, scientist and educationist. Born at Hawes in Yorkshire. Educated at John Gough's School, Kendal, and Trinity College, Cambridge. 4th wrangler and BA, 1817, MA, 1820. Fellow, mathematical tutor and bursar of Downing College, from 1818. Vicar of Tadlow, Cambridgeshire, a college living, 1819–36. In 1836 Dawes became rector of King's Somborne, Hampshire where he became aware of the deficiencies in educational provision for the lower and lower-middle classes. In 1842 National Society schools were established there under his personal control, which achieved great success and public acclaim. The curriculum included not only religious observance but also emphasis upon language skills and practical scientific knowledge. Dean of Hereford from 1850 where he restored the cathedral, took much interest in the city's schools, and in 1861 became master of St Catherine's Hospital, Ledbury. Vice-President of the British Association, 1864. Writer of several works on contemporary educational issues. See, for example, his *Suggestive Hints toward improved*

Secular Instruction (1849); *Schools and other similar Institutions for the Industrial Classes* (1853); *Mechanics' Institutes and Popular Education* (1856), and Henry, W.C., *A Biographical Notice of the Late Very Revd Richard Dawes* (1867); Layton, D., *Science for the People* (1973).

Dawson, George (1821–76). Theologian and reformer. Born London, son of a schoolmaster. Educated by his father until the age of 17 and at Glasgow University, MA, 1841. Became minister, Baptist Chapel, Rickmansworth, Buckinghamshire, 1843, moving to Birmingham the following year as minister, Graham Street Baptist Chapel. Dawson was strongly opposed to evangelicalism; together with a considerable section of his congregation, Dawson broke away to become minister of 'The Church of the Saviour', Birmingham in 1847. An outstanding orator, he lectured in all parts of the United Kingdom for some 30 years and in the USA in 1874. Editor, *Birmingham Morning News* from 1871. Strong advocate of municipal government. Dawson was a radical in politics and served on the Birmingham School Board from 1871. He took a keen interest in foreign affairs and was a friend of Mazzini and Kossuth. See his *Sermons on daily life and duty* (1878), *Shakespeare and other lectures* (1878), and Dale, R.W., 'George Dawson: Politician, Lecturer and Preacher', *Nineteenth Century*, ii, 1877; Wilson, W.W., *The Life of George Dawson* (1905).

Denison, George Anthony (1805–96). Clergyman. Born Ossington, Nottinghamshire, fourth son of John Denison, MP, Colchester, 1802–6 and for Minehead, 1807–12. Educated at Eton and at Christ Church, Oxford. First class in *literae humaniores*, 1827, MA, 1830. Fellow, Oriel College, Oxford, 1829. Ordained, 1832 and vicar of Broadwinsor, Dorset in 1830. Appointed to the living at East Brent, Somerset in 1845 remaining there for the next 50 years. Archdeacon of Taunton, 1851. A firm High Churchman, Denison was deeply concerned about State intervention in schooling. In 1852, he fought for school management to be exclusively in the hands of the clergy and actively opposed Gladstone's Oxford University election in 1853 to draw attention to the latter's views on the management issue. Denison became involved in a number of ecclesiastical *causes célèbres*, in one instance in 1856 narrowly escaping deprivation of his living. Editor, *Church and State Review*, 1862–5. He opposed the religious compromise effected in the 1870 Education Act and continued to campaign against the erosion of Church influence in education by the civil power which, as he wrote in 1893, 'has confounded education for another world with instruction for this'. See his *Notes on my Life* (1878, supplement, 1893), and Denison, L.E. (ed.), *Fifty Years at East Brent. The Letters of George Anthony Denison* (1902).

Derby *see* **Stanley.**

Deverell, Edith Mary (1872–1937). School inspector. Educated at Somerville College, Oxford, 1893–6 and member of a select discussion group, which inlcuded Margery Fry, Hilda Oakeley and **Eleanor Rathbone** which met weekly to discuss 'social subjects'. Assistant to A.L. Bowley, the statistician, 1898–1900, in research for his classic book *Wages in the United Kingdom in the 19th Century* (1900). She was appointed to the Inspectorate in May 1900, joining five other women sub-inspectors who had been appointed since 1896 to assist HMIs in inspecting girls' and infants' departments in elementary schools. Apart from an initial year in Liverpool, Edith Deverell spent her entire service in London at West Ham. She campaigned vigorously to improve the health and welfare of children in schools. On the question of health and hygiene she suggested that the system operating in French schools might be adopted whereby 'all children leave the classroom and march or run round the playground (mid morning)'. She also campaigned to secure the interest and co-operation of parents in the work of the school. In April 1901, along with her women colleagues, Miss Deverell became a junior inspector. She was employed on the inquiry by the Board of Education into the arrangements made in elementary schools for children between three and five, begun in 1904. Before the work was completed, she had left the Inspectorate on her marriage to a fellow HMI, **F.S. Marvin.** Her energies were subsequently canalized into a number of causes, including women's suffrage and the betterment of conditions of women workers. See Gordon, P., 'Edith Mary Deverell: An Early Woman Inspector', *History of Education Society Bulletin*, 22, 1978.

Devonshire, *see* **Cavendish.**

Dicey, Albert Venn (1835–1922). Jurist. Born Claybrook Hall, near Lutterworth, Leicestershire, third son of proprietor of the *Northamptonshire Mercury*. Educated King's College, London, 1852–4, and Balliol College, Oxford, 1854–8, first class in classical moderations and *literae humaniores*. President, Oxford Union, 1859 and one of the founders of the small influential club entitled the Old Mortality, which included amongst its members **T.H. Green**, A.C. Swinburne and **J. Bryce**. Fellow, Trinity College, Oxford, 1860–72. Barrister, Inner Temple, 1863. Vinerian professor of Law, Oxford University, 1882–1909. His most famous books were *Introduction to the Study of the Law of the Constitution* (1885), 9th edn. 1939, and *Lectures on the relation between Law and Public Opinion in the Nineteenth Century* (1905). He defended **Gladstone**'s conversion to home rule, publishing *England's Case Against Home Rule* in 1886. An admirer of **T.H. Green**, Dicey shared his compassion for the state of the poorer classes. Principal, Working Men's College, London, 1899–1912. See Rait, R.S., *Memorials of Albert Venn Dicey* (1925).

Dickens, Charles John Huffam (1812–70). Novelist. Born Portsmouth. Educated at a dame school and at a classical, mathematical and commercial school in Chatham where the family had moved in 1816. In 1822 moved to London, and at the age of twelve Dickens began work in a blacking factory. After his father's release from imprisonment for debt Dickens attended Wellington House Academy, 1824–7. For the next five years worked in a solicitor's office and as a law court reporter; and from 1832 to 1836 as a parliamentary reporter and contributor to newspapers and journals. *Sketches by Boz* and *Pickwick Papers* were published 1836–7. Dickens was the first English novelist in whose works children regularly occupied the central place. These little heroes and heroines suffered in unpleasant schools, such as Dotheboys Hall, Salem House Academy and the Minerva House Finishing Establishment for Young Ladies, at the hands of vicious and incompetent teachers, for example Wackford Squeers, Bradley Headstone, Messrs Creakle, Gradgrind and M'Choakumchild. Dickens cared deeply about children and their education; he helped many schools, especially for the orphaned, handicapped and destitute, gave readings and lectures for adult education establishments and argued for a State system of education. See his novels, particularly *Oliver Twist*, *Nicholas Nickleby* and *David Copperfield*, and Forster, J., *The Life of Charles Dickens* (3 vols., 1872–4); Hughes, J.L., *Dickens as an Educator* (1900); Carter, J.A., *Dickens and Education: The Novelist as Reformer* (1956); Collins, P., *Dickens and Education* (1963); Mackenzie, N. and J., *Dickens, A Life* (1979).

Diggle, Joseph Robert (1840–1917). Chairman of the London School Board. Born Astley, Lancashire, and educated Manchester Grammar School and Wadham College, Oxford, first class honours in modern history, 1873. Curate, St Mary's, Bryanston Square, London, 1876–9, when resigned to devote himself to public service. Stood unsuccessfully as parliamentary candidate for West Marylebone, 1885, to test eligibility of clergy to be nominated. Member, London School Board, Marylebone division, 1879–97 and chairman of the Board, 1885–94. Dominated the proceedings by his personality and as leader of the Moderate Party, filled the committees with his followers. His domination led the Progressive Party to coin the word 'Diggleism' and produce a booklet of articles entitled *The Case Against Diggleism* (1894). It was claimed that there had been a neglect of accommodation, teachers and equipment in order to save voluntary schools from Board competition. Diggle was in fact a sincere and prodigious worker for the cause of education and retired from the chairmanship of the Board in 1894. Once more attempted to enter Parliament, standing as Unionist candidate for North Camberwell in 1900 where he was heavily defeated by a School Board opponent, **T.J. Macnamara**. Member, Kent County Council, 1898. Chairman, Elementary Schools Education Committee, Kent, 1903. See his *The School Board for London. A Plea for Better Administration* (1881), and Gautrey, T., *'Lux Mihi Laus': School Board Memories* (1937).

Dixon, George (1820–98). Educational reformer and politician. Born Gomersal, near Bradford, Yorkshire. Educated Leeds Grammar School. Entered firm of foreign merchants, 1838, becoming partner, 1844. Spent three years in Australia, and on his return took up the cause of municipal reform. Councillor, Edgbaston Ward, Birmingham, 1863, mayor, 1866. Initiated series of conferences in Birmingham early in 1867 which called for an Act of Parliament which would allow a rate to be levied by municipal authorities for education, for delaying the age at which children could enter employment and for education to be compulsory. This led to the formation of the Birmingham Aid Society, whose object was to provide additional schools and pay fees of poor children. It was at Dixon's house that the National Education League was founded in 1869, with the co-operation of **Joseph Chamberlain**, **R.W. Dale** and **George Dawson**. At the League's first conference in October 1869, Dixon was president. Liberal MP, Birmingham, 1867–76, when retired because of his wife's ill-health. Returned for Edgbaston division, 1885, becoming a Liberal Unionist, and remaining MP until his death. Played prominent part in the debates on the 1870 Education Bill, opposing the proposal to allow school boards to determine the question of religious instruction. Member, Birmingham School Board, 1870, chairman, 1876–97, succeeding **Chamberlain**. Promoted high standards in Board Schools, subscribing liberally to scholarship for promising pupils. See Marcham, A.J., 'The Birmingham Education Society and the 1870 Education Act', *Journal of Educational Administration and History*, 8 (1), 1976.

Dodd, Catherine Isabella (1860–1932). Educationist. Born Birmingham. Educated privately and abroad. Studied pedagogy at Zurich, Jena, Göttingen, Berlin, Vienna and Budapest. At Jena in 1896, she came under the influence of Herbartianism through the teachings of Wilhelm Rein. One of the earliest day training colleges for men was opened at Owens College, Manchester in 1890. Two years later, a similar department was opened there for women students and she was appointed as Mistress of Method, the only member of staff. A lively, able and original teacher, Catherine Dodd instigated an interesting experiment in 1902, opening an elementary school and kindergarten near the college where experiments in new methods of teaching could be made. Students were able to observe and carry out in practice these methods. Headmistress, Milham Ford Secondary School, 1905–17, then principal, Cherwell Hall, a training college for secondary school teachers in Oxford, 1917–21. See her *Introduction to the Herbartian Principles of Teaching* (1898); *The Child and the Curriculum* (1906); *The Department of Education in the University of Manchester 1890–1911* (1911) and Wilson, E.C., *Catherine Isabella Dodd* (1936).

Donnelly, Sir John Fretcheville Dykes (1834–1902). Soldier and educational administrator. Born Bombay, son of an army officer. Educated at Highgate School, 1843–8, and Royal Military Academy, Woolwich, 1849–53. On active service in the Crimean War. Donnelly was placed in charge of a detachment of soldiers in London on his return, preparing for building a permanent museum and centre of science and art in South Kensington. **Sir Henry Cole**, who was in charge of the scheme, as Secretary of the Department of Science and Art, appointed Donnelly Inspector of Science in March 1859. Donnelly, promoted to the rank of captain, was seconded to the Department for ten years, though he never returned to the Army. A man of great energy, he was responsible for a minute issued in 1859 which ensured that grants made to certified teachers were dependent on the result of the examinations of their pupils, an early example of 'payment by results'. In 1874, Donnelly was appointed Director of Science, responsible for the expansion of science schools and classes nationally as well as important scientific institutions. Three years later his scheme for a central technical training institution, the City and Guilds Industrial University, became a reality. In 1881 he became an Assistant Secretary to the Science and Art Department and was also promoted to a full colonel. He became permanent head in 1884 and built up the Science School at South Kensington. Donnelly was largely responsible for the vocationally-orientated Royal Society of Arts examinations from 1871; the higher grade school was also his creation. Major-general, 1887, knight, 1893. Retired, 1899. See Armytage, W.H.G., 'J.F. Donnelly: Pioneer in Vocational Education', *Vocational Aspects of Secondary and Further Education*, 4 (2), 1950; Bishop, A.S., *The Rise of a Central Authority for English Education* (1971); Butterworth, H., 'The Science and Art Department Examinations: Origins and Achievement' in Macleod, R. (ed.), *Days of Judgement* (1982).

Dunn, Henry (1801–76). Educationist. Born in Nottingham where at an early age he revealed 'great zeal for mental improvement'. Little is known about his early life. He spent some time at Borough Road College, and after brief service as master of a monitorial school in Guatemala, 1827–8, became master of the Borough Road School. Secretary of the British and Foreign School Society, 1830–56, and member of the committee until his death. Dunn gave evidence to the 1834 Select Committee on Education which showed how the students at Borough Road were occupied from five in the morning until ten at night. In his *Annual Reports* he emphasized the need for better candidates, longer training, and improved pay and status for teachers. Dunn saw the success of the training institution as the key to the Society's work both at home and overseas. See his *Popular Education or the Normal School Manual* (1837); *National Education* (1838), and Bartle, G.F., *A History of Borough Road College* (1976); Bartle, G.F., 'Henry Dunn and the Secretaryship of the British and Foreign School Society, 1830–1856', *Journal of Educational Administration and History*, 18 (1), 1986.

Dyke, Sir William Hart, 7th Bt. (1837–1931). Politician. Born Orpington, Kent, son of Sir Percyvall Hart Dyke. Educated at Harrow, 1851–5, and Christ Church, Oxford, 1855–9. Excellent rackets player, playing for the University against Cambridge for four years, winning every match. One of the founders of lawn tennis. Elected Conservative MP, West Kent, 1865–8, Mid Kent, 1868–85 and Kent (Dartford), 1885–1906. Whip, 1868, Chief Whip, 1874. Chief Secretary, Ireland in Salisbury's government, 1885–6 and Vice-President, Committee of Council on Education, 1887–92. During his time in office, Dyke played a leading part in promulgating the 1890 Education Code, which paved the way for the ending of the system of 'payment by results'; he was also in charge of the 1891 Free Education Bill in the Commons. Its successful passage opened the way to provide free elementary education to children. Succeeded as 7th Bt., 1875.

Ede, James Chuter, Baron Chuter-Ede (1882–1965). Teacher and politician. Born Epsom, Surrey. Educated at Epsom National School, Dorking High School, Battersea Pupil-Teacher Centre, and Christ's College, Cambridge. Ede taught in schools, 1905–14 and was secretary to the Surrey County Teachers' Association, 1919–45. His interests in local government included membership of Surrey County Council, 1914–49, of which he was chairman, 1933–7, the mayoralty of Epsom and Ewell, and the presidency of the County Councils Association, 1953–61. Also president of the International Association for Liberal Christianity and Religious Freedom, 1955–8. Ede entered Parliament in 1923 as Labour member for Mitcham. Sat for South Shields, 1929–31, and 1935–64 when he was granted a life peerage as Baron Chuter-Ede. Parliamentary Secretary to the Board of Education, 1940–4, and to the Ministry of Education, 1944–5. Home Secretary, 1945–51. Trustee of the British Museum, 1951–63 and deputy chairman of BBC General Advisory Council, 1952–9. Ede's many services to education, particularly in respect of the 1944 Education Act were recognized by honorary degrees from the Universities of Bristol, Cambridge, Durham and Sheffield. PC, 1944, CH, 1953. See his *Mutual Relations of Industry and Education* (1944); *Knowledge, Wisdom and Freedom* (1949), and Barker, R., *Education and Politics 1900–51, A Study of the Labour Party* (1972).

Edgeworth, Maria (1767–1849). Novelist and educationist. Born at Black Bourton, Oxfordshire. Daughter of **R.L. Edgeworth** and the second of his 21 children by four wives. Educated at schools in Derby, 1775–80, and in London, 1780–2. Small of stature she was subjected to several mechanical attempts, including hanging by the neck, to increase her height. A good French and Italian scholar, she translated de Genlis' *Adèle et Théodore*. Her educational writings included a defence of female education, *Letters to Literary Ladies* (1795); *The Parent's Assistant* (6 parts, completed 1800); *Practical Education* (2 vols., 1798) with her father, which modified the educational theories of Rousseau, and *Early Lessons* (1801) and *Moral Tales* (1801). In addition to writing stories and plays for children her novels – *Castle Rackrent* (1800) and *Belinda* (1801) were the first – brought her fame and fortune. She published her father's *Memoirs* in 1820. She had always taken a keen interest in the family's Irish estate and was very active in organizing relief during the famine of 1845–6. See her own writings and Butler, M.S., *Maria Edgeworth: a literary Biography* (1972); Colvin, C., *Maria Edgeworth in France and Switzerland* (1979).

Edgeworth, Richard Lovell (1744–1817). Author, inventor and educationist. Born in Bath. Educated at schools in Warwick, Drogheda and Longford. A student for six months at Trinity College, Dublin in 1761, and then transferred to Corpus Christi College, Oxford. Keener on mechanical inventions – he designed a telegraph, a one-wheeled carriage and a turnip cutter – than on bookish study. Became friendly with Thomas Day, author of *Sandford and Merton* (1783). Edgeworth's eldest son was brought up on Rousseauian principles, and they met Rousseau in Paris in 1771–2. MP for Longford in the last Irish Parliament, 1798–1800, and served on a board inquiring into Irish education, 1806–11. See his educational writings including *Practical Education* (2 vols., 1798, with his daughter); *Professional Education* (1808); *Memoirs* (2 vols., 1820, with his daughter), and Clarke, D.J., *The Ingenious Mr Edgeworth* (1965).

Edwards, Sir Owen Morgan (1858–1920). Educationist and school inspector. Born Coedypry, Llanuwchllyn, Merionethshire. Educated at parish school and Bala Grammar School where he became a friend of T.E. Ellis and D.R. Daniel. In 1875, Edwards attended the Bala Theological College as a lay student and acted as lecturer; Aberystwyth University College, 1880–3, where he took a London BA; Glasgow University, 1883–4 and in 1885, elected a Brackenbury scholar in modern history at Balliol College, Oxford, obtaining a first, 1887. Fellow, Lincoln College, Oxford and lecturer in modern history, 1889–1907. His great interest in Welsh nationalism

which dated from his undergraduate days led him in 1889 to become editor of five Welsh journals. Succeeded **T.E. Ellis** as Liberal MP, Merionethshire, unopposed in May 1899, but resigned his seat in 1900. Edwards' chance to further his promotion of Welsh culture and education came in 1907 when he was appointed Chief Inspector, Wales, Board of Education, when the Welsh Department was set up. He recruited HMI who were able 'to discharge a particular responsibility for the traditional language and culture of Wales'. Edwards encouraged the Intermediate Schools to flourish, promoting science teaching. In 1909 he ordered that 'Every HMI will see that Welsh is put in its right place in the curriculum of every school'. Knight, 1910, for services to Welsh literature. Member, Royal Commission on University Education in Wales, 1916–18. See his *England before the Conquest. A School History of England* (1901); *A Short History of Wales* (1906) and Lloyd, W., 'Owen M. Edwards 1858–1920', in Gittins, C. (ed.), *Pioneers of Welsh Education* (1964).

Eicholz, Alfred (1869–1933). School and medical inspector. Born Manchester, son of a cotton merchant. Educated Manchester Grammar School and Emmanuel College, Cambridge, first class honours in natural science tripos, 1891 and 1892. MB, BC and MA, 1895, MD, 1898, and at St Bartholomew's Hospital, London. Fellow, Emmanuel College, 1893, the first Jew to be elected fellow of a Cambridge college, and lectureship, 1895. HMI, 1898–1907, Inspector, Medical Department, 1908–19, Chief Medical Officer, Board of Education, 1919–30. Gave evidence before a number of official commissions, including those on wage-earning children (1902), physical deterioration (1903), and the feeble-minded (1908). Member, Departmental Committee on the Causes and Prevention of Blindness, 1922. CBE, 1919.

Eldon, John Scott, 1st Earl of Eldon (1751–1838). Lawyer. Born at Newcastle upon Tyne. Educated by a Scottish dominie named Warden, at Newcastle Grammar School, and at University College, Oxford. Fellow, 1767; BA, 1770; MA, 1773; DCL, 1802. In 1801 was appointed High Steward of the University. Called to the bar at Middle Temple, 1776; Bencher, 1783; treasurer, 1797. First entered Parliament in 1783 as member for Weobley, Herefordshire and from 1796 sat for Boroughbridge, Yorkshire. Solicitor-General and knighted in 1788. In 1792 created Baron Eldon and entered the House of Lords. Lord Chief Justice of the Common Pleas, 1799–1801, and Lord Chancellor, 1801–6, and 1807–27. In 1805 his decision that the Leeds Grammar School was a school 'for teaching grammatically the learned languages' slowed the reform of grammar school curricula. Created Earl, 1821. Eldon was honoured by the University of Oxford, for example in the Eldon Law scholarship founded in 1829. He was FRS, FSA, a governor of the Charterhouse and a trustee of the British Museum. See Twiss, H., *The Public and Private Life of Lord Chancellor Eldon* (3 vols., 1844); Surtees, W.E., *A Sketch of the Lives of Lords Stowell and Eldon* (1846); Tompson, R.S., 'The Leeds Grammar School Case of 1805', *Journal of Educational Administration and History*, 3 (1), 1970.

Ellis, Thomas Edward (1859–1899). Statesman. Born Llandderfel, Merionethshire, son of a tenant farmer. Educated Bala Grammar School, 1870–5, where he made friends with D.R. Daniel and **O.M. Edwards,** and University College of Wales, Aberystwyth, 1875–9, where he became more conscious of the Welsh language and culture and joined forces with other nationalists; New College, Oxford, 1880–4, where he read history. Ellis was much influenced by **T.H. Green** who emphasized the moral duties of the citizen as servant of the state and **Arnold Toynbee,** then a Balliol don, and participated in activities connected with guild socialism. Elected Liberal MP, Merionethshire, 1886, remaining its member until his death. Supported Gladstone's home rule policy. Ellis's friendship with **A.H.D. Acland,** struck up at Oxford bore fruit with their active campaigning for free education in 1890 and for leasehold enfranchisement in Wales. With the coming of county councils in 1888, Ellis played a conspicuous part in ensuring that the measure to establish a system of intermediate schools which provided secondary education throughout Wales (1889) received Liberal support. Known as 'the Parnell of Wales', Ellis was made Lord of the Treasury and Parliamentary Charity Commissioner, 1892–4, and Parliamentary Secretary to the Treasury, (Junior Whip), 1894–5, during the Gladstone and Rosebery ministries, and was chief Opposition Whip, 1895–9. See Ellis, T.I., *Thomas Edward Ellis* (2 vols., 1944–8); Masterman, N., *The Forerunner* (1972).

Ellis, William (1800–81). Economist and educator. Born London. Son of a French Huguenot father and an Italian mother. Educated at a school in Bromley and at the age of 14 became assistant to his father, a Lloyd's underwriter. In 1826 he became chief underwriter of the Indemnity Marine Insurance Company, a position he held until 1876. A most successful man of business (he did not take a holiday for 30 years), Ellis nevertheless devoted much time to education and particularly to teaching political economy to children. He was a friend of **John Stuart Mill** and associated with him in the Utilitarian Society and in other groups interested in economic questions, and contributed to the *Westminster Review*. Ellis saw the necessity of a national system of education. He believed in teaching useful knowledge, in learning by enquiry rather than by memorization, and in founding schools to provide examples. The first, which used the Mechanics' Institute premises in Chancery Lane, London, he named the Birkbeck School, in honour of **George Birkbeck**. The 11 schools founded by Ellis were known as Birkbeck Schools. They were secular and catered for pupils from the artisan and tradesmen classes. Buildings were rented rather than constructed for the purpose. The William Ellis School was founded in North London in 1862. Ellis gave lectures to the royal children at the invitation of the Prince Consort, and also wrote a series of textbooks, some of which were translated and used in schools in France. See his *Outlines of Social Economy* (1846); *Education as a Means of Preventing Destitution* (1851), and Ellis, E., *Memoir of William Ellis and an account of his conduct-teaching* (1888); Blyth, E.K., *Life of William Ellis* (1889); Wickenden, T.D., *The William Ellis School* (1962).

Elmhirst, Leonard K. (1893–1974). Educational innovator. Born Laxton, Yorkshire, son of a landowner. Educated at Repton and Trinity College, Cambridge, studying history and theology, 1912–14. Worked with Young Men's Christian Association in India during the war followed by army service, 1918–19. Cornell University, 1919–21, obtaining a degree in agriculture, then returned to India to work with Rabindranath Tagore, the poet. Elmhirst helped to found the Institute of Rural Reconstruction at Sriniketar, where students were trained in many aspects of rural life which harmonized with modern society. These ideas were translated to England after Elmhirst's marriage to Dorothy Whitney Straight in 1925. They purchased Dartington Hall in Devon, an old manor house with extensive land. A Trust was formed in 1931–2 with Elmhirst as chairman, responsible for the many activities which had been established, ranging from cider-making to sawmilling. One of Elmhirst's best known ventures was the setting up of a progressive coeducational boarding school. The arts were strongly represented. Besides an Arts Centre for training talented locals, there was a music college, a theatre, an adult education centre and Summer School of Music which has gained an international reputation. Dorothy Elmhirst died in 1968. See Young, M., *The Elmhirsts of Dartington* (1982).

Ewart, William (1798–1869). Politician. Born Liverpool, educated at Eton and Christ Church, Oxford. Second class honours in classics, 1821. Called to the bar in 1827 and first entered Parliament for Bletchingley in 1828. MP for Liverpool, 1830–7, for Wigan, 1839–41, and for Dumfries, 1841–68. An advanced Liberal, he advocated a number of measures to improve the lot of the working classes. These included the opening of public museums and galleries without charge or other restriction. From 1841 he regularly moved for an annual statement upon education by a minister of the Crown, and also called for the examination of candidates for the civil service (1845), for the army (1847) and for the diplomatic service (1852). These and others of his proposals were eventually achieved, but his name is particularly connected with the establishment of the Schools of Design from 1837, and his successful Bill of 1850 for establishing free public libraries supported from local rates. In 1867 he also secured the admission of 'unattached' students to universities. See Munford, W.E., *William Ewart MP* (1960).

Farrar, Frederic William (1831–1903). Schoolmaster, scholar and cleric. Born at Bombay, India. Educated in England at a Latin school at Aylesbury, at King William's College, Isle of Man, and at King's College, London, where he graduated first in the honours examination BA, 1852. Trinity College, Cambridge from 1850, graduating BA, 1854; MA, 1857; DD, 1874. Ordained deacon, 1854; priest, 1857. Fellow of Trinity from 1856. Assistant master at Marlborough 1854–5 and Harrow, 1855–71; headmaster of Marlborough, 1871–6; canon of Westminster and rector of

ESSAYS

ON

A LIBERAL EDUCATION.

EDITED BY

REV. F. W. FARRAR, M.A. F.R.S.

ASSISTANT-MASTER AT HARROW, LATE FELLOW OF TRINITY COLLEGE, CAMBRIDGE, AND
HON. FELLOW OF KING'S COLLEGE, LONDON.

London:

MACMILLAN AND CO.

1867.

St Margaret's, 1876–83; Archdeacon of Westminster, 1883–95; Dean of Canterbury, 1895–1903. Farrar was a prolific writer. His first fictional work *Eric, or Little by Little* (1858), a partly autobiographical work about schoolboy life, went through 36 editions in his own lifetime. *Julian Home* (1859) and *St Winifred's* (1862) were also bestsellers with more than 40 editions of the two before his death. Farrar's scholarly works were in the field of philology, education and theology. He was an evolutionist in philology, and became a close friend of **Darwin**, securing his burial in Westminster Abbey and preaching the funeral sermon. He was an advocate of science teaching and a critic of the defects of classics teaching, and put these principles into practice as headmaster at Marlborough. He had a considerable influence upon the religion and culture of the middle classes; his *Life of Christ* went through 12 editions in its first year of publication. See his (ed.), *Essays on a Liberal Education* (1867); *Life of Christ* (1874); *Language and Languages* (1878), and Farrar, R.A., *The Life of Frederic William Farrar* (1904).

Fawcett, Henry (1833–84). Politician and academic. Born Salisbury, son of a draper. Educated Queenswood College, 1847–9, King's College School, London, 1849–52, Peterhouse, Cambridge, 1852–3 and Trinity Hall, Cambridge, 1853–6, where he graduated 7th wrangler in mathematics. Fellow, Trinity Hall, 1856. He published his *Manual of Political Economy* in 1863 and in the same year was elected professor of Political Economy at Cambridge. Earlier, in 1858, he had been blinded in both eyes by his father in a shooting accident. Despite this handicap, Fawcett also embarked on a political career. He was Liberal MP, Brighton, 1865–74, and Hackney, 1874–84, and was appointed Postmaster-General in **Gladstone**'s second ministry in 1880. A social reformer with a great interest in educational issues, Fawcett introduced a bill into the Commons in 1867 which proposed that agricultural children should be made to attend school on alternate days, and which gave magistrates the power of ordering schools to be built at ratepayers' expense. He joined the Birmingham Education League in 1869 and vigorously addressed a congress that year, advocating universal compulsory education, rate-supported if necessary, and looked forward to a complete system of graduated education from elementary school to the university. Fawcett also campaigned to open fellowships at Trinity College, Dublin, to all denominations. In 1873 when Gladstone introduced an Irish Universities Bill which would have amalgamated various bodies but left courses in theology, moral philosophy and history to separate colleges, Fawcett attacked the measure. The government was defeated on the second reading in March 1873, and Gladstone resigned; Disraeli refused to take office, but Fawcett's action proved fatal to the government. See Stephen, L., *Life of Henry Fawcett* (1885).

Fawcett, Philippa (1868–1948). Scholar and administrator. Born London, the only child of **Henry** and Millicent **Fawcett**. Educated at home, at Miss Macleod Smith's at Cambridge, at Clapham High School, and at Newnham College, Cambridge. Winner of the Gilchrist scholarship for her results in the higher local examination. In 1890 her fame was ensured when the tripos lists were read out, when she was placed 'above Senior Wrangler'. Leading articles in *The Times* and other newspapers proclaimed the significance of this result for the women's cause. In 1901 accompanied her mother on a tour of the concentration camps in South Africa, and in the following year returned to assist in the establishment of public elementary education in the Transvaal. As private secretary to the acting Director of Education she helped to develop a system of farm schools. Briefly taught mathematics at Newnham. In 1905 Fawcett was appointed principal assistant in the executive officers' department of the London County Council (LCC). From 1920 as Assistant Officer for Higher Education Fawcett was concerned with setting up the training colleges of Furzedown and Avery Hill, for which she also acted as principal. She retired from the LCC in 1934. Fawcett combined exceptional ability with humility. She established good relationships between the LCC and London University, and the LCC and the governing bodies of existing secondary schools. In 1949 the former Clapham and Streatham Hill Training College was renamed Philippa Fawcett College. See her *The Colonial Problem* (1932), and Strachey, R., *Millicent Garrett Fawcett* (1931).

Fearon, Daniel Robert (1835–1919). Civil servant. Born Assington, Suffolk, son of a vicar. Educated Marlborough and Balliol College, Oxford, 1854–60, gaining firsts in classical moderations and *literae humaniores* and a fourth in law and history. Barrister, Lincoln's Inn, 1874. Assistant Inspector of Schools, 1860–4, HMI, 1864–70. The only non-clergyman to inspect Anglican schools before 1870. His ten years as an inspector were recorded in *School Inspection* (1876). The book gives a vivid account of schooling under 'payment by results', of which he was a stout supporter. Useful advice for young inspectors included, 'There is only one way to stop copying, and that is to make it impossible'. Assistant Commissioner, Royal Commission on Middle Class Education (Taunton), 1865. Special Commissioner, together with **Joshua Fitch**, to investigate the state of elementary education in four major cities, reporting on Birmingham and Leeds, 1869. Assistant Charity Commissioner, 1875–86. Secretary, Charity Commission, 1886–1900. Charity Commissioner, 1900–3. CB, 1894. See Leese, J., *Personalities and Power in English Education* (1950).

Findlay, Joseph John (1860–1940). Educationist and author. Son of Wesleyan minister and educated Kingswood School, Bath, Wadham College, Oxford, 1880–3, gaining firsts in mathematics and history, and Jena and Leipzig, where he was awarded a doctorate, 1891–3. It was there that he became influenced by the ideas of Herbart. Taught at Bath College, 1884–5 and Rugby, 1888, 1893–4, for short periods. Headmaster of two Wesleyan proprietary schools, Taunton and Wesley College, Sheffield, 1885–91, and headmaster, Cardiff High School for Boys, 1898–1903. Professor of Education, University of Manchester, 1903–25. Unsuccessful Labour Party candidate, Combined English Universities, 1923 and 1924. Publications include *Arnold of Rugby* (1897); *Principles of Class Teaching* (1902); *The School* (1912, revised edition, 1932); *The Children of England* (1923); *The Foundations of Education* (2 vols., 1925, 1927).

Fisher, Herbert Albert Laurens (1865–1940). Historian and statesman. Born London. Educated at Winchester and New College, Oxford. BA first class in classical moderations and *literae humaniores*, 1888, and elected to a fellowship in the same year. Studied also at the Universities of Paris and Göttingen. As a tutor in modern history at Oxford he published several books including *Bonapartism* (1908), *The Republican Tradition in Europe* (1911) and *Napoleon* (1913). In 1912 Fisher was appointed to the Royal Commission on the public services in India, and in 1914 was elected Vice-Chancellor of the University of Sheffield. Won considerable support both within the university and in the city for his work in arts, sciences and in the war effort. In December 1916 was invited by Lloyd George to become President of the Board of Education and entered Parliament as member for the Hallam division of Sheffield. He was a successful minister, and his name is particularly associated with the Education Act of 1918. Fisher remained in the Cabinet until 1922. Member for the Combined English Universities, 1918–26,

British delegate to the League of Nations, 1920–2. In 1925 he became Warden of New College, Oxford. Continued his writings which culminated in his last and best work, the *History of Europe* (3 vols., 1935). President of the British Academy, 1928–32; fellow of the Royal Society; trustee of the British Museum; honorary degrees from Edinburgh, Sheffield, Manchester, Cambridge, Liverpool and Oxford. OM, 1937. See his *An Unfinished Autobiography* (1940), and Ogg, D., *Herbert Fisher, 1865–1940* (1947); Sherington, G., *English Education, Social Change and War, 1911–20* (1981).

Fitch, Sir Joshua Girling (1824–1903). School inspector. Born Southwark, London, son of a clerk. Educated privately and Borough Road School, Southwark, becoming pupil teacher there 1838, full assistant, 1842. Headmaster, Kingsland Road School, Dalston, 1844. External University of London BA, 1850, MA, classics, 1852. Taken on the staff of Borough Road Training College the same year, Fitch became principal, 1856. A gifted teacher. HMI, County of York, 1863–5, Assistant Commissioner, Schools Inquiry Commission, Yorkshire and Durham, 1865–7, Special Commissioner on elementary education in Manchester and Liverpool. Assistant Commissioner, Endowed Schools, 1870–7, HMI, East Lambeth, 1877–83, Chief Inspector, eastern division, 1883–5, Chief Inspector, Training Colleges, 1885–94. Fitch devoted much time to promoting the education of women: assisted with the establishment of the College of Women, Hitchin, 1874, which became Girton College, Cambridge and helped in the founding of the Girls' Public Day School Company, 1874. He was also involved in the setting up of Holloway College, Egham, Maria Grey Training College and the Cambridge Training College for women secondary school teachers. He lectured at the latter, 1879–80, publishing his course as *Lectures On Teaching* (1881). As a result of a visit to USA, he prepared a report *Notes on American Schools and Training Colleges* (1890). He was also involved in a public controversy concerning the 'overpressure' issue in London schools in 1884 with Dr Crichton-Browne. His advocacy of well-trained elementary school teachers is best seen in *Educational Aims and Methods* (1900). Knight, 1896. See Lilley, A.L., *Sir Joshua Fitch* (1906), and Leese, J., *Personalities and Power in English Education* (1950).

Fitzroy, Sir Almeric William (1851–1935). Civil servant. Son of country gentleman and great-grandson of 3rd Duke of Grafton. Educated Cheam and Balliol College, Oxford, 1870–4, with a first in

LECTURES ON TEACHING

DELIVERED IN THE

UNIVERSITY OF CAMBRIDGE

DURING THE LENT TERM, 1880,

BY

SIR JOSHUA FITCH, M.A., LL.D.

LATE HER MAJESTY'S INSPECTOR OF TRAINING COLLEGES;
AND ASSISTANT COMMISSIONER TO THE
ENDOWED SCHOOLS COMMISSION.

STEREOTYPED EDITION

CAMBRIDGE:
AT THE UNIVERSITY PRESS.
1902

modern history. HMI in Wiltshire, 1876–84. Junior Examiner, Education Department, 1884–5, then private secretary to three Vice-Presidents of the Council, Hon. Edward Stanhope, Sir Henry Holland and **Sir William Hart-Dyke**, 1885–92. Returned to ordinary work at Education Department, then appointed private secretary to **Duke of Devonshire**, Lord President of the Council, 1895–8. Clerk to the Privy Council, 1898–1923. Chairman, Interdepartmental Committee on Physical Deterioration, 1903–4. Author of *The History of the Privy Council* (1928) and the entertaining *Memoirs* (2 vols., 1925).

Fleming, David Pinkerton, Lord Fleming (1877–1944). Judge. Born Rutherglen, near Glasgow, fourth son of a writer (Scottish equivalent of a solicitor). Educated at Glasgow High School and Glasgow University, MA, 1895, LL.B, 1896, and Edinburgh University, where studied procedure and evidence. Barrister-at-law, Scotland, 1902. Served as officer in France and Belgium in First World War and seriously wounded, 1918. Awarded Military Cross and Belgian Croix de Guerre. Conservative, unsuccessfully contested Dumbartonshire, 1923, but elected MP there, 1924, sitting until 1926 when appointed a Judge of the Court of Session with judicial title of Lord Fleming. Solicitor-General, 1922–3 and 1924–5. King's Counsel, 1921. Fleming's wide interests were usefully employed in his capacity as chairman of a committee on public schools, appointed by **R.A. Butler**, then President of the Board of Education, in June 1942. The Fleming Report, isued in 1944, suggested constructive ways in which links could be forged between public schools and the state sector of education. The Report received only a lukewarm reception and its recommendations were not implemented.

Fletcher, Joseph (1813–52). School inspector. Born Rennes, France. Entered Middle Temple, 1838, barrister, 1841. From the age of 19 Fletcher was involved in investigations connected with the health and welfare of the people. Secretary to two royal commissions, on hand loom weavers, 1841, and on children's employment, 1843. Secretary, Statistical Society of London and editor of the *Statistical Journal*. Member of the Council of the British Association. Appointed HMI, 1844. Greatly interested in relationship between crime and the provision of education. In 1850, published *The Moral Statistics of England and Wales*, and *Education:*

National, Voluntary and Free (1851) in which he advocated rate aid for schools. Fletcher died at the early age of 39.

Forster, William Edward (1818–86). Statesman. Born Bradpole, Dorset. Brought up in a Quaker family and received a Quaker  education at Fishponds House, Bristol, and Grove House, Tottenham which he left in 1835. Learnt the trade of wool manufacture and in 1842 became a partner in a woollen business at Bradford. A free trade supporter, he visited famine districts in Ireland in 1846 and 1847. Knew **Robert Owen**, Thomas Cooper, and **F.D. Maurice**. In 1850 married Jane the eldest daughter of **Thomas Arnold** and left the Society of Friends. In 1861 elected Liberal MP for Bradford which he represented till the end of his life. Under-Secretary for the Colonies, 1865–6; Vice-President of the Committee of Council on Education, 1868–74. Responsible for carrying through the House of Commons the Elementary Education Bill of 1870. Rate-aided School Boards were established in areas where there was a deficiency of elementary school provision. The chief Parliamentary opposition came from some of the Government's own supporters who argued that such education should be compulsory, secular and free. Chief Secretary, Ireland, 1880–2, where his policies also came under considerable criticism. Reid, T. Wemyss, *Life of the Rt. Hon. W.E. Forster* (2 vols., 1888); Murphy, J., *The Education Act 1870* (1972).

Fortescue, Hugh, 3rd Earl Fortescue (1818–1905). Politician and reformer. Born London, educated at Harrow and Trinity College, Cambridge. Private secretary to his father, then Lord Lieutenant of Ireland, 1839–40, and to Lord Melbourne the Prime Minister, 1840–1. Whig MP for Plymouth, 1841–52; and Marylebone, 1854–9, when he was raised to the peerage on the death of his father. Differed from Gladstone on the Eastern Question in the 1870s, sat on the cross benches thereafter, and declared himself a Liberal Unionist in 1886.

Fortescue was an ardent social reformer. Secretary to the Poor Law Board, 1847–51; chairman of the Metropolitan Consolidated Commission on Sewers, 1849–51. He advocated sanitary reform, particularly in respect of conditions for the army, and local government reform in London. His educational work included lectures to mechanics' and other institutes, liberal subscriptions to schools, and support for a plan to establish a university in Devon. See his *Public Schools for the Middle Classes* (1864); *State and Rate-paid Education* (1886), and Allsobrook, D., *Schools for the Shires* (1986).

Foster, Vere Henry Lewis (1819–1900). Educationist and philanthropist. Born in Copenhagen where his father was the British minister. Educated at Eton and Christ Church, Oxford. Served in the diplomatic service in South America from 1842–7, but a trip to Ireland in 1847, coupled with his Irish ancestry, determined him to work for the improvement of the conditions of the Irish poor. He secured reform of the regulations governing emigrant ships and also gave financial aid to many emigrants. His final years were spent in Belfast working with the sick. His contribution to education was twofold. Foster gave a large part of his fortune to building hundreds of parish schools. He also wrote and published a series of copybooks which taught writing, drawing and colouring. The *Vere Foster Copybook* was used in Irish schools until the 1920s. See MacNeill, M., *Vere Foster, 1819–1900, an Irish benefactor* (1971).

Fox, William Johnson (1786–1864). Politician, preacher and writer. Born Wrentham, Suffolk. Went to a chapel school and after other jobs, in 1799 became a clerk in a bank, studying hard in his own time. By 1812 became minister of the Unitarian chapel at Chichester. Began writing for periodicals and contributed to the first issue of the *Westminster Review* in 1824. Fox became one of the most renowned orators of his day and a leading speaker for the Anti-Corn Law League. He gave Sunday evening lectures to the working classes in Holborn 1844–6, which were published in four volumes in 1849. In 1847 he was returned to Parliament as member for the working-class constituency of Oldham. His championship of the cause of national education reached a peak in 1850 with his introduction of an unsuccessful Bill for establishing compulsory secular education. See Garnett, R., *The Life of W.J. Fox, public teacher and social reformer 1786–1864* (1910).

Fraser, James (1818–85). Cleric. Born Prestbury, Gloucestershire, eldest of seven children of a retired Indian merchant. Educated at Heavitree, Exeter, Bridgnorth School, Shropshire, 1832–4 and Shrewsbury, 1834–6 and Lincoln College, Oxford, 1837, obtaining first class in classics 1839, and fellow, Oriel College, Oxford, 1840–60. Ordained as priest, 1847, with living of Cholderton, Wiltshire. Assistant Commissioner, Newcastle Commission, 1858–61, making reports for Dorset, Devon, Somerset, and Herefordshire. In 1865, appointed a commissioner to report on education in the United States and Canada, published 1866. Rector, Upton Nervet, Berkshire, 1860–70. Prepared report for the Commission on the Employment of Children in England for the south-eastern district, 1867. **Gladstone** offered Fraser the see of Manchester in January 1870 because of his interest in education. The new bishop quickly became known for his enthusiasm for schooling and other social movements addressing many meetings in halls, factories and workplaces. Member of the governing bodies of Manchester and Shrewsbury Grammar Schools and Owens College, visitor of the Manchester Girls' High School and president of the College of Women. A liberal in church matters he was known as 'the bishop of all denominations'. See Hughes, T., *James Fraser, Second Bishop of Manchester. A Memoir* (1887).

Freud, Dr Anna (1895–1982). Pioneer of child analysis. Born Vienna, youngest of Sigmund and Anna Freud's six children. Educated at the Cottage Lyceum, Vienna and subsequently taught there for five years. A great admirer of her father's work, she became an international figure in her own right, making important contributions in the fields of child analysis, child development and child psychology. Anna Freud published her first paper, on the family life of children, in 1922, to be followed by many other works, including *The Ego and the Mechanisms of Defence* (1938). After the Nazi occupation of Austria, she left with her father and settled in Hampstead, London. With Dorothy Burlingham, she opened the residential Hampstead War Nurseries: their observations led to two books, *Young Children in War Time* (1942) and *Infants Without Families* (1943). She also established the Hampstead Child Therapy Course and Clinic after the war for training, teaching and research purposes. In later years, she also became interested in family law and related problems. CBE, 1967. See *The Psycho-Analytical Treatment of Children. Technical lectures and essays* (1944); *Normality and Pathology in Childhood Assessment of Development*

(1966); *Beyond the Best Interests of the Child* (1973), and *Before the Best Interests of the Child* (1980), both with Goldstein, J. and Solnit, A.J.; and Solnit, A.J., 'Anna Freud: The Child Expert', in *The Psychoanalytic Study of the Child,* Vol. 39 (1984); Peters, U.H., *Anna Freud. A Life Dedicated to Children* (1985).

Fry, Elizabeth (1780–1845). Prison reformer and educationist. Born at Earlham, Norfolk, daughter of John Gurney of the well-known Quaker banking family. In 1798, inspired by the American Quaker evangelist Savery, she visited the poor and taught their children. Opened a Sunday school, and in 1809 became a Quaker minister. In 1813 Fry first visited Newgate prison. Established an Association for the Improvement of Female Prisoners run by a Committee of Quaker ladies. A school was set up and women were provided with work. Her rehabilitative ideas were outlined in *Observations . . . on Female Prisoners* (1827). Fry's concerns for the poor included prisons, transport, housing and employment. She helped to found a model district visiting society in Brighton and to provide libraries for Sussex coastguards. In Germany and in London she was involved in setting up institutions for training nurses. An assiduous diarist. See Fry, K. and R., *Memoirs of the Life of Elizabeth Fry* (1847), and Rose, J., *Elizabeth Fry: a biography* (1980).

Galloway, Janet Ann (1841–1909). Promoter of higher education for women. Born at Campsie near Glasgow. Educated at various schools in Scotland, France, Germany and Holland. Employed in her father's surveyor's office and in 1877 became secretary of the Glasgow Association for the Higher Education of Women. Galloway, who had studied the establishment of higher educational institutions for women in England and Europe, made arrangements for lectures, tutorial classes and correspondence courses. She was supported by **John Caird**, principal of Glasgow University, and in 1883 Queen Margaret College was established. In 1893 Glasgow University took over the College and it became a separate Women's Department. Galloway resisted the trend towards coeducation, but by 1909 all honours courses were attended by men and women together. Galloway's concern for student welfare continued and a female hall of residence was opened in 1894. She was also prominent in the Queen Margaret Settlement Association, 1897, which led to students undertaking voluntary social work in deprived areas of Glasgow, and to the establishment of an invalid school. A member of the Teachers' Guild and of the Glasgow Provincial Committee for the Training of Teachers. Awarded an honorary LL.D by Glasgow University in 1907. See Murray, D., *Miss Janet Galloway and the Higher Education of Women in Glasgow* (1914).

Galton, Sir Francis (1822–1911). Scientist. Born Birmingham, son of a banker. Educated at private schools, King Edward's School, Birmingham, 1836–8, King's College, London, 1839–40, where he studied medicine, and Trinity College, Cambridge, 1840–4, where he read mathematics but took an *aegrotat* degree because of illness. The death of his father in 1844 provided Galton with an income, so he abandoned his medical studies and toured Africa. His book, *Tropical South Africa* (1853) made him known as an explorer. FRS, 1856. General Secretary, British Association, 1863–7. He published a work on meteorographics in 1863 which laid the basis for weather forecasting. His interest in the laws of heredity led him to establish an 'anthropometric laboratory' in connection with the International Health Exhibition, 1884–5, and collected data of the senses and physical dimensions of humans. Galton demonstrated that human types could be generalized: for example, he made a map to show the distribution of beauty in Great Britain. He also made contributions to psychology, including work on visual memory. Galton was greatly impressed by *The Origin of Species* (1859) written by his cousin, **Charles Darwin**; this led him to devote the rest of his working life to tracing the effect of heredity on human beings. The fruits of this research are contained in his books *Hereditary Genius* (1869), *Inquiries into Human Faculty* (1883) and *Natural Inheritance* (1889). He promoted the notion of eugenics, i.e. that inferior human stock should be restricted, and set up eugenic societies, a eugenics laboratory and a research fellowship at University College, London in 1907 and a journal devoted to the subject. He influenced a number of later psychologists who investigated children's mental development and intellectual ability, notably **Cyril Burt**. Knight, 1909. See his *Memories of My Life* (2 vols., 1908), and Forrest, D.W., *Francis Galton, The Life and Work of a Victorian Genius* (1974).

Garnett, Dr William (1850–1932). Scientist and educator. Born Portsea. Educated at the City of London School, the Royal School of Mines, London, and St John's College, Cambridge. The first Whitworth Scholar, 1869, and bracketed 5th wrangler, 1873. Fellow of St John's College, 1874–9, lecturer in physics at St John's College and on mechanics and physics at Newnham College. Garnett was the first demonstrator of Physics at the Cavendish Laboratory,

Cambridge under James Clerk-Maxwell. Professor of Mathematics, Physics and Mechanics, University College, Nottingham, 1882; principal and professor of Mathematics in the Durham College of Science, Newcastle upon Tyne, 1884; Secretary and educational adviser to the London Technical Education Board, 1893–1904; educational adviser to the London County Council, 1904–15. During the war Garnett was chairman of the Educational Reform Council, 1916–17, and organizer of technical training for interned British prisoners of war in Switzerland. Secretary to the London District University Committee for Higher Education of ex-service students, 1919–23. Hon. DCL, University of Durham. Author of several basic works on dynamics, heat and mechanics. Garnett College for training teachers of technical subjects, established in London in 1953 after an earlier foundation in 1946, was named after him. See his *Heroes of Science. Physicists* (1868), and Allen, B.M., *William Garnett. A memoir* (1933).

Garrett *see* **Anderson.**

Gathorne-Hardy, Gathorne, 1st Earl of Cranbrook (1814–1906). Statesman. Born Bradford. Educated at preparatory schools, Shrewsbury School and Oriel College, Oxford. BA, classics, 1836. Called to the bar at the Inner Temple, 1840 and joined the Northern circuit. Conservative MP for Leominster, 1856–65; for Oxford University, 1865–78. Created first Viscount Cranbrook in 1878 and advanced to an earldom in 1892. President of the Poor Law Board, 1866–7; Home Secretary, 1867–8; Secretary for War, 1874–8; Secretary for India, 1878–80. Lord President of the Council, 1885–6 and 1886–92. A sincere churchman, he sat on the Royal Commission on cathedral churches, 1879–85. Cranbrook was keen to protect the voluntary schools. He gave only qualified support, therefore, to the Education Bill of 1891 which extended the provision of free elementary schooling: 'I have not been a hearty "free schooler" '. Opposed rate aid for Church schools in the belief that this would lead to secular interference and control. See Gathorne-Hardy, A.E., *Gathorne Hardy, first Earl of Cranbrook, a memoir* (2 vols., 1910); Johnson, N.E. (ed.), *The Diary of Gathorne Hardy* (1981).

Geddes, Sir Eric Campbell (1875–1937). Politician, administrator and businessman. Born Agra, India, eldest son of a civil engineer. Educated Merchiston Castle School, Edinburgh, Edinburgh Academy and Oxford Military College, Cowley. Travelled, at age of 17, to USA and later India. Returning to England in 1906, joined the North Eastern Railway Company and by 1914, was deputy general manager. Deputy Director of Munitions, 1915–16, Director-General of military railways, War Office, and Director General of transportation to Commander-in-Chief, France and Inspector-General of transportation for all theatres of war. Honorary major-general, 1916–17. Controller, Board of Admiralty. Honorary vice-admiral, 1917. Conservative MP, Cambridge Borough, 1917–22. Member, War Cabinet, in charge of demobilization, 1918. First Minister of Transport, 1919–21. Best remembered as chairman of Committee on National Expenditure, 1921 which recommended economies which would yield £70m. This included £18m from education, a sum reduced by the Cabinet in the following year to £6m. The so-called 'Geddes Axe' affected the implementation of many of the provisions of the 1918 Education Act. Knight, 1916. See his *Mass Production: the revolution which changes everything* (1931), and Simon, B., *The Politics of Educational Reform 1920–1940* (1974).

Gilkes, Revd Arthur Herman (1849–1922). Schoolteacher. Born Leominster, Herefordshire, son of a chemist. Educated Shrewsbury School and Christ Church, Oxford, gaining first class honours in classical moderations and *literae humaniores*, 1872. Assistant master, Shrewsbury, 1873–85, headmaster, Dulwich College, 1885–1914. An impressive if austere person, Gilkes considerably raised Dulwich's reputation with only modest financial resources. By the 1890s the College had no fewer than five sides – classical, mathematical and army, modern, science and engineering. Continued to teach (classics) as well as to administrate. Accepted London County Council scholars from elementary schools, thus attracting Science and Art Department grants. Author of a number of books, including *Boys and Masters* (1887) and *A Day at Dulwich* (1905); see also Hodges, S., *God's Gift. A Living History of Dulwich College* (1981).

Gittins, Charles E. (1908–70). Educational administrator and academic. Born Wrexham and educated at Grove Park School, Wrexham and Aberystwyth University College, gaining first class honours in history, 1928, followed by postgraduate work. Taught in Wales, and St James' Grammar School, Bishop Auckland, Durham, becoming deputy head in 1938. Administrative Assistant, Durham County Council, 1939–42, West Riding County Council, 1942–4, and Director of Education, Monmouthshire, 1944–56. Professor of Education, Swansea University College, later Vice-Principal and Dean of Faculty of Arts, 1956–70. Chairman, Central Advisory Committee for Education (Wales), 1964–7. In England in 1963, this Committee, chaired by Lady Plowden, was asked to consider primary education in all its aspects and the transition to secondary education. The Welsh Committee, under Gittins, was given the same remit for Wales. The Report, published in 1968, attracted wide interest: besides advocating a major reorganization of primary education in Wales, it reflected Gittins' own opinions, recommending the teaching of Welsh at the primary stage and the establishment of bilingual schools. Editor, *Pioneers of Welsh Education* (1964).

Gladstone, William Ewart (1809–98). Statesman. Born Liverpool, son of a corn merchant. Educated Eton and Christ Church, Oxford, 1828–31, double first in classics and mathematics. Conservative MP, Newark, 1832–46, Peelite MP, Oxford University, 1847–65, Liberal MP, South Lancashire, 1865–68, MP, Greenwich, 1868–80, MP, Midlothian, 1880–95. Posts included President of Board of Trade, 1841–3, 1843–5, Master of the Mint, 1841–5, Colonial Secretary, 1845–6, Chancellor of Exchequer, 1852–5, 1859–66, 1873–4 and 1880–2. Leader of Commons, 1865–6, Prime Minister, 1868–74, 1880–5, 1886 and 1892–4. It was during his first ministry that the 1870 Education Act was formulated. Much of the burden of ensuring its passage through the Commons fell on the shoulders of **W.E. Forster,** though Gladstone paid close attention to its progress. His own religious views were that the state had a duty to support the Church, but that the former should deal with secular aspects of schooling, the latter with the spiritual. In 1869, he suggested to Forster that the state or locally-provided elementary schools should be confined to secular instruction. In the event, after strong opposition in the Commons to the provision of religious teaching in schools, Gladstone allowed the **Cowper-Temple** clause which provided that no catechism or formulary distinctive of any particular denomination should be taught. Gladstone later regretted making this concession. See Feuchtwanger, E.J., *Gladstone* (1975).

Gleig, George Robert (1796–1888). Pioneer of army education. Born Stirling, his father was Bishop of Brechin. Educated at Stirling Grammar School, Glasgow University, Balliol College, Oxford and Magdalen Hall, Oxford. His studies were interrupted by service in the Peninsular War, at Waterloo and in the United States. He was wounded six times. BA, 1818, ordained 1820, chaplain of the Royal Hospital, Chelsea from 1834, and Chaplain-General to the forces, 1844–75. Regimental schools which catered for both adults and children had existed since the seventeenth century, and Gleig instructed chaplains to visit the schools weekly. His concern led to Gleig's appointment in 1846 additionally as Inspector-General of Military Schools, a post he held until 1857. Gleig's initiatives included the establishment of a Corps of Army Schoolmasters, and of Inspectors, improvements in school accommodation, an attempt at grading soldiers by means of intelligence tests, and the production of a 42-volume library called *Gleig's School Series*. He also wrote novels and biographies. See White, A.C.T., *The Story of Army Education, 1643–1963* (1963).

Gore, Bishop Charles (1853–1932). Scholar and theologian. Educated at Harrow and Balliol College, Oxford. Fellow of Trinity College, Oxford, 1875–95; vice-principal of Cuddesdon College, 1880–3; librarian of Pusey Library, Oxford, 1884–93; vicar of Radley, 1893–4; canon of Westminster, 1894–1902; Bishop of Worcester, 1902–4; of Birmingham, 1905–11; of Oxford, 1911–19. Gore also served as chaplain to Queen Victoria and to King Edward VII. In addition to MA, DD and DCL degrees of his own university he received honorary doctorates from the Universities of Athens, Birmingham, Cambridge, Durham and Edinburgh, and honorary fellowships from Balliol and Trinity, Oxford and from King's College, London. He wrote widely on moral and religious questions. See for example his *The Mission of the Church* (1891);

(ed.), *Good Citizenship* (1899); *Christian Moral Principles* (1921); *The Philosophy of the Good Life* (1930), and Crosse, G., *Charles Gore* (1932); Prestige, G.L., *The Life of Charles Gore* (1935); Ramsey, A.M., *Charles Gore and Anglican Theology* (1955).

Gorst, Sir John Eldon (1835–1916). Lawyer and politician. Born Preston. Educated there at the grammar school and at St John's College, Cambridge. Third wrangler, 1857 and fellow of his college, 1857–60. Studied law; assistant master at Rossall School, 1858–9 to be near his ailing father. On his death sailed to New Zealand, arriving in 1860. In 1861 appointed inspector of native and missionary schools in Waikato. In 1862 became civil commissioner for the district and edited a newspaper, but narrowly escaped with his life during the Maori uprising of 1863. Returned to England and called to the bar at the Inner Temple, 1865, took silk ten years later. Conservative MP for Cambridge, 1866–8; Chatham, 1875–92; Cambridge University, 1892–1906. Reorganized the Conservative party machinery, 1868–74; in the 1880s was a member of the 'Fourth Party', a ginger group of Conservatives led by Lord Randolph Churchill. Solicitor-General and knighted, 1885; Under-Secretary of State for India, 1886; Financial Secretary to the Treasury, 1891–2; the last Vice-President of the Committee of the Privy Council on Education, 1895–1902. Gorst broke with the Conservative Party over the issue of protection and in his later years devoted his energies to the causes of health and education, particularly the health of children. As Vice-President, Gorst who was genuinely interested in education clashed frequently with the President the **8th Duke of Devonshire** who was not. In 1896 the Duke informed him, 'Gorst, your damned Bill's dead'. See his *The Children of the Nation* (1906); *Education and Race-Regeneration* (1913), and Gorst, H.E., *The Fourth Party* (1906).

Gould, Frederick James (1855–1938). Moral educator. Born Brighton. Choirboy at St George's Chapel, Windsor. Village schoolmaster and London Board School teacher, 1877–96. Worker in the Ethical Movement, 1896–9. A member of the Leicester School Board and Town Council, and secretary of the Leicester Secular Society, 1899–1908. Gould achieved fame as a lecturer on and demonstrator of moral education. In 1911 he first toured the USA, and visited India in 1913. He brought the ideal of the League of Nations to young audiences, and was secretary to the Inter-

national Moral Education Congress, 1919–27 and 1930. See his several writings for young people, and particularly *Moral Instruction: its Theory and Practice* (1913); *British Education after the War* (1917); *The Life story of a Humanist* (1923) (his autobiography); *This England, and other Things of Beauty* (1930), and Hayward, F., and White, E., *The Last Years of a Great Educationist* (1942).

Gould, Sir Ronald (1904–86). Teachers' union representative. Born Midsomer Norton, Somerset, son of Fred Gould, a Labour MP. Educated Shepton Mallet Grammar School and Westminster Training College, where he took a London degree. Assistant teacher, Radstock Council School, 1924–41 and headmaster, Welton County School, Bath, 1941–6. Executive committee, National Union of Teachers, 1937 and president, 1943–4. Succeeded **Sir Frederick Mander** as General Secretary, 1947, serving until his retirement in 1970. Although Gould was an effective leader, he was a reluctant advocate of militancy by teachers, preferring to see his role as keeping together a membership of over 200,000. Knight, 1955. See his *The Changing Pattern of Education* (1965), and an autobiography, *Chalk Up the Memory* (1976).

Graham, Sir James Robert George (1792–1861). Statesman. Born at Netherby, Cumberland. Educated at a private school in Dalston, Cumberland, at Westminster and Christ Church, Oxford. Left university without a degree in 1812 and travelled in Spain and Sicily where he became private secretary to the British minister. Whig MP for Hull, 1818–20; Carlisle, 1826–7; county of Cumberland, 1827–37; Pembroke, 1838–47; Ripon, 1847–52; and thereafter for Carlisle. Resigned over the Irish Church question in 1834, took office under Peel in 1841, became leader of the Peelites in 1850 and was First Lord of the Admiralty, 1852–5, in the Aberdeen coalition. Elected Rector of Glasgow University in 1838. Graham as Home Secretary, 1841–6, was keen to advance government aid to education but, as he wrote to **Brougham** in 1841, 'Religion, the keystone of education, is, in this country the bar to its progress'. The education clauses of his Factory Bills of 1843 and 1844 were defeated by the opposition outside Parliament of the Nonconformists, particularly the Methodists. See Parker, C.S., *Life and Letters of Sir James Graham 1792–1861* (2 vols., 1907); Erickson, A.B., *The Public Career of Sir James Graham* (1952); Ward, J.T., 'A Lost Opportunity in Education: 1843', *Leeds Researches and Studies in Education*, 20, 1959.

Granville, Leveson-Gower, George, 2nd Earl Granville (1815–91). Statesman. Born London, educated at Eton and Christ Church, Oxford, BA, 1839. Whig MP for Morpeth, 1837–41, Lichfield, 1841–6, when on the death of his father he succeeded to the peerage and moved to the House of Lords. Vice-President of the Board of Trade, 1848, Secretary of State for the Colonies, 1868–70 and 1886, Secretary of State for Foreign Affairs, 1851–2, 1870–4, 1880–5. Granville took a prominent part in promoting the Great Exhibition of 1851 and was vice-president of the Royal Commission in charge of the arrangements. Lord President of the Council, 1852–4, and 1859–65, and thus presided over the controversies surrounding the introduction and implementation of the Revised Code in 1862. In 1856 received Oxford DCL, was elected a Fellow of the Royal Society and became Chancellor of the University of London, a post which he held for 35 years. In this capacity he presided regularly at the annual prize day and advanced the cause of admission of women to examinations and degrees. He founded elementary schools in Cobridge, Staffordshire, and took a keen interest in the Wedgwood Institute. Supported prize schemes and continuation classes. A fluent French speaker he urged that modern languages should be taught by the conversational method. The most popular after-dinner speaker of his day. See Fitzmaurice, Lord E., *The Life of Granville George Leveson-Gower* (2 vols., 1905).

Graves, Alfred Perceval (1846–1931). Author and school inspector. Born Dublin, second son of Bishop of Dublin. Educated Windermere College and privately, and Trinity College, Dublin, studying English literature, classics and history. Clerk, Home Office, 1869–75, HMI, 1875–1910, serving in Manchester, Huddersfield, Taunton and Southwark, London. Published *Songs of Killarney* (1873), and later, *Songs of Old Ireland* (1882) and *Songs of Erin* (1892), collaborating with his friend, the composer Charles Villiers Stanford. His most famous song was *Father O'Flynn*, written in 1875, which attained worldwide fame. An essayist, editor and poet on Irish musical and literary subjects, Graves also contributed to *Punch*. Chairman, representative managers, London County Council, 1911–19, and promoted the supply of playing fields for town children. His autobiography, *To Return To All That* (1930) was a reply to the autobiography of his son, Robert, entitled *Goodbye To All That* (1929).

Graves, John James (1832–1903). Schoolmaster. Began teaching in London in 1846 at St Anne's School, Soho, moving to Cambridge in the following year, Saleby, Lincolnshire, in 1848 and Hanging Houghton endowed school, in the parish of Lamport, Northamptonshire, in 1851. In his first year there Graves joined the Northampton and Northamptonshire Church Schoolmasters and Mistresses Association and gave addresses on aspects of elementary teachers' work. Graves became secretary of a national organization, the General Associated Body of Church Schoolmasters in England and Wales in 1857. The National Union of Elementary Teachers was founded in 1870 with Graves as its first President. He addressed its first conference that year, held at King's College, London, stressing the importance of unity in the teaching profession and calling for proper training and a registration system for teachers. He was an active member of the Union as a member of its Executive until 1900. He remained at Hanging Houghton for 50 years, retiring in 1901. See Tropp, A., *The School Teachers* (1957), and Seaborne, M., and Isham, G., 'A Victorian Schoolmaster, John James Graves', *Northamptonshire Past and Present*, 4, 1972.

Green, John Alfred (1867–1922). Educationist. Educated at Firth College, Sheffield and at the Borough Road College where he was a junior tutor. BA London; MA Sheffield. Assistant master in a London pupil teachers' school, 1893–4; head of the teacher training department and lecturer in education at Bangor, 1894. Green made a particular study of the educational systems of Austria, Germany and Switzerland. Member of the Central Welsh Board, 1898–1906; professor of Education at Bangor, 1900–6 and thereafter professor of Education at Sheffield, where he was also a member of the Sheffield Education Committee. Green played a major part in such ventures as the Teachers' Guild and the Teachers' Registration Council, and chaired committees concerned with the development of museums and educational institutions and with educational hand work. He was editor of the *Journal of Experimental Pedagogy* and author of major works on psychology, teaching practice and a particular expert on Pestalozzi. See for example his *Educational Ideas of Pestalozzi* (1905); *Educational Writings of Pestalozzi* (1912); *Life and Works of Pestalozzi* (1913).

Green, Thomas Hill (1836–82). Idealist philosopher. Born Birkin, Yorkshire. Educated at home by his father, an evangelical clergyman, and at Rugby School and Balliol College, Oxford. BA, 1859; MA, 1862. Fellow of Balliol, 1860–82; senior dean, 1865; ethical tutor, 1869; classical tutor, 1875; Whyte Professor of Moral Philosophy, 1877–82. In 1864 appointed an Assistant Commissioner to the Taunton Commission and took a deep interest in the work. Member of the governing body of King Edward's School in Birmingham, one of the schools on which he had reported. He took an active part in Oxford life, and in 1874 was elected to the Oxford School Board. He joined the Temperance Alliance in 1872 and in 1875 set up a coffee house at St Clement's. He contributed £200 to the Oxford High School building of 1877, and founded a scholarship of £12 a year for boys from elementary schools. He also made bequests to the University and to Balliol. Green was an idealist who believed that the state was a spiritual entity, and that it was essential to provide a coherent educational system. As a teacher and social reformer he drew heavily upon the Christian Socialist tradition and inspired a generation of public servants including **Asquith, Morant** and **Toynbee**. See Nettleship, R.L. (ed.), *The Works of T.H. Green* (3 vols., 1885–8); Fairbrother, W.H., *The Philosophy of T.H. Green* (1896); Cacoullos, A.R., *T.H. Green: philosopher of rights* (1974); Gordon, P., and White, J., *Philosophers as Educational Reformers* (1979).

Gregory, Robert (1819–1911). Cleric and educationist. Born Nottingham, son of a merchant. Educated privately. Orphaned at the age of five, he later worked in a Liverpool shipping office, 1835–7, before deciding to enter the ministry. Admitted to Corpus Christi College, Oxford, 1840, BA, 1843, MA, 1846 and DD, 1891. Ordained as priest, 1844, serving as a curate in Gloucestershire, Lincolnshire and London, 1843–53; vicar, St Mary-the-Less, Lambeth, 1853–73, where he built elementary schools and a school of art. Canon of St Paul's Cathedral, 1868, and Dean, 1890, occupying the post until four months before his death. He was a controversial figure in Church matters playing a prominent part in 1880 over the Burial Bills controversy and in 1881 supported the memorial favouring the toleration of ritual. Gregory stoutly

101

defended the role of the Church in providing elementary schools. Treasurer of the National Society; member, London School Board, 1873–6, the Royal Commission on Elementary Education, 1886–8 and of City Parochial Churches Commission, 1888. See his *Elementary Education: Some Account of its Rise and Progress in England* (1895), and Hutton, V.H. (ed.), *The Autobiography of Robert Gregory* (1912).

Grey, Maria Georgina (1816–1906). Campaigner for women's education. Daughter of Rear-Admiral Shirreff. Educated privately. Much of her childhood was spent abroad. In 1834 returned to England and in 1841 married her first cousin William Grey. She had a very close relationship with her older sister **Emily Shirreff** and together they published *Thoughts on Self Culture addressed to Women* (1850). After the death of her husband in 1864 Grey became increasingly involved in the campaign to improve the education of girls and women. She founded the National Union for the Improvement of the Education of Women of All Classes, which later became the Women's Educational Union, 1871, and established the Girls' Public Day School Company (later Trust), 1872, and the Teachers' Training and Registration Society, 1877. Gave numerous lectures on women's education, addressed the British Association and the National Association for the Promotion of Social Science on the subject and published many articles. She also wrote in favour of women's suffrage and, towards the end of her life, became interested in the co-operative movement and in Socialism. In 1878, the Teachers' Training and Registration Society established the Maria Grey College in Bishopsgate to train women for teaching in secondary schools. See her *On the Education of Women* (1871); *Last words to Girls on Life in School and after School* (1889), and Kamm, J., *Indicative Past* (1971).

Grier, Lynda (1880–1967). Economist and educationist. Educated at home and at Newnham College, Cambridge. Economics tripos, 1908. Fellow and lecturer at Newnham, and acting head of Economics department, Leeds University, during absence of professor of Economics on war service, 1915–19. Principal of Lady Margaret Hall, Oxford, 1921–45. Member of the Consultative Committee of the Board of Education, 1924–38. President of the Economics Section of the British Association in 1925 and of the Education Section, 1946. British Council representative in China, 1948–50. Hon. LL.D Cambridge, 1953. Grier investigated the substitution of men by women in industry during the First World War and was a member of Wages Councils until 1948. See her *Life of Winifred Mercier* (1937); *Achievement in Education. The work of Michael Ernest Sadler* (1952).

Grote, George (1794–1871). Politician and historian. Born at Beckenham, Kent. Educated at a school in Sevenoaks, and at Charterhouse. Acquired a deep love of learning, but at the age of 16 joined his father's banking house in the City. Knew **Bentham**, Ricardo and **James Mill**. In the 1820s he was with Mill, **Brougham** and Campbell one of the founders of the new University of London (University College). Grote's business experience helped to raise money and he served on the finance and education committees and on the Council. Liberal Member of Parliament for the City of London, 1832–41, where he was one of the leaders of the 'philosophical radicals', and a particular advocate of the ballot. Treasurer of University College, London from 1860 and its president from 1868. On his death he left £6,000 to endow the chair of philosophy of mind and logic. From 1850 Grote was also concerned with the wider University of London and became a member of its Senate. Was prominent in the campaign to reform its examinations, achieved in 1858, and became Vice-Chancellor in 1862. In 1868 he secured the admission of women to its examinations. Trustee of the British Museum, 1859; Fellow of the Royal Society, 1857; professor of Ancient History to the Royal Academy, 1859; DCL, Oxford, 1853; LL.D Cambridge, 1861. Declined a peerage from Gladstone in 1869. See his *History of Greece* (12 vols., 1846–56); *Plato and other companions of Socrates* (3 vols., 1865), and Grote, H., *The personal life of George Grote* (1873); Clarke, M.L., *George Grote* (1962).

Hadow, Sir William Henry (1859–1937). Educationist, scholar and music historian. Born Ebrington, Gloucestershire, son of a curate. Educated at Malvern College, Worcester College, Oxford, 1878–82, with first class in classical moderations and *literae humaniores*. Lecturer, Worcester College, Oxford, 1884. Fellow, tutor and dean, 1889. Lectured in both classics and music. Hadow wrote two important books which set new standards for music criticism, *Studies in Modern Music* (1892 and 1895), and contributed to the Oxford History of Music a volume on *The Viennese Period* (1904) as well as many other works. Principal, Armstrong College, Newcastle upon Tyne, 1909; Vice-Chancellor, University of Durham, 1916–18. Knight, 1918. Director of Education, Young Men's Christian

Association in France, 1918. Vice-Chancellor, University of Sheffield, 1919–27. A very able administrator, Hadow made a notable contribution to education as chairman of the Consultative Committee of the Board of Education, 1920–34. The best known of the reports *The Education of the Adolescent* (1926), which recommended the separation of primary and secondary education at the age of about eleven and some form of secondary education for all, is widely called the 'Hadow Report'. Other reports which were issued under his chairmanship include one on Differentiation of the Curriculum for Boys and Girls in Secondary Schools (1923), The Primary School (1931) and The Infant School (1933). See also *Music* (1924) and with Hadow, G.E., *The Oxford Treasury of English Literature* (1906), and Kogan, M., and Packwood, T., *Advisory Councils and Committees in Education* (1974).

Hahn, Kurt Matthias Robert Martin (1886–1974). Educator. Born Berlin, Germany, educated at the Wilhelmgymnasium, Berlin, Christ Church, Oxford, and the Universities of Berlin, Heidelberg, Freiburg and Göttingen. Lector of English newspapers for the German Foreign Office and Supreme Command, and then private secretary to the last Imperial Chancellor, Prince Max von Baden, and to Dr Melchior, a delegate at Versailles. In 1920 helped Prince Max to found the Salem School (coeducational) at Salem Castle, and became its headmaster. Hahn was arrested by the Nazis in 1933 but Ramsay MacDonald secured his release and emigration to Britain. In 1934 Hahn founded Gordonstoun School at Elgin in Scotland from which he himself retired in 1953. He was co-founder of the Outward Bound Sea School at Aberdovey, Wales in 1941, and was the moving spirit behind the Duke of Edinburgh Award Scheme and of the Atlantic Colleges project. The United World College of the Atlantic, Wales was founded in 1962. Gordonstoun, with its emphasis on a broad education, including land and sea expeditions and adventures, community activities and exchange visits with pupils from other countries, achieved fame as the school attended by Prince Philip, Duke of Edinburgh and by Prince Charles, the heir to the throne. See, Röhrs, H., and Tunstall-Behrens, H. (eds.), *Kurt Hahn* (1970).

Haldane, Richard Burdon, Viscount Haldane of Cloan (1856–1928). Statesman and philosopher. Born Edinburgh, son of a writer to the signet (similar to a solicitor) of strong Calvinist convictions. Educated Edinburgh Academy, entering Edinburgh University at

16, interrupting to study at Göttingen University, 1874 under R.H. Lotze, the philosopher, graduating in arts, MA, 1876, first class in philosophy. Barrister, Lincoln's Inn, 1879. QC, 1890, remaining in practice until 1905. Liberal MP, East Lothian, 1885–1911. Home ruler and Liberal Imperialist. Secretary of State, War, 1905–12. Created Viscount Haldane, 1911. Lord Chancellor, 1912–15 and again in 1924, when he joined the Labour Party. Leader of Party, House of Lords, 1925–8. Haldane's main interest was in higher education and he worked with the Webbs on a programme of national efficiency. Visits to Germany convinced him of the need for a 'British Charlottenberg' which led to the establishment of the Imperial College of Science and Technology. Haldane continued with **Sidney Webb** in negotiating for a University of London Act, 1898, which gave the University teaching as well as examining functions. A believer in providing a network of regional universities, Haldane's advocacy before the Privy Council in 1902 resulted in separate charters being granted to Liverpool and Manchester Universities and paved the way for further university expansion. In the following year, he headed a small group whose deliberations were responsible for the creation of the University Grants Committee in 1919. Chairman, Royal Commissions on university education, London (1909–13) and Wales (1916–18). Haldane was also a firm advocate of adult education involving himself in the work of the Workers' Educational Association and was the driving force behind the setting up of the British Institute of Adult Education in 1921. Haldane, more than many of his contemporaries, had a Hegelian strain of idealism tempered by the milder versions of **T.H. Green**. His vision of the world as objectified reason and of knowledge as the remedy for societal ills proved to be over-optimistic. See his Gifford lectures *The Pathway to Reality* (2 vols., 1903–4); *Universities and National Life* (1911); *An Autobiography* (1929), and Sommer, D., *Haldane of Cloan* (1960); Ashby, E., and Anderson, M., *Portrait of Haldane* (1974).

Hamilton, Lord George Francis (1845–1927). Statesman. Born Brighton, third son of 1st Duke of Abercorn. Educated Harrow and entered the Rifle Brigade in 1864. Lieutenant, Coldstream Guards, 1868 in which year he was invited to stand as Conservative MP for Middlesex. Hamilton was elected, remaining as Member until 1885. Sat for the Ealing division, Middlesex, 1885–1906. Under-Secretary of State for India, 1874–8, Vice-President of the Committee of Council on Education, 1878–80, First Lord of the Admiralty, 1885–

6, and 1886–92, and Secretary of State for India, 1895–1903. He later wrote of his time as Vice-President of the Council, 'The work of the Education Department was terribly meticulous and dull after the India Office. I had to administer about three Acts of Parliament under a code. That code consisted of 157 regulations and seven schedules. It dealt with the minutest detail connected with school life, and so tied the managers and teachers with red-tape regulations that all individuality and initiative was knocked out of them.' Hamilton was governor of Harrow School. Chairman of the Royal Commission on Poor Law and Unemployment, 1905–9. See his *Parliamentary Reminiscences and Reflections, 1868–85* (1916) and a second volume, *1886–1906* (1922).

Hamilton, Sir William (1788–1856). Philosopher and university teacher. Born Glasgow. Educated briefly at Chiswick and Bromley, also at the grammar school at Glasgow and in university classes there and at Edinburgh. Student at Balliol College, Oxford from 1807, BA, 1811, MA, 1814; DD, of Leyden, 1840. Called to the Scottish bar, 1813. Professor of Civil History at the University of Edinburgh from 1821, and professor of Logic and Metaphysics from 1836 until his death. Hamilton's reputation was established by a series of articles in the *Edinburgh Review* ranging from such subjects as the 'Philosophy of Perception' and 'Logic', to attacks upon the abuses of the University of Oxford and a plea for the admission of Dissenters. He was a very widely-read man and after his death his library of some 9,000 volumes was purchased by the University of Glasgow. Ill health after 1844 restricted his activities. In addition to his editions of the works of Thomas Reid (1846) and Dugald Stewart (10 vols., 1854–8), see his *Discussions on Philosophy and literature, education and university reform* (1852); *Lectures on metaphysics and logic* (4 vols., 1859–60), and Veitch, J., *Memoir of Sir William Hamilton* (1869); Monck, W.H.S., *Sir William Hamilton* (1881); Rasmussen, S.V., *The Philosophy of Sir William Hamilton* (1925).

Harrison, Frederic (1831–1923). Positivist. Born London, son of a wealthy merchant, with a country seat at Sutton Place, Surrey. Educated King's College School, London, 1842–9 and Wadham College, Oxford, 1849–54, obtaining a first class honours in *literae humaniores*, second class in classical moderations and fourth class in law and history. Fellow, Wadham College, 1854–6. Barrister, Lincoln's Inn, 1858, practising from then until 1873. Became attracted to Positivism through his tutor, Richard Congreve, and accepted it as a religion. President, English Positivist Committee, 1880–1905 and founded the *Positivist Review*. Harrison was a Liberal in politics. He taught at the Working Men's College, together with **F.D. Maurice** and **Tom Hughes**. Member, Royal Commission on Trades Unions, 1867–9 and Secretary, Royal Commission for digesting the law, 1869–70. Professor of Jurisprudence, Constitutional and International Law, Council of Legal Education, 1877–89. Alderman, London County Council from 1888. Unsuccessful parliamentary candidate, London University, 1886. He was a prolific writer; among his works are *Cromwell* (1888), *Ruskin* (1902), *Chatham* (1905) and edited *The New Calendar of Great Men* (1892). See his *Autobiographic Memoirs* (2 vols., 1911), and Vogeler, M., *Frederic Harrison* (1984).

Hartog, Sir Philip Joseph (1864–1947). Educationist. Born London, educated at University College School, London, Owens College, Manchester, and the Universities of Paris and Heidelberg. Lecturer in Chemistry at Owens College, subsequently the Victoria University, Manchester, 1891–1903. Academic Registrar of the University of London, 1903–20. Hartog's administrative experience which began with his secretaryship of the Moseley Commission of Educational Enquiry, 1902–3, was broadened by his secretaryship of the Treasury Committee on the Organization of Oriental Studies in London, 1907–9, and of the India Office committee on the same subject, 1910–17. Membership of the Viceroy's Commission on the University of Calcutta, 1917–19 took him to India where he became first Vice-Chancellor of the University of Dacca, Bengal, 1920–5; a member of the Indian Public Service Commission, 1926–30; and chairman of the Auxiliary Committee on Education of the Indian Statutory Commission, 1928–9. Director of the International Institute Examinations Enquiry, 1932. Knighted in 1926. Hartog's interests in India, scientific and literary subjects, and examinations were reflected in his many writings. See for example, *Examinations in their bearing on National Efficiency* (1911); *The Relation of Poetry to Verse* (1926); *Priestley* (1931); *Some Aspects of Indian Education* (1939), and Hartog, M.H., *A Memoir of Sir Philip Hartog* (1949).

Hawtrey, Edward Craven (1789–1862). Headmaster. Born at Burnham. Educated at Eton College, and at King's College, Cambridge. Scholar, 1807, BA and fellow, 1810. Private tutor to the sons of the Earl of Shrewsbury. Hawtrey's family had been connected with

Eton for some 300 years. In 1814 was appointed by **Dr Keate** as an assistant master at Eton. During the next 20 years he devoted himself to his pupils and to the study of modern languages. In 1834 he succeeded Keate as headmaster and in 1853 became provost, which post he held till his death. Rector of Ewhurst, Sussex, 1835–53; of Eton, 1853–4; of Mapledurham, Oxfordshire, 1854–62. As headmaster Hawtrey increased the number of boys to 777, presided over the construction of new buildings including a sanatorium, and restored the college chapel. He suppressed outdated practices and bullying, and fostered academic study. He was the last person to be buried in Eton College chapel. He published volumes of translations and of chapel lectures. See Lyte, M., *A History of Eton College* (1875); Thackery, F. St John, *Memoir of E.C. Hawtrey* (1896); How, F.D., *Six Great Schoolmasters* (1904).

Hayward, Frank Herbert (1872–1954). School inspector and author. Educated London University, BA, 1894, B.Sc. and MA, 1898 and D. Litt., 1901. Admitted to Gonville and Caius College, Cambridge, as an advanced student, 1900. BA, moral science, 1901, gaining the Moral Science Prize. Assistant master, St George's School of Science, Bristol, 1897–9. Lecturer, Cambridge Day Training College, 1899–1900, Organizing tutor, Mid-Devon, 1902–4, principal, Torquay Pupil Teacher Centre, 1904–5. Inspector of Schools, London County Council, 1905–37. Hayward, a close friend of **F.J. Gould**, was a supporter of the secularist movement, especially in relation to education. In 1907, the Rationalist Press Association circulated his *Science of Education.* He was a leading member of the Moral Instruction League, founded in 1897 to further ethical and civic teaching on a non-theological basis in schools. From 1903, Hayward was a powerful champion of Herbartianism. Between 1903 and 1909, he wrote six popular books on this topic including *The Secret of Herbart* (1904) and *The Meaning of Education* (1907). See also his *The Psychology of Educational Administration* (1912); *An Educational Failure* (1938), and Connell, W.F., *A History of Education in the Twentieth Century World* (1980).

Headlam, Revd Stewart Duckworth (1847–1924). Clergyman and educational reformer. Born at Wavertree near Liverpool. Educated at Wadhurst, Eton, and Trinity College, Cambridge where in 1869 he was placed last but one in the third class of the classical tripos. Ordained, 1870, curate at St John's, Drury Lane, 1870–3, where he became interested in popular education in the St Martin's National Schools. At St Matthew's, Bethnal Green, Headlam who had at Cambridge become a follower and friend of **F.D. Maurice**, founded the Guild of St Matthew which became the centre of Christian Socialism. Headlam also became editor and leading writer of the *Church Reformer*. Headlam's work at Bethnal Green and later at St Thomas's, Charterhouse, 1879–81, and St Michael's, Shoreditch, 1881–4, convinced him of the importance of education. He was a member of the London School Board, 1888–1904 and advocated higher grade schools, free school dinners, smaller classes and the provision of pianos and swimming lessons. Chairman of the Evening Schools Committee and a strong supporter of teachers. Member of the London County Council, 1907–24. See his *The Laws of Eternal Life* (1884); *The Place of the Bible in Secular Education* (1903); *The Socialist's Church* (1907) and Bettany, F.G., *Stewart Headlam* (1926); Leech, K., 'Stewart Headlam' in Reckitt, M. (ed.), *For Christ and the People* (1968).

Headlam-Morley, Sir James Wycliffe (1863–1929). School inspector and author. Born Barnard Castle, son of a clergyman. Assumed the name of Morley by royal licence, 1918. Educated Eton, King's College, Cambridge, classical tripos, 1883–7, first class honours part one and second class part two. Fellow, King's College, 1890–6, and Berlin University. Lecturer, Cambridge University Extension. Honorary Assistant Commissioner, Royal Commission on Secondary Education (Bryce), 1894–5. Professor, Greek and Ancient History, Queen's College, London, 1894–1900. Temporary Inspector, Board of Education, 1902–4. Published report in 1903 deploring the predominance of technical education in secondary schools at the expense of literary subjects. The Secondary School Regulations issued in the following year redressed the balance between the two elements. Staff Inspector, Secondary Schools, Board of Education, 1904–20. Member, Prime Minister's Committee on Modern Languages, 1918. Assistant Director, Political Intelligence, Department of Information, 1917–18. Assistant Director of Intelligence, Foreign Office, 1918–20. CBE, 1920. Knight, 1929. See his *Life of Bismarck* (1899), and *Studies in Diplomatic History* (1930).

Heath, Sir Henry Frank (1863–1946). Academic and scientific administrator. Born London, son of Henry Heath, miniature painter to Queen Victoria. Educated Westminster School and

109

University College, London, BA, mental and moral science, 1886, and University of Strasbourg for three years. Professor of English Literature and Language, Bedford College, London, 1890–6. Assistant registrar and librarian, University of London, 1891–1901 and academic registrar and acting treasurer, 1901–3. Director of Special Inquiries and Reports, Board of Education, 1903–16, succeeding **Michael Sadler**, making a special study of scientific and technical education. Joint secretary, Royal Commission on University of London, 1910–13. Principal Assistant Secretary, Board of Education, in charge of administration of the new branch dealing with financial grants to universities, 1911. Knight, 1917. Worked towards the establishment of a University Grants Committee, independent of the Board, which was created in 1919. The Department of Scientific and Industrial Research was established with Heath as Secretary, 1916–27.

Heller, Thomas Edmund (1837–1901). Teachers' leader. Son of a schoolmaster. Trained at Cheltenham where he came under the influence of Revd C.H. Bromby. Began teaching in London in 1862. Heller was a founder member of both the London Church Teachers' Association and of the National Union of Elementary Teachers (NUT from 1889). Secretary of the NUET, 1873–91, a full-time paid post. He also served on the London School Board from 1874, and on the Cross Commission, 1886–8. Heller advocated the total abolition of payment by results and a wider training for elementary teachers, with training colleges linked to universities. He urged that teacher training courses should lead to university degrees and that registration of school teachers should be provided by legislation. See the annual editions of *The New Code for Day Schools* which he edited, and Tropp, A., *The School Teachers* (1957).

Henslow, Revd John Stevens (1796–1861). Botanist. Born at Rochester, Kent. Educated there at the grammar school and at St John's College, Cambridge. BA, 1818, MA, 1821. Fellow of the Linnean Society, 1818, and of the Geological Society, 1819. In 1819 with Adam Sedgewick founded the Cambridge Philosophical Society. Ordained deacon and priest, 1824. Professor of Mineralogy at Cambridge, 1822–7; professor of Botany, 1825 to his death. As a result of his work botany became a popular subject and **Darwin**, Berkeley and Babington were amongst his students. He recommended Darwin for the *Beagle* and took charge of all the specimens he sent home during the five-year voyage. Member of the

British Association from 1832, of the Senate of London University from 1836, examiner there in botany from 1838, and a founder of the Ipswich Museum in 1848. As rector of Hitcham, Suffolk from 1837 he established botany as a subject in schools which he had himself founded, and encouraged benefit and sports clubs, flower shows and parish excursions. He gave lectures and published *Letters to the Farmers of Suffolk* to improve their agricultural practices. In 1843 he discovered beds of phosphatic nodules in the Suffolk Crag which could be used as manure. He contributed to the museums at Kew. See his *Catalogue of British Plants* (1829); *A dictionary of botanical terms* (1857), and Jenyns, L., *Memoir of J.S. Henslow* (1862); Darwin, C.R., *Darwin and Henslow* (1967); Layton, D., *Science for the People* (1973); Russell-Gebbett, J., *Henslow of Hitcham* (1977).

Hetherington, Sir Hector (1888–1965). University statesman. Born Cowdenbeath, Scotland. Educated at Dollar Academy and the University of Glasgow. Lecturer in moral philosophy at Glasgow, 1910–14; lecturer in philosophy, Sheffield, 1914–15; professor of Logic and Philosophy, University College, Cardiff, 1915–20. Principal of the University College of the South West in Exeter, 1920–4. Professor of Moral Philosophy, Glasgow, 1924–7; Vice-Chancellor of Liverpool University, 1927–36; Principal and Vice-Chancellor of Glasgow University, 1936–61. Knighted in 1936; KBE, 1948; GBE, 1962. Hetherington guided Glasgow through the difficult days of depression, war and post-war expansion. Chairman of the Committee of Vice-Chancellors and Principals, 1943–7, 1949–53; Vice-Chairman of the Central Advisory Committee on Adult Education in the Forces, 1942–8; and Chairman of the Commonwealth Universities Grants Committee, 1946–64. He also served on many public bodies including the National Arbitration Tribunal, 1940–8, and the Industrial Disputes Tribunal, 1948–59. Honorary degrees from some 20 universities. See Illingworth, C.F.W., *A University Statesman, Sir Hector Hetherington* (1971).

Hetherington, Henry (1792–1849). Radical reformer. Born London and apprenticed as a boy to Luke Hansard the parliamentary printer. Became a committee member of the London Mechanics' Institution and a friend of **George Birkbeck**. In the 1820s he also became a member of the British Association for Promotion of Co-operative Knowledge, and of other associations which sought to promote political and social emancipation. Hetherington's main contribution to the radical movement was as an educator of the working classes by means of the printed word. In 1822 he registered his first press and types, and published pamphlets of his own and for others. His most famous publication, the *Poor Man's Guardian*, was the longest lived of the unstamped press, appearing from 1831 to 1835. He was a founder member and treasurer of the London Working Men's Association in 1836 from which Chartism sprang, and supported Lovett as opposed to O'Connor. Hetherington was frequently prosecuted, and imprisoned on three occasions in his campaign for a free press which would give the working classes genuine knowledge and enable them to become politically active. See his several pamphlets and papers and Holyoake, G.J., *The Life and Character of Henry Hetherington* (1849); Barker, A.G., *Henry Hetherington* (1938); Wiener, J.H., *The War of the Unstamped* (1969) and Hollis, P., *The Pauper Press* (1970).

Hewins, William Albert Samuel (1865–1931). Political economist and politician. Born Wolverhampton, son of an iron merchant. Educated Wolverhampton Grammar School and Pembroke College, Oxford, 1884–7, graduating in mathematics. After undertaking extensive university Extension work in the North of England, he was invited by **Sidney Webb** to become Director of the London School of Economics, a post he held from 1895 to 1903 and was also Tooke professor of Economic Science and Statistics, King's College, London, 1897–1903. A believer in Imperial economic unity, Hewins turned to politics. Unionist MP, Hereford, 1912–18, and Under-Secretary, Colonial Office, 1917–19. See his autobiography, *The Apologia of an Imperialist* (2 vols., 1929).

Hickson, William Edward (1803–70). Educational writer. Born London, brought up as a boot-maker in the family business from which he retired in 1840 to devote himself to philanthropic pursuits. He was in particular a pioneer of national education and of popular music culture. His interests were aroused by membership of the Royal Commission on Hand Loom Weavers. He visited all the main seats of the industry in Great Britain and Northern Ireland, and, whilst signing the joint report in 1841, published a separate report in 1840 which advocated the improvement of elementary education and the abolition of the Corn Laws as more fundamental remedies for distress. Studied national school systems in Belgium, Germany and Holland, 1839. As editor and proprietor of the *Westminster Review*, 1840–52, he expounded his educational policy in this organ of philosophic radicalism, and effected the link between the radicalism of Westminster and that of Manchester. See his *The Singing Master* (1836); *Dutch and German Schools* (1840); *Part Singing* (1842); *Time and Faith* (2 vols., 1857), and Aldrich, R., 'W.E. Hickson and the *Westminster Review*, 1840–51' in Lowe, R., (ed.), *Biography and Education* (1980).

Higdon, Annie Catharine (1864–1946). Schoolteacher and Socialist. Born near Wallasey, Cheshire, daughter of Samuel and Jane Schollich. In 1896 she married Thomas George Higdon (1869–1939). Both were by then schoolteachers but details of their early lives are not clear. In 1902 Annie Higdon became mistress of the Wood Dalling Council School in Norfolk, with her husband as her assistant. The Higdons sympathized with the village poor and their children, and incurred the anger of the local landowners and school managers, particularly in respect of their opposition to children being withdrawn from school to work on the land. In 1911 after an inquiry conducted by the Norfolk Education Committee the Higdons were moved to another school at Burston. In 1914 following similar complaints by the Burston School managers the Higdons were dismissed. This led to the Burston School Strike whereby the children refused to attend school and were taught by the Higdons on the village green. The Higdons' case was taken up by the National Union of Teachers and the Independent Labour Party, and funds were raised for a new village school, opened in 1917, in which Annie Higdon taught for many years. Her husband became active in the farm workers' union. See van der Eyken, W., and Turner, B., *Adventures in Education* (1969); Edwards, B., *The Burston School Strike* (1974).

Hill, Matthew Davenport (1792–1872). Legal reformer. Born Birmingham, eldest son of Thomas Wright Hill. Educated at his father's school at Hill Top and at Wolverhampton, and until the age of 23 assisted his father in his school. Entered Lincoln's Inn, called to the bar, 1819 and worked in the Midland circuit until 1846. The publication of his *Public Education* (1822) which described the Hazlewood system of schooling brought him the acquaintance of **Bentham** and other radicals, and he was a founder of the Society for the Diffusion of Useful Knowledge. MP for Hull, 1832–5; QC, 1834. Recorder of Birmingham, 1839–66. In this office and in his work with the National Association for the Promotion of Social Science and the co-operative movement he worked for the reform of criminal law and for the rehabilitation of offenders. Juvenile criminals occupied much of his attention. He advocated free day or ragged schools for neglected children, industrial schools for those on the brink of criminal life, and reformatories for young criminals, based on the family principle as at Mettray in France. Several conferences were held in Birmingham to advance these causes. See his *Public Education* (1822); *Suggestions for the Repression of Crime* (1857), and Hill, R., and F.D., *The Recorder of Birmingham, a memoir of M.D. Hill* (1878); Dobson, J.L., 'The Hill family and educational change in the early nineteenth century', *Durham Research Review*, 2 (10), 3 (11), 3 (12), 1959–60.

Hill, Octavia (1838–1912). Housing reformer. Born Wisbech, Cambridgeshire. Daughter of Caroline Smith, a writer on educational theory, and granddaughter of Thomas Southwood Smith, the sanitary reformer. Educated at home. In 1852 began work in London at the Ladies' Guild, a Christian Socialist co-operative association where she was put in charge of teaching ragged school children. Influenced by **F.D. Maurice** and by **John Ruskin** who encouraged her artistic talent. In 1856 Hill became secretary to the classes for women at the Working Men's College and subsequently with her sisters started a school for poor girls. From 1864 her main energies were devoted to purchasing and improving dwellings for the poor. Her recommendations influenced the Artisans' Dwellings Bill of 1875 and she gave evidence to the Royal Commission on Housing in 1884. In the same year the Ecclesiastical Commissioners appointed her to manage much of their property in Southwark. In 1889 Hill joined the Committee of the Southwark Women's University Settlement, a scheme whereby educated women lived and worked in poor districts. At the Southwark Settlement women were given a training in social work to help them to qualify for professional or voluntary work. Supported the Charity Organisation Society and in 1895 was one of the founders of the National Trust. She opposed female suffrage. See her *Homes for the London Poor* (1875, repr. Cass 1970); *Our Common Land* (1877), and Maurice, C.E. (ed.), *Life of Octavia Hill as told in her Letters* (1913); Bell, E.M., *Octavia Hill* (1942); Hill, W.T. *Octavia Hill* (1956).

Hill, Rosamond Davenport (1825–1902). Reformer of schools and prisons. Born in Chelsea, London, eldest daughter of **Matthew Davenport Hill**, Recorder of Birmingham and social reformer. Educated at home and at boarding school in Clapton, London.

From 1851 assisted **Mary Carpenter** in her ragged school at Bristol, and also established her own industrial school for girls. Travelled widely inspecting schools and prisons, after her father's death in 1872 in the company of her sister Florence. They wrote an account of their travels in Australia (1875) and a biography of their father (1878). Whilst in Australia they gave evidence on the English system of boarding out paupers to a New South Wales Public Charities Commission. From 1879 the sisters settled in London where Rosamond served on the London School Board for 18 years. Chairman of its Cookery and later Domestic Sciences Committee and member of the Industrial Schools Committee. The Brentwood Industrial School was reorganized and in 1896 renamed the Davenport-Hill Home for Boys. In the same year she gave evidence to the Departmental Committee on Reformatory and Industrial Schools. In 1895 she was appointed a life governor of University College, London. See her *Lessons in Cookery* (1885), and Metcalfe, E.E., *Memoir of Rosamond Davenport Hill* (1904).

Hill, Sir Rowland (1795–1879). Schoolmaster and inventor of the penny post. Born Kidderminster, third son of Thomas Wright Hill. In 1803 entered his father's school at Hill Top, Birmingham. Became a teacher there at the age of 12, taught himself mathematics, astronomy and land surveying and made several ingenious machines. He designed and built a new school house called Hazlewood. He established a new system of school management – government by boys under a constitution, with a court of justice, and the abolition of corporal punishment. The system was described by his brother **Matthew Davenport Hill** in *Public Education: Plans for the Government and Liberal Instruction of Boys in Large Numbers, drawn from Experience* (1822). The leading radicals, **Bentham, Grote**, and Hume declared their approval, and pupils came from the newly-founded republics of South America. In 1827 the main body of the school was transferred to Bruce Castle, Tottenham. In 1826 Hill was one of the founders of the Society for the Diffusion of Useful Knowledge. Inventor of a rotary printing press; Secretary to the South Australian commission, 1835–9; founder of the penny post, 1840; director of the London and Brighton Railway, 1843, chairman, 1845–6; Secretary to the Postmaster General, 1846–54; Permanent Secretary to the Post Office, 1854–64; by which date he had transformed the whole service. FRS, 1857; KCB, 1860; DCL, Oxford, 1864. See Hill, G.B., *The life of Sir Rowland Hill* (1880); Smyth, E.C., *Sir Rowland Hill* (1907); Hill, H.W., *Rowland Hill*

(1940); Dobson, J.L., 'The Hill family and educational change in the early nineteenth century', *Durham Research Review*, 2 (10), 3 (11), 3 (12), 1959–60.

Hobhouse, Arthur, 1st Baron Hobhouse of Hadspen (1819–1904). Endowed School Commissioner and judge. Born Hadspen House, Somerset, son of Henry Hobhouse, Under-Secretary of State, 1817–27. Educated privately, Eton, 1830–7, and Balliol College, Oxford, 1837–40, gaining a first in classics. Barrister, Lincoln's Inn, 1845. QC, 1862. Because of severe illness Hobhouse retired from practice and was appointed Charity Commissioner, 1866. Hobhouse, an advanced Liberal, advocated reform of the law governing charitable endowments. When the Endowed Schools Act, 1869 set up a Commission to carry out this task, Hobhouse was chosen as one of the three Commissioners along with **4th Baron Lyttelton** and **Canon H.G. Robinson**. He discharged his duties with great vigour in remodelled schemes of endowed schools but received a setback when, in 1871, the Lords rejected the new scheme for Emanuel Hospital, Westminster. Law member of the council of the Governor-General, India, 1872–7. Unsuccessfully contested Westminster as a Liberal, 1880. Member, Judicial Committee of the Privy Council, 1881–1901. Knight, 1877. Peer, 1885. A social reformer, Hobhouse helped to establish and further the aims of the London Municipal Reform League, 1880, which looked to a single government for the metropolis. Member, London School Board, 1882–4. Alderman, London County Council, 1888. An important address to the Social Science Association at Birmingham 1868 on the law of married women's property was later published. A collection of addresses on endowments and the settlements of property appeared under the title *The Dead Hand* (1880). See also Hobhouse, L.T., and Hammond, J.L., *Lord Hobhouse, a Memoir* (1905).

Hodgson, William Ballantyne (1815–80). Educational reformer and political economist. Born Edinburgh and educated there at the High School and University but left without taking a degree. Lectured in Fifeshire on education and phrenology and in 1839 appointed secretary to the Liverpool Mechanics' Institute. From 1844 principal of the Liverpool Institute to which a girls' school had been added on his advice. Principal of the Chorlton High School, Manchester, 1847–51. Travelled abroad 1851–3, and returned to Edinburgh where he gave popular lectures on physiology. From

1854 lectured on economic science at the Royal Institution, London. Assistant Commissioner to the Newcastle Commission, 1858–61. Examiner in political economy at the University of London, 1863–8, and served on the Council of University College. Professor of Commercial and Political Economy and Mercantile Law at Edinburgh University, 1871–80. President of the Education section of the National Association for the Promotion of Social Science, 1873; president of the Educational Institute of Scotland, 1875. A lucid lecturer and prolific writer on a range of topics. See Meiklejohn, J.M.D. (ed.), *Life and Letters of W.B. Hodgson* (1883); Graff, H.J., *'Exaggerated Estimates of Reading and Writing, as Means of Education* (1867) by W.B. Hodgson', *History of Education Quarterly*, 26 (3), 1986.

Hogben, Lancelot Thomas (1895–1975). Scientist and popular educator. Born Southsea, Hampshire, son of a drysalter. Educated Trinity College, Cambridge (senior scholar), natural science tripos, 1915. During the 1914–18 war, Hogben went to prison as a conscientious objector. A brilliant scientist, especially in the fields of genetics and endocrinology. Lecturer in zoology, Imperial College, London, 1919–22, during which time he campaigned actively for the Labour Party in the East End. Assistant professor of Zoology, McGill University, Montreal, 1922–7 and professor of Zoology, University of Cape Town, 1927–30, where he championed the black cause. In 1930, a new chair in Social Biology was created for him at the London School of Economics. It was during his term of office there that Hogben wrote *Mathematics for the Million* (1936) which explained the subject in simple language. This was followed by *Science for the Citizen* (1938). Both books were well received by a large audience. Regius professor of Natural History, Aberdeen University, 1937–41 and Mason professor of Zoology, Birmingham University, 1941–7. Hogben's interest in medieval statistics led to his occupying a new chair which was established at Birmingham in Statistics, 1947–61. Vice-Chancellor, Ghana University, 1963–5. FRS, 1936.

Hogg, Quintin (1845–1903). Philanthropist. Born London, educated at Eton where he was prominent at association football, in later years playing in some of the first international matches. In 1863 he entered the City and became senior partner in a firm of sugar merchants. In the winter of 1864–5 he started a ragged school, to which was soon added a Youths' Christian Institute. In 1878 this

latter was transferred to new premises with 500 members and courses in technical education an a sports ground at Mortlake, Surrey. In 1882 Hogg purchased a lease on the buildings of the Royal Polytechnic Institution in Regent Street which had closed in the previous year. The new Polytechnic opened in September 1882 with 2,000 members and by the winter these numbers had risen to 6,800. Hogg's aim was to provide young men and women of the lower middle classes with instruction, recreation and social intercourse. Technical classes, sports facilities, a debating society, volunteer corps, savings bank and Christian workers' union were organized. In 1891 a labour bureau was established. Hogg's financial contributions totalled some £100,000 and further money was raised by public subscription and grants from the London parochial charities. As an Alderman of the first London County Council, 1889–94, Hogg encouraged the formation of other London polytechnics. See his *The Story of Peter* (1900) and Hogg, E.M., *Quintin Hogg* (1904) (revised and enlarged in 1932 as *The Polytechnic and its founder Quintin Hogg).*

Holland, Henry Scott (1847–1918). Theologian and academic. Born Ledbury, Herefordshire. Educated private school, Allesley, near Coventry. Eton, 1860–4 and Balliol College, Oxford, 1866–70, first class in classical moderations and *literae humaniores*, becoming a close friend of **T.H. Green** and **R.L. Nettleship**. Senior student, Christ Church, Oxford, 1870–86. Ordained, 1872. Tutor, 1872, Censor, 1882–4. Canon, St Paul's Cathedral, 1884–1910. A man of deep social conscience, Holland regarded the Church as a social organism or universal brotherhood which should look to spiritual equality and brotherly fellowship. In an age of industrialism, he argued, the Church had hitherto failed to give a lead in protesting against the conditions under which the working classes lived. These views were propagated by a group of like-minded clerics, including Holland, through the Christian Social Union, founded in 1889. Their beliefs, set out in a book *Lux Mundi* that year, caused an uproar in theological circles. Professor of Divinity, Oxford University, 1910–18. See also his *Logic and Life* (1882); *Personal Studies* (1905); *A Bundle of Memories* (1915), and Paget, S. (ed.), *Henry Scott Holland: Memoirs and Letters* (1921).

Hollowell, James Hirst (1851–1909). Congregationalist minister. Born Northampton. Left school early but continued his studies independently and aged 18 became a temperance agent and lecturer. Studied for the Congregationalist ministry at Nottingham, 1871 and at Cheshunt, 1872–4. Pastor at Bedford Chapel, Camden Town, London, 1875–82; Park Hill Congregational church, Nottingham, 1882–9; Milton church, Rochdale, 1889–96. At Nottingham he was chairman of the School Board, and in 1896 became secretary of the Northern Counties Education League for promoting unsectarian state education. He was a leader of the movement against the payment of rates and taxes on the grounds that the 1902 Education Act gave unfair support to Church schools to teach Church doctrines at public expense, and a tireless speaker and writer in the cause of unsectarian education. See his *National Elementary Education* (1888); *Education and Popular Control* (1898); *What Nonconformists stand for* (1901), and Evans, W., and Claridge, W., *James Hirst Hollowell and the Movement for Civic Control in Education* (1911).

Holman, Henry (1859–1919). University professor and school inspector. Born Hurstpierpoint, Sussex. Admitted to Gonville and Caius College, Cambridge, as a non-collegiate student, 1889, scholar, 1890, obtaining first class honours in moral science tripos the same year. The University College of Aberystwyth housed the first Welsh day training college from 1892. It consisted of 15 men and 15 women. Holman was appointed lecturer, head of department and Master of Method in 1892; professor of Theory of Education, 1893–4. Holman insisted that the pupil teachers, with five years' experience but no formal examination qualifications, should be respected. HMI, 1894–1919. See his *Education, an introduction to its principles and their psychological foundations* (1896); *English National Education, a sketch of the rise of public elementary schools in England* (1898), and *Seguin and his physiological method of education* (1914).

Holmes, Edmond Gore Alexander (1850–1936). School inspector and writer. Born in mid-Ireland. Came to London at the age of 11.

WHAT IS AND WHAT MIGHT BE

A STUDY OF EDUCATION IN GENERAL AND ELEMENTARY EDUCATION IN PARTICULAR

EDMOND HOLMES

"THE CREED OF CHRIST," "THE CREED OF BUDDHA," "THE SILENCE
OF LOVE," "THE TRIUMPH OF LOVE," ETC.

LONDON

CONSTABLE & CO. LTD.

1911

Educated at Merchant Taylors' School and St John's College, Oxford. First class honours in classics. Left Oxford in 1874 and in the following year became one of Her Majesty's School Inspectors, 'a calling which without being too absorbing or exacting would provide me with the means of subsistence'. Served in Yorkshire from 1875, Kent from 1879, Oxford from 1897 and Northumberland as Divisional Inspector from 1903. Chief Inspector for elementary schools, 1905–10. Holmes was critical of the system of payment by results and in 1907 came upon the 'revelation' of the school at Sompting in Sussex and its headmistress Harriet Finlay-Johnson, his 'Egeria'. In *What Is and What Might Be* (1911), Holmes condemned the formal, systematized, examination-ridden education system and advocated co-operation, self-expression and activity methods. Thus in education as in his poetry and his philosophical writings Holmes committed himself to the pursuit of ideal truth. See his several writings including *The Tragedy of Education* (1913); *Sonnets and Poems* (1920); *In Quest of an Ideal* (1920), and Gordon, P., 'The writings of Edmond Holmes: a reassessment and bibliography', *History of Education*, 12 (1), 1983.

Holmes, Sir Maurice Gerald (1885–1964). Civil servant. Son of **Edmond Holmes**, HMI. Educated at Wellington and Balliol College, Oxford, 1904–8 in classical moderations and jurisprudence. Barrister, Inner Temple, 1909, entering Board of Education in the same year. Served in the Army, Europe, Egypt and Palestine as Lt.-Col. OBE (Military), 1919. Rejoined Board of Education. Private secretary, then Director of Establishments, 1923–6, Principal Assistant Secretary, 1929, Deputy Secretary 1931, Permanent Secretary, 1937–45, succeeding **Sir Henry Pelham**. After the outbreak of the Second World War, Holmes, who had moved with the Board to Bournemouth, was given the task of preparing the Green Book which paved the way for the new education policy embodied later in the Butler Act 1944. He returned to London 1942 to work with great energy on preparing the Bill itself. Knight, 1938. Author of *Some Bibiographical Notes on the Novels of George Bernard Shaw* (1929), and *An Introduction to the Bibliography of Captain Cook* (1936).

Holyoake, George Jacob (1817–1906). Author, lecturer and co-operative pioneer. Born Birmingham. Little formal education and started work at the age of nine at the Eagle Foundry. Between 1834 and 1840 attended classes at the Old Mechanics' Institution. In 1841 having already done some lecturing he moved to Sheffield as a lecturer and schoolmaster at the Hall of Science. Imprisoned and fined for blasphemy and for his general advocacy of secularism which substituted the piety of usefulness for the usefulness of piety. Worked as a Socialist lecturer in London, Glasgow and Paisley. In 1846 Holyoake began the *Reasoner* which he issued weekly until 1861. There was a circulation of 5,000 and local branches of atheists were formed. In the 1860s Holyoake became increasingly interested in the co-operative movement. He was a supporter of Gladstonian Liberalism and opposed state socialism and a separate Labour party. He was a printer and publisher and a leading opponent of the taxes on knowledge. Holyoake was a leading advocate of secular education. See his *The History of Co-operation in England* (2 vols., 1875, 1877); *Sixty Years of an Agitator's Life* (2 vols., 1892); *Essentials of Co-operative Education* (1898), and Goss, C.W.F., *A Descriptive Bibliography of the Writings of G.J. Holyoake with a Brief Sketch of his Life* (1908); MacCabe, J., *Life and Letters of G.J. Holyoake* (1908).

Hook, Walter Farquhar (1798–1875). Cleric. Born London, educated at schools at Hertford and Tiverton, and subsequently at Winchester and Christ Church, Oxford. BA, 1821, MA, 1824, BD and DD, 1837. Served as his father's curate at Whippingham, Isle of Wight, 1821–5, when he became perpetual curate of Moseley near Birmingham where he established a village school. In 1827 also appointed to a lectureship at St Philip's, Birmingham. Vicar of Holy Trinity, Coventry, 1828–37, where his sermons and lectures attracted great attention and where he established a Religious and Useful Knowledge Society. From 1837–59 as vicar of Leeds he became a prominent and controversial national figure. His sermon, preached before the Queen in 1838, 'Hear the Church', sold over a hundred thousand copies. In 1846 his *On the means of rendering more efficient the education of the people* outlined his scheme for national education. Hook argued that the state must establish rate-supported schools in which all children could receive secular elementary education, with religious instruction provided at specified times by the ministers of the respective flocks. This provoked a considerable outcry from the Church party in education. Hook was interested in the welfare of the working classes, accepted Chartists as his churchwardens in 1842 and 1843 and frequently lectured at mechanics' institutes and similar institutions. In 1859 he became Dean of Chichester, 'having found Leeds with three schools and left it with thirty'. Prodigious worker and earnest writer, he wrote a *Lives of the Archbishops of Canterbury* (12 vols., 1860–76), whilst his sermons were published as *The Church and her Ordinances* (2 vols., 1876). See Stephens, W.R.W. (ed.), *Life and Letters of W.F. Hook* (2 vols., 1878).

Horner, Leonard (1785–1864). Educational reformer and geologist. Born Edinburgh and educated at the Edinburgh High School where **Brougham** was a fellow pupil and friend. Studied sciences and philosophy at Edinburgh University. Elected fellow of the Geological Society, 1808, secretary, 1810, vice-president, 1828 and president, 1846. In 1821 took the lead in establishing the Edinburgh 'School of Arts for the better Education of the Mechanics of Edinburgh, in such branches of physical science as are of practical advantage in their several trades'. This developed ultimately into the Heriot-Watt University. Horner was also one of the two major founders (with Henry Cockburn) of the Edinburgh Academy in 1824. In 1827 he moved to London to become Warden of London University (University College) but resigned in 1831 after considerable opposition from the professors. In 1838 Horner translated Cousin's *State of Education in Holland as regards the Working Classes* into English and advocated educational legislation in Britain. From 1833–59 served as one of the inspectors appointed under the Factory Acts and advocated half-time education for factory children in a paper written in 1840. Throughout his long career as an inspector Horner attempted to safeguard the interests of children at work and to ensure that they received some education. See Brown, C.M., 'Leonard Horner, 1785–1864; his contribution to education', *Journal of Educational Administration and History*, 17 (1), 1985.

Horsbrugh, Florence Gertrude, Baroness (1889–1969). Conservative politician. Born Edinburgh, educated at Lansdowne House, Edinburgh, and St Hilda's, Folkestone. MBE for work in canteens and national kitchens, 1916–18. Conservative member for Dundee, 1931–45, and for Manchester (Moss Side), 1950–9, when she was made a Life Peeress. In 1936 she was the first woman to move the address in reply to the King's Speech, and her private member's bill of 1939 became law as the Adoption of Children (Regulation) Act. As Parliamentary Secretary to the Ministry of Health, 1939–45, she was responsible for arranging the evacuation of children from major cities during the war. In 1951 became Minister of Education, and in

1953 a member of the Cabinet. She resigned in 1954. Delegate to the Council of Europe and Western European Union, 1955–60. Honorary degrees from Mills College, California, and Edinburgh University. CBE, 1939, GBE, 1954. See Vallance, E., *Women in the House: a study of Women Members of Parliament* (1959).

Houghton, Sir William Frederick (1909–71). Educational administrator. Educated Christ's College, Cambridge, history tripos, second

class honours, 1931. Taught at Methodist College, Belfast and Wirral Grammar School, 1932–6. Assistant to Secretary, East Suffolk Education Committee, 1936–8, Deputy Director of Education, West Sussex, 1938–41, Chief Education Officer, Darlington, 1941–7, Deputy Education Officer, Birmingham, 1947–52, Deputy Education Officer, London County Council, 1952–6 and Education Officer, 1956–65. Education Officer, Inner London Education Authority, 1965–71. Knight, 1967. Author of *Greeks and Romans* (1935).

Hubback, Eva Marion (1886–1949). Educationist and social reformer. Born London and educated St Felix School, Southwold and Newnham College, Cambridge, economics tripos first class honours, 1908. Director of Economic Studies, Newnham and Girton during First World War, 1916–17. Parliamentary Secretary (later President), National Union for Equal Citizenship, 1918–27, which successfully campaigned for legislative reforms affecting women and children. Honorary Secretary, Association for Education in Citizenship and one of its founders; member, Population Investigation Committee and Council of the Eugenics Society. Elected councillor, London County Council, 1946–49. Principal, Morley College for Working Men and Women, 1927–49. See her *Training for Citizenship* (with Sir Ernest Simon) (1935); *A New Plea for Family Allowances* (1943); *The Population of Britain* (1947), and Hopkinson, D., *Family Inheritance: A Life of Eva Hubback* (1954).

Hughes, Thomas (1822–96). Lawyer and author. Born Uffington, Berkshire. Educated at a private school near Winchester, at Rugby and at Oriel College, Oxford. Was a friend of **Matthew Arnold** and **Arthur Hugh Clough**. Graduated BA in 1845 and called to the bar at the Inner Temple, 1848. QC in 1869 and Bencher of his inn in 1870. In 1848 joined the Christian Socialist group centred around **F.D. Maurice** and **Charles Kingsley** and contributed to its conferences, journals and tours. Became a supporter of the co-operative movement, particularly in respect of the full participation of workers in business. In 1854 Hughes helped to found the Working Men's College established in Great Ormond Street, London. Was active in its social work, as commander of its volunteer corps, and as its principal, 1872–83. A reforming member of Parliament he sat for Lambeth, 1865–8, and Frome, 1868–74. Hughes was best known for his novel *Tom Brown's School Days* published anonymously in April 1857 which went through five editions in nine months. Tom Brown, according to the author's preface, 'the commonest type of English boy of the upper middle class', reflected much of Hughes himself, and helped to endorse the reputation of **Thomas Arnold**, headmaster of Rugby School. See his other works including *The Scouring of the White Horse* (1859); *Tom Brown at Oxford* (1861), and Mack, E.C., and Armytage, W.H.G., *Thomas Hughes* (1952).

Hullah, John Pyke (1812–84). Teacher and school inspector. Born Worcester. Educated at schools in Harlow, Essex, High Wycombe, Buckinghamshire, and Brixton, London, 1817–26. Studied piano and composition privately, 1829–33. Royal Academy of Music, 1833–5. His opera, 'The Village Coquettes' to a text by Dickens, completed 1836, achieved success in London. Organist, Croydon Church, 1835. Conceived the idea after travelling abroad of forming a school for instruction in vocal music based on the Wilhem 'fixed doh method' of sight-singing. In February 1840, began teaching at Dr James Kay's (later **Kay-Shuttleworth**) Normal School for schoolmasters at Battersea and visited schools in Paris with Kay in August. From then on, Hullah demonstrated and lectured in singing method throughout the country. By 1844, 50,000 people had attended sessions. Professor of Vocal Music, King's College, London, 1847–74. Active supporter of women's education, Hullah was one of the founders of Queen's College, Harley Street, London, in 1847 and was also concerned with the establishment of Bedford College two years later, teaching at both institutions. Campaigned for the election of women to the London School Board, canvassing successfully for Miss Garrett, MD (later **Mrs Garrett Anderson**). Elected committee of management Royal Academy of Music, 1869, and conductor of choral and orchestral concerts, 1870–3. Appointed HMI for music in training colleges, 1872. Hullah continued to compose throughout his life and was author of a number of influential books on various aspects of music. Those relating to education include *Wilhem's Method of Teaching Singing, adapted to English Use* (1840), *A Grammar of Vocal Music* (1843), *Time and Tune in the Elementary School* (1874) and *Music in the House* (1876). See also Hullah, F.R., *Life of John Hullah* (1886).

Huxley, Thomas Henry (1825–95). Scientist, humanist and educator. Born Ealing, London. Received only two years' schooling, from eight to ten, but read widely and taught himself Latin, Greek, French, German and Italian. Free scholarship at Charing Cross Medical School. Graduated MB, 1845 with the gold medal for anatomy and physiology. Enrolled as an assistant surgeon in the Royal Navy. During a voyage on HMS *Rattlesnake* 1846–50, he engaged in marine research. His scientific papers led to his being elected FRS in 1851, and to an appointment as professor of Natural History at the Royal School of Mines in London in 1854. Huxley became a firm supporter of **Darwin**'s theories and invented the word 'agnostic' to describe his own position in respect of religion. He wrote innumerable research papers, essays and articles, and some textbooks, on subjects ranging from anthropology, botany and zoology to education and religion. Huxley was a member of the first London School Board of 1871 and was keenly interested in working-class education. He served on a number of royal commissions and strongly influenced the teaching of science, particularly biology, in schools. Rector of Aberdeen University, 1872–5, and a governor of Eton College; University College, London; the London Medical School; Owens College, Manchester; president of the British Association and of numerous scientific societies; Hunterian Professor at the Royal College of Surgeons, 1863–9; and Fullerian Professor at the Royal Institution, 1863–7. Huxley emphasized the importance of physical and moral culture in the elementary school curriculum, and argued that the curriculum of the University of London should not include the technical specialities of medicine, law and theology, but rather the broader study of 'art (literary and other), history, philosophy and science'. See his several writings especially the *Collected Essays* (9 vols., 1893–4) (Volume III is entitled *Science and Education*), and Huxley, L., *Life and Letters of T.H. Huxley* (2

SCIENCE & EDUCATION

ESSAYS

BY

THOMAS H. HUXLEY

London

MACMILLAN AND CO.

1893

vols., 1900); Bibby, C., *T.H. Huxley, Scientist, Humanist and Educator* (1959).

Iles, John Cyril (1865–1915). School inspector. Born Stafford, son of a minister. Educated Lancing and Trinity College, Cambridge, Senior wrangler, 1887. Appointed HMI, 1892, Warwickshire; Preston division of Lancashire, 1894–1905; Liverpool, 1905–9, Divisional Inspector, north-west division, 1909–12 and Divisional Inspector, Staffordshire, 1912–15. Although his own studies were mainly in mathematics and applied science, he was greatly interested in the teaching of English, claiming that the best way to improve the teaching of arithmetic was to improve the teaching of English. See Dale, F.H., *J.C. Iles, H.M. Inspector of Schools 1892–1915* (1915).

Isaacs, Susan Sutherland (1885–1948). Child psychologist. Born Bromley Cross, near Bolton, Lancashire, daughter of a journalist.

Left school at 14, later entering Manchester University for a two-year infant course; proceeded to a BA in philosophy, gaining first class honours, 1912. MA, 1913. Research student, University of Cambridge Psychological Laboratory, where her interest in child development flourished. Lecturer, Darlington Training College, 1913–14, when she married, and lecturer in logic, Manchester University, 1914–15. Her second marriage to Nathan Isaacs in 1922 was an important factor in the development of her educational thinking and subsequent career. Much of her writing was stimulated by her time as principal of the Malting House School, Cambridge, 1924–7, an independent establishment which furthered the individual development of children. D.Sc., Manchester, 1931. Head of Child Development Department, University of London Institute of Education, 1933–43. CBE, 1948. See her *Intellectual Growth of Young Children* (1930); *The Children We Teach* (1932); *Social Development in Young Children* (1933), and Gardner, D.E.M., *Susan Isaacs* (1969).

Jacks, Lawrence Pearsall (1860–1955). Man of religion and philosopher. Born Nottingham, son of an ironmonger. Educated Nottingham University School, leaving school at 17. Entered Manchester New College, London, 1882. BA, 1883, MA, 1886. After a year at Harvard, appointed assistant to Stopford Brooke, who had renounced his Anglican orders to become a Nonconformist at Bedford Chapel, Bloomsbury, 1886–7. He participated in university extension work, lecturing on political economy and was part of a circle which included **George Bernard Shaw, Beatrice** and **Sidney Webb** and Oscar Wilde. Unitarian minister, Liverpool, 1888–94 and at Birmingham, 1894–1903. Jacks was the first editor of the *Hibbert Journal* (1902), which provided a forum for religious and allied topics. Lecturer in philosophy, Manchester College (now at Oxford), 1903–15 and principal, 1915–31. Jacks was a prolific writer; among his books are *The Alchemy of Thought* (1910) and *The Education of the Whole Man* (1931) and two volumes of autobiography, *The Confessions of an Octogenarian* (1942) and *Near the Brink* (1952).

Jackson, Sir Cyril (1863–1924). Educationist. Born Bodiam, Sussex, son of a City broker. Educated Charterhouse and New

College, Oxford, obtaining second class in classical moderations, 1883 and *literae humaniores*, 1885. Attracted to the ideals of Toynbee Hall, a settlement in the East End of London which provided evangelical opportunities to educate the working classes, Jackson was resident there, 1885–95. Barrister, Inner Temple, 1893, Secretary, Children's Holiday Fund, 1888–96 and member of the London School Board, 1891–6. In 1896, became Inspector-General of Schools and permanent head of the education department, Western Australia, completely reorganizing the school system in the state. Returned to England 1903 and appointed first Chief Inspector, Elementary Schools, Board of Education, following the restructuring of the Inspectorate by **Robert Morant**. Resigned in December 1905 after

129

disagreement with Morant over transfer of his inspectors to the new Secondary Branch. Investigator, Royal Commission on the Poor Law, 1906. Member for Limehouse, London County Council, 1907–13, alderman, 1913–16 and 1919 and chairman, London County Council Education Committee, 1908–10 and 1922. Leader, Municipal Reform Party and chairman, London County Council, 1915. He supported the notion of central schools and compulsory continuation education and introduced a scheme for reducing the size of elementary school classes in London. Jackson also took a great interest in non-provided schools and was a keen advocate of religious instruction. Senator, London University, 1908–21. Created knight, 1917. See his *The Religious Question in Public Education* (1911) with Sadler, M. and Riley, A., and *Outline of Education in England* (1913).

Jackson, Sir Percy Richard (1869–1941). Administrator. Born Huddersfield. Educated at Huddersfield Collegiate School. Business interests in the textile industry, and a Methodist Church member. The moving spirit behind the West Riding Religious Instruction Syllabus of 1922. Elected to the West Riding Council in 1904 and served until 1937, being chairman of the Education Committee from 1917. President of the Association of Education Committees, 1924, and chairman of the County Councils Association, 1929–35. Jackson was also a member of the Council and Court of Leeds University from 1918, and trustee and vice-chairman of the United Kingdom Carnegie Trust from 1924. His national work for education was particularly associated with his membership of the Consultative Committee of the Board of Education, 1922–38. He was a member of the Burnham Committee on teachers' salaries from 1919, and served on the departmental committee under **Burnham** which reported in 1925 on the training of teachers for public elementary schools. He was a member of the Hadow committees which reported in 1926, 1931 and 1933 on the education of the adolescent and primary schools, and of the Spens committee which reported in 1938 on secondary education with special reference to grammar and technical high schools. Honorary doctorates from Leeds and Sheffield in 1924, and knighted in 1925. See Gosden, P.H.J.H., and Sharp, P.R., *The Development of an Education Service: The West Riding 1889–1974* (1978).

Jeffery, George Barker (1891–1957). Educationist. Born Lambeth, London, son of a corresponding clerk. Educated Strand School,

King's College, London, Wilson's Grammar School, Camberwell and King's College, London, London Day Training College and University College, London. B.Sc. in mathematics, 1911. Assistant lecturer, applied mathematics, at University College, London, 1912–21. Published many papers on mathematics and mathematical physics. MA, London University, 1914, D.Sc., London, 1921. Reader in mathematics, University College, London, 1921–2, professor, King's College, London, 1922–4, and Astor Professor of Mathematics, University College, London, 1924–45. FRS, 1925. Became increasingly interested in aspects of teaching and administration. Chairman, Matriculation and School Examination Council, London University, 1939. Jeffery succeeded **Sir Fred Clarke** as Director, University of London Institute of Education, in 1945. Following the establishment of Area Training Organizations after the War, Jeffery, an able administrator, was responsible for more than 30 teacher training establishments in the London area. The Institute itself was expanding and the creation of new chairs in education was successfully carried out. Jeffery also took a great interest in West African education, and was instrumental in establishing a West African examination council to control all examinations there. Member, Secondary School Examinations Council from 1946; member, National Advisory Council on Training and Supply of Teachers from 1949; Chairman, Executive Committee, National Foundation for Educational Research from 1949; President, New Education Fellowship from 1952; President, Association of Teachers in Colleges and Departments of Education, 1954–7. See his *Relativity for Physics Students* (1924), *African Education, A Study of Educational Policy and Practice in British Tropical Africa* (1953), and Dixon, C.W., *The Institute: A History of the University of London Institute of Education, 1932–72* (1986).

Jex-Blake, Sophia (1840–1912). Physician. Born at Hastings. Educated at various boarding schools and at Queen's College, London.

Taught mathematics there, 1859–61, and subsequently taught in Germany and the USA. In Boston she became interested in medicine and in 1869 returned to England to study for a medical degree. Studied at Edinburgh University, 1869–72, but harassment by male undergraduates and staff and refusal to sit the final MD degree thwarted her purpose. In 1874 Jex-Blake opened the London School of Medicine for Women. In 1877 she obtained an MD from Queen's University, Belfast and was entered on the register of the General Medical Council. In 1878 London University admitted women to all its degrees. Jex-Blake returned to Edinburgh where she practised, 1878–99. In 1885 she opened the Edinburgh Hospital and Dispensary for Women and Children and a medical school in the following year. See her *Medical Women* (1872); *The Care of Infants* (1884), and Todd, M.G., *The Life of Sophia Jex-Blake* (1918); Bell, E. *Storming the Citadel* (1953).

Jex-Blake, Thomas William (1832–1915). Schoolmaster and cleric. Born London, son of a gentleman. Educated at Rugby and University College, Oxford, obtaining first class in classical moderations, 1853, and first class in *literae humaniores*, 1855. Fellow, Queen's College, Oxford, 1855 and ordained priest at Winchester two years later. Jex-Blake served as schoolmaster in public schools for the next 32 years. After a brief spell at Marlborough, he was assistant master at Rugby under **Frederick Temple**, 1858–68, principal of Cheltenham College, 1868–74 and headmaster of Rugby, 1874–87. His strong conviction in the value of the arts in the public school curriculum led to the foundation of the first art museum in an English school (at Rugby), donating many items himself. He also started the modern side there and built workshops for boys. His sermons, given at Cheltenham and Rugby, were published as *Life in Faith* (1876). Rector, Alvechurch, Worcestershire, 1887–91. Dean of Wells Cathedral, 1891–1910.

Johnson-Marshall, Stirrat Andrew William (1912–81). Architect. Born in India. Educated at Liverpool University School of Architecture, graduating with first class honours. ARIBA, 1936. Served in the Royal Engineers, 1939–45, and made a daring escape from Singapore by rowing boat and launch in 1942. Deputy County Architect for Hertfordshire, 1945–8 where he helped to pioneer the design and production of efficient and elegant prefabricated school buildings. Chief Architect at the Ministry of Education, 1948–56. He established a Development Group within the new Architects and Building Branch and inspired teams of architects, educators and builders. The Ministry became the centre of research and innovation in school design and building. Partner in Robert Matthew, Johnson-Marshall and Partners, 1956–78. Johnson-Marshall himself was particularly involved with the design and building of the new University of York. Member of the council of the Royal Institute of British Architects and of the Medical Research Council. CBE, 1945; Knight, 1971. See Saint, A., *Towards a social architecture: the role of schoolbuilding in postwar England* (1987).

Jones, Emily Elizabeth Constance (1848–1922). Scholar. Born Ross, Herefordshire, the eldest of ten children, she was a descendant of David Lewis the first principal of Jesus College, Oxford, 1571. Educated at home, both in Britain and South Africa, at Alston Court, Cheltenham and at Girton College, Cambridge. Jones stated that from her childhood onwards she had 'an inexplicable love of books and hunger for knowledge'. First class in moral science tripos of 1880. Lecturer in moral sciences at Girton, 1884–1903; Vice-Mistress, 1896–1903; Mistress, 1903–16. Jones showed great skill in administration. A debt of £50,000 was repaid, accommodation for a further 50 students was provided, scholarships were increased and a system of fellowships instituted. After 1916 devoted herself to moral philosophy. Governor of the University College of Wales, Aberystwyth and D.Litt. of the University of Wales. See her *Elements of Logic* (1890); *A New Law of Thought* (1910); *Girton College* (1913); *As I Remember* (1922).

Jones, Sir Henry (1852–1922). Philosopher. Born Llangernyw, Denbighshire, son of village shoemaker. Educated at local school, leaving at the age of 12, but returned on a half-time basis five years later, and Bangor Normal College, 1870–3. Appointed headmaster of Ironworks School, Brynamman, South Wales, 1873–5, during which time he also became a Calvinist Methodist preacher. Entered Glasgow University, 1875 to study philosophy. A fellowship enabled him to study in Germany, 1878–82. Lecturer in philosophy, University College, Aberystwyth, 1882–4, professor of Philosophy and Political Economy, University College, Bangor, 1884–91, professor of Logic, Rhetoric and Metaphysics, St Andrews University, 1891–4 and succeeded **Edward Caird** as professor of Moral Philosophy, Glasgow University, 1894–1922. Caird had been a leading influence on Jones from the 1870s, introducing him to Hegelian

idealism. His books *Idealism as a Practical Creed* (1909) and *Philosophical Landmarks* (1917) set out clearly his own philosophy. He was deeply interested in educational affairs. Jones drafted the constitution in 1883 for the new college in North Wales at Bangor, and played a leading part in the movement for intermediate education in Wales, culminating in the Act of 1889 which established such schools. Member, Royal Commission on University in Wales, 1916–17 and the Departmental Committee on Adult Education, 1918. Knight, 1912, Companion of Honour, 1922. See his *The Principles of Citizenship* (1919); *Old Memories. Autobiography* (1923) Jones, T. (ed.), and Hetherington, H.J.W., *The Life and Letters of Sir Henry Jones* (1924).

Jones, John Viriamu (1856–1901). Physicist and educationist. Born at Pentre Poeth, near Swansea, son of Thomas Jones, the noted Welsh poet–preacher. Educated at Oakley House, Reading and University College School, London. Returning to Wales, he attended Swansea Normal School, 1870–2, then University College, London (B.Sc. in geology, 1875) and Balliol College, Oxford, 1876–81, first class honours in mathematics, 1879, and natural science, 1880. Appointed principal, Firth College, Sheffield, and professor of Physics and Mathematics, 1881–3. First principal, University College of South Wales at Cardiff, 1883–1901. Jones was a distinguished scientist, making contributions in many fields. FRS, 1894. He was passionately devoted to the ideal of creating a national University of Wales and poured much of his energies into this cause. In 1893 and for the following three years he was the first Vice-Chancellor of the new University of Wales. The Physical Research Laboratory at Cathays Park, Cardiff, was later erected in his memory. See Jones, K.V., *Life of John Viriamu Jones* (1915).

Jones, Thomas (1870–1955). Academic and civil servant. Born Rhymney, Monmouthshire, a Welsh mining village. Educated at

134

Lewis School, Pengam. Began work at 14 in the local iron company, but continued to study in his spare time. Attended the University College of Wales at Aberystwyth and the London School of Economics, and graduated from Glasgow University in 1901. Lectured in economics in Belfast and Glasgow, employed as a special investigator by the Poor Law Commission, 1906–9, professor of Economics, Queen's University, Belfast, 1909–10. Secretary to the Welsh National Campaign against Tuberculosis, 1910–11, and Secretary to the National Health Insurance Commissioners (Wales), 1912–16. Assistant, then Deputy-Secretary to the British Cabinet, 1916–30; Secretary of the Pilgrim Trust, 1930–45, and Chairman, 1952–4. President of the University College of Wales, Aberystwyth from 1944 until just before his death. Jones supported the Workers' Educational Association, and encouraged the University of Wales to develop more tutorial classes. In 1927 he founded Coleg Harlech in North Wales, the first adult residential college in the principality. Its Council included trade unionists and industrialists as well as academics. See his many publications, particularly *A Theme with Variations* (1933); *Leeks and Daffodils* (1942); his diaries edited by Middlemass, K., as *Whitehall Diary* (3 vols., 1969–71), and White E., *Thomas Jones* (1978).

Jowett, Benjamin (1817–93). Scholar. Born in Camberwell, London. Educated at St Paul's School and Balliol College, Oxford. Won the Hertford scholarship in 1837, was elected a fellow in 1838 and graduated BA first class in 1839 and MA in 1842. Awarded the Chancellor's Latin essay prize in 1841. Was a college tutor at Balliol, 1842–70, and Master, 1870–93. Took deacon's orders in 1842, and priest's in 1845. Was Regius professor of Greek, 1855–93 and Vice-Chancellor, 1882–6. Honorary degrees from Leyden, Edinburgh, Dublin and Cambridge. Jowett was a successful lecturer and tutor but his Broad Church theological views were frequently attacked and he was even formally charged with heresy. He enlarged the college buildings and encouraged the founding of more scholarships and exhibitions. He was involved in reform of the university as a whole, and contributed to the development of secondary education and to university extension, particularly to the University College at Bristol. He was fascinated by India, involved in a scheme of examinations for the Indian Civil Service, arranged to receive candidates as students at Balliol, and helped to establish a school of oriental languages. Jowett influenced generations of students, notably **T.H. Green**, and his *bon mots* such as 'Respectability is a great foe to religion', 'The practice of divines has permanently lowered the standard of truth' reflected his critical approach to theology and philosophy. See his several religious commentaries and translations from classical authors, and Abbot, E., and Campbell, L., *Life and Letters of Benjamin Jowett* (2 vols., 1897); Faber, G., *Benjamin Jowett* (1958).

Kandel, Isaac Leon (1881–1965). Comparative educationist. Born Romania but parents moved to England. Educated Manchester Grammar School, Manchester University and Columbia University, USA. Assistant classical master, Royal Academical Institution, Belfast, 1906–8, assistant editor, Monroe's *Cyclopaedia of Education*, 1909–13. Lecturer, Teachers' College, Columbia University, 1913–23, Professor, 1923–46, Simon Research Fellow, Manchester University, 1947–8. Professor of American Studies, Manchester University, 1948–50. A pioneer in the field of comparative education, Kandel in his seminal work *Studies in Comparative Education* (1933) discussed 'the meaning of general education, elementary and secondary, in the light of forces, political, social and cultural – which determine the character of national systems of education'. In the book, six of the 'leading educational laboratories of the world', England, France, Germany, Italy, Russia and the United States were investigated. See also his *History of Secondary Education* (1930); *Conflicting Theories of Education* (1938); *Cult of Uncertainty* (1943), and *The New Era in Education* (1955).

Kane, Sir Robert John (1809–90). Scientist. Born Dublin. Educated there at Trinity College, BA, 1835; LL.D, 1868. Professor of Chemistry at the Apothecaries Hall, Dublin, 1831. In 1832 Kane founded the *Dublin Journal of Medical Science*. His *Elements of Chemistry* (1841) attracted attention both in Britain and in the USA. *Industrial Resources in Ireland* published in 1844 led to the establishment in 1846 of a Museum of Irish industry with Kane as director. First president of Queen's College, Cork, and a member of the commission appointed in 1845 to inquire into the Irish famine. Knighted in 1846. FRS, 1849. In 1873 Kane left Queen's College to take up the post of Commissioner of National Education, and in 1880 became first Chancellor of the newly-created Royal University of Ireland. See O'Raghallaigh, D., *Sir Robert Kane* (1942).

STUDIES IN
COMPARATIVE
EDUCATION

BY

I. L. KANDEL

M.A., Manchester; Ph.D., Columbia
Professor of Education and Associate
International Institute, Teachers College
Columbia University

GEORGE G. HARRAP & CO. LTD.
LONDON   BOMBAY   SYDNEY

Kay, Joseph (1821–78). Educationist and economist. Born at Salford. Educated at a private school and by private tutors, and at Trinity College, Cambridge. BA, 1845 and appointed in that year as the travelling bachelor of the university. In the next four years he visited Austria, France, Germany, Holland and Switzerland and reported upon the social conditions (including education) of their poorer classes. Kay was able to compare and contrast these educational systems with that of England with which he was well acquainted through the work of his elder brother **James Kay-Shuttleworth**. Called to the bar in 1848; QC, 1869. Twice unsuccessfully contested Salford as a Liberal. See his writings on free trade in land and the law relating to shipping, and *The Education of the Poor in England and Europe* (1846); *The Condition and Education of Poor Children in English and in German Towns* (1853).

Kay-Shuttleworth, Sir James Phillips (1804–77). Pioneer of English popular education. Born at Rochdale. Worked there in a bank, but  in 1824 entered Edinburgh University to study medicine. MD, 1827 and became a physician and secretary to the board of health in Manchester. Here he was made aware of the sufferings of the poor, especially during the cholera outbreak of 1832, and became a supporter of the parliamentary reform and anti-corn law league movements. In 1835 he became an Assistant Poor Law Commissioner working both in East Anglia and in the metropolitan district. In 1839 he was appointed the first Secretary of the new Committee of the Privy Council on Education. For ten years he worked tirelessly to advance the work of this department, resigning in 1849 as a result of a breakdown brought on by overwork. In this year he was created a baronet. Kay-Shuttleworth (he assumed the suffix Shuttleworth upon his marriage in 1842) also established in 1839–40 the training college at Battersea, to which pupil teachers were transferred from the Norwood Pauper School, which became the model for nineteenth-century training colleges for elementary school teachers.

Though there has been some reaction against the excessive praise heaped upon him by his biographer and writers of educational textbooks, he remains a key figure in the development of nineteenth-century elementary education. High Sheriff of Lancashire, 1863; DCL, Oxon, 1870; served on the Devonshire Commission on Scientific Instruction, 1870–3; unsuccessfully contested north-east Lancashire for the Liberals in 1874. See his *Public Education* (1853); *Four Periods of Public Education* (1862), and Smith, F., *The Life and Work of Sir J. Kay-Shuttleworth* (1923); Paz, D.G. 'Sir James Kay-Shuttleworth: The man behind the myth', *History of Education*, 14 (3), 1985.

Keate, John (1773–1852). Headmaster. Born Wells. Educated at Eton and King's College, Cambridge. Brilliant classical scholar, winning four Browne's medals and the Craven scholarship. BA, 1796; MA, 1799; DD, 1810. Took holy orders and elected a fellow of King's. Assistant master at Eton, 1797–1809; headmaster, 1809–34. A small figure, little more than five feet in height, he had great presence and a powerful voice. His principal method of control was flogging, amounting on average to some ten boys a day. Upon his retirement there were 570 boys in the upper school with nine masters. In spite of his combative manner Keate appears to have enjoyed a considerable popularity with many of his pupils. Canon of Windsor from 1820, rector from 1824 of Hartley Westpall, Hampshire, where he lived after his retirement from Eton. See Lyte, M., *History of Eton* (4th edn. 1911); Chandos, J., *Boys Together* (1984).

Keenan, Sir Patrick Joseph (1826–94). Educational administrator. Born Phibsborough, Dublin. At the age of 22, appointed inspector of national education, Ireland, 1848; head inspector, 1854–9 and chief inspector, 1859–71. The Royal Commission of inquiry into primary education (Ireland), the Powis Commission, 1869–70, recommended the introduction of 'payment by results' and Keenan was requested to draw up a scheme. This was less severe than the system operating in England as teachers were paid a basic salary irrespective of results. Earlier in his official reports Keenan had recommended the use of Irish in schools in Irish-speaking areas. Resident Commissioner of national education, Ireland, 1871–94, establishing denominational training colleges and attempting to enforce compulsory education in schools. Member, Commission to inquire into the state of education in Trinidad, 1869, and of the Commission to inquire into university lyceums and primary schools in Malta, 1878. CB, 1871, Knight, 1881, Privy Councillor, Ireland, 1885. See his *Model Schools, a sketch of their nature and objects* (1857), and Akenson, D.H., *The Irish Education Experiment. The National System of Education in the Nineteenth Century* (1970).

Kekewich, Sir George William (1841–1921). Educational administrator, son of Samuel Kekewich, MP for South Devon, 1858–73. Educated at Eton and Balliol College, Oxford, gaining first class honours in classical moderations and *literae humaniores*, 1863. Spent two years studying at Lincoln's Inn for the Bar before joining the Education Department as Examiner, 1867–71; then Senior Examiner, 1871–90, succeeded **Cumin** as Secretary to the Department, 1890–1900 and Secretary, Science and Art Department, 1899–1900. Secretary, Board of Education, 1900–3. Kekewich stated in his autobiography: 'My creed was that the children came first, before everything and everybody.' He was also much respected by teachers for his sympathetic attitude towards them. He was closely involved in the promulgation of the enlightened 1890 Education Code which led to the ending of 'payment by results'. After retirement, he was elected as a Liberal MP for Exeter, 1906–10. Knight, 1895. See his lively and amusing autobiography, *The Education Department and After* (1920).

Kennedy, Benjamin Hall (1804–89). Schoolmaster, academic and cleric. Born Summer Hill, near Birmingham, son of Rann Kennedy, poet and a schoolmaster. Educated at King Edward's School, Birmingham and Shrewsbury, 1819–23, where **Samuel Butler** was then headmaster and St John's College, Cambridge, 1823–8; senior optime in mathematical tripos and Senior Classic and first Chancellor's medallist. A member of the 'Apostles' where he formed a friendship with **F.D. Maurice**. 1827, assistant master, Shrewsbury School; fellow, St John's College, 1828, and ordained priest, 1830. Assistant master, Harrow School, 1830–6, when he succeeded Butler as headmaster of Shrewsbury, remaining there for exactly 30 years. A brilliant classics teacher, Kennedy built up the reputation of his school, producing many pupils who became distinguished scholars of Latin and Greek at Oxford and Cambridge. Following the deliberations of the Clarendon Commission on the nine public schools in England, which recommended the use of standard Latin and Greek grammars in these schools, Kennedy was one of the three authors of *The Public School Latin Primer* (1866) and his own *The Public School Latin Grammar* (1871). He also published many

140

translations from Greek and Roman authors in verse. After his retirement, he was appointed Regius professor of Greek at Cambridge, 1867 and in the same year became canon of Ely Cathedral, holding both posts until his death. See his *Between Whiles, or Wayside Amusements of a Working Life* (1st edn., 1877, 2nd edn., 1882).

Kennedy, William James (1814–91). School inspector. Born Birmingham, son of a vicar. Educated King Edward's School, Birmingham, and St John's College, Cambridge. Porson Prize for Greek iambics, 1835, BA, 1837, MA, 1844. Ordained 1839, curate, St Martin-in-the-Fields, London, 1842–3. Secretary, National Society, 1844–8. HMI, Manchester district, 1848–78. Vicar, Barnwood, Gloucestershire, 1878–91. See his *On the principles to be observed in promoting school attendance* (1857); 'The conscience clause', read at Manchester Social Science Congress (1866).

Kimmins, Charles William (1856–1948). School inspector. Educated Owens College, Manchester, University College, Bristol, London B.Sc., 1883 and Downing College, Cambridge, natural science tripos, first class honours, 1886. Chief science master, The Leys School, Cambridge. Staff lecturer, Cambridge University Extension. Inspector of Schools for **H. Llewellyn Smith**'s report on technical education to the London County Council, 1892. Inspector of Science, London Technical Education Board, 1894–5. Director, London University Extension, 1895–1900. Chief Inspector, Technical Education Board, London County Council, 1900–4, and for the Education Department, London County Council, 1904–23, where he promoted progressive methods in schools. Deputy Vice-Chancellor, London University, 1933. See his *Children's Dreams* (1920); *The Mental and Physical Welfare of the Child* (1927), and *The Triumph of the Dalton Plan* (1932), with Rennie, B.

King, Bolton (1860–1927). Educational administrator. Born Chadshunt, Warwickshire, son of E. Bolton King, Liberal MP, Warwick. Educated at Eton and Balliol College, Oxford, 1879–83, obtained firsts in classical moderations and modern history. Secretary of the Committee which bought the premises for Toynbee Hall, Whitechapel and resident there, 1884–92. A great admirer of **Arnold Toynbee** and a radical, King carried out co-operative ventures in farming and investigated economic conditions in South Warwickshire villages. He also supported the Warwickshire Agricultural and General Workers' Union. Alderman, Warwickshire County Council, 1892–1904 and chairman of the Technical Education Committee, 1890–1900. Unsuccessfully contested Stratford-upon-Avon for the Liberals in 1901. Director of Education, Warwickshire, 1904–28. King was an enlightened administrator. He encouraged curriculum change and self-government in schools and set up rural central schools in large villages. An enthusiast for the day continuation schools scheme following the 1918 Education Act, King established the first two such schools in the country, at Rugby and Stratford-upon-Avon. See his *Schools of Today* (1929), and also Browne, J.D., 'The Formation of an Educational Administrator', *History of Education*, 10 (3), 1981.

Kingsley, Charles (1819–75). Author. Born at Holne, Devon. Educated at Helston Grammar School under **Derwent Coleridge**, King's College, London, and Magdalene College, Cambridge. Very keen sportsman but obtained a first class in classics, 1842. In that year he was ordained and became curate and subsequently rector of Eversley in Hampshire. He worked hard to promote education within the parish, threw himself with vigour into various works to improve the lot of the working classes, particularly in association with **F.D. Maurice** and the Christian Socialist group, and became professor of English Literature at Queen's College, London. He wrote dramatic poetry, pamphlets, articles and a series of novels including *Alton Locke* (1850), *Westward Ho!* (1855) and *The Water Babies* (1863). Kingsley was professor of Modern History at Cambridge, 1860–9. In 1869 he presided over the education section of the National Association for the Promotion of Social Science. His inaugural address was printed by the National Education League and some 100,000 copies were distributed. Kingsley's wide-ranging interests and talents made him one of the best known and most controversial figures of Victorian England. His collected works (1879–81) fill some 28 volumes. See Kingsley, F.E. (ed.), *Letters and Memories of Charles Kingsley* (2 vols., 1877); Kendall, G., *Charles Kingsley and his Ideas* (1946); Pope-Hennessy, U., *Canon Charles Kingsley* (1948); Colloms, B., *Charles Kingsley* (1975); Harrison, S., *Charles Kingsley, a Reference Guide* (1981).

Klein, Melanie (1882–1960). Psychoanalyst. Born Vienna. Studied medicine. In 1903 married her second cousin Stephan Klein, divorced in 1923. In Budapest before the First World War she became interested in psychoanalysis and worked in the children's clinic of Sandor Ferenczi, a follower of Freud. In 1921 she moved to Berlin and in 1926 settled permanently in England, becoming naturalized in 1934. Klein employed 'free play' techniques with children and drew conclusions about their impulses and neuroses which were strongly criticized by other psychoanalysts, including **Anna Freud**, as being unscientific. They argued that she attributed to the infant mind processes for which there was no real evidence. Her work, nevertheless, was extremely important. She was the pioneer of knowledge about the mental life of infant children, and influenced general attitudes to young children. In her own lifetime, however, she remained a thoroughly controversial figure. See her *The Psycho-Analysis of Children* (1932); *Narrative of a Child Analysis* (1961), and Segal, H., *Introduction to the Work of Melanie Klein* (1964); Geets, C., *Melanie Klein* (1971); Segal, H., *Klein* (1979).

Knox, Vicesimus (1752–1821). Headmaster and scholar. Born at Newington Green, Middlesex. Educated at Merchant Taylors' School and St John's College, Oxford. BA, 1775, MA, 1779. Fellow of his college and in residence 1775–8. Ordained priest in 1777. In 1779 Knox succeeded his father (also Vicesimus) as headmaster of Tonbridge School and held the post until 1812, when he was in turn succeeded by his younger son Thomas who was headmaster until his death in 1843. Knox was a good scholar, impressive preacher and a voluminous writer. He held several ecclesiastical livings, and had the degree of DD conferred upon him by the University of Philadelphia. See his *Works* (7 vols., 1824), and Rivington, S., *The History of Tonbridge School* (1910); Leinster-Mackay, D.P., and Goldsmith, P., 'Vicesimus Knox II of Tonbridge School: A Case of Unfulfilled Promise', *Journal of Educational Administration and History*, 13 (1), 1981; Bantock, G.H., *Studies in the History of Educational Thought II: The Minds and the Masses 1760–1980* (1984).

Labouchere, Henry, Baron Taunton (1798–1869). Politician. Born in London and educated at Winchester and Christ Church, Oxford, first class in classics, 1820. MP, St. Michael's, 1826–30 as a Whig, then Taunton, 1830–59. Lord of the Admiralty, 1832–4, Vice-President, Board of Trade and Master of the Mint, 1835–9, President, Board of Trade, 1839–41 and 1847–52, Chief Secretary for Ireland, 1846–7 and Secretary of State, Colonies, 1855–8. Created Baron, 1859. Taunton was a good administrator, serving as a commissioner for the Great Exhibition, 1851 and chairman of Commission to inquire into the state of the Corporation of London, 1853. He also served as chairman of the Schools Inquiry Commission, 1864–8, known as the Taunton Commission, which was given the task of investigating some 800 endowed grammar schools. Its report, published in 1868, recommended that a system of efficient secondary schools corresponding to the three grades of society should be created. Girls' education was shown to be grossly inadequate but little action was taken. See Allsobrook, D., *Schools for the Shires* (1986).

Lancaster, Joseph (1778–1838). Pioneer of monitorial schooling. Born Southwark, London. Probably educated at the local Dissent

ing Charity School. Between 1792 and 1797 worked as an usher in local schools and as an occasional preacher. In 1798 set up a school and by 1801 was receiving subscriptions from local patrons. Large numbers of pupils were attracted and Lancaster devised a system of monitors to teach them. The system was described in *Improvements in Education*, published in 1803. By 1805, Lancaster's Borough Road School was becoming well known; teachers were coming there to be trained in the monitorial method and Lancaster secured royal patronage after an interview with King George III. Many of his earlier supporters were Quakers, like Lancaster, and the two Societies which carried on his work were non-denominational. Religious instruction was confined to the study of passages from the Bible. In the following year he travelled extensively in the United Kingdom, and Lancasterian committees were established in several areas. The Royal Lancasterian Society was established in 1808 and in 1814 it was transmuted into the British and Foreign School Society. Lancaster travelled in the United States, Canada and South America from 1818 to 1838. By 1851 some 826 British schools had been established in Britain itself and it had become recognized as one of the two major educational societies. Borough Road also became the earliest teacher training institution. Although Lancaster was ousted from the organization which he had begun, largely as a consequence of his financial mismanagement and for other faults of character, and although the monitorial system as such fell into disrepute, he can be counted as one of the founders of mass schooling for the poor in the industrial age. See Lancaster's own pamphlets and Corston, W., *A brief sketch of the life of Joseph Lancaster* (1840); Salmon, D., *Joseph Lancaster* (1904); Bartle, G., 'Joseph Lancaster and his biographers: some unfamiliar aspects of his character', in Lowe, R. (ed.), *Biography and Education* (1980); Dickson, M., *Teacher Extraordinary: Joseph Lancaster, 1778–1838* (1986).

Lane, Homer (1875–1929). Progressive educationist. Born Hudson, New Hampshire, USA. Educated Framingham, Massachussetts. Worked on the railways as a delivery man and other occupations. Teacher of Sloyd (manual training), Southboro, Massachussetts, and began a self-governing club for youths, Detroit. Superintendent, Ford Junior Republic, Farmington, a home for difficult and delinquent boys, 1912–13. Invited by George Montagu, later 9th Earl of Sandwich, to be Superintendent of the Little Commonwealth, a community of delinquent children in Dorset, 1913–18. Working on psychoanalytical lines, Lane believed that it was possible to reform delinquents by means of trust and mutual respect coupled with freedom and self-government. Lane influenced other progressivists, particularly **A.S. Neill** and **J.H. Simpson**. Following a scandal, the Little Commonwealth was disbanded. He subsequently lectured on education and some of the talks were gathered in a volume *Talks to Parents and Teachers* (1928). See also Bazeley, E.T., *Homer Lane and the Little Commonwealth* (1928) and Willis, W.D., *Homer Lane. A Biography* (1964).

Lansdowne, Petty-Fitzmaurice, Henry, 3rd Marquess of Lansdowne (1780–1863). Statesman. Born at Lansdowne House and educated at Westminster School, the University of Edinburgh and Trinity College, Cambridge where he graduated MA in 1801. Awarded LL.D in 1811. At Westminster he had attended debates in the House of Commons; at Edinburgh he was a contemporary of **Brougham**, Palmerston, Jeffrey, **Horner** and Sydney Smith. Entered Parliament as Whig member for Calne at the age of 22, and by 1806 was Chancellor of the Exchequer at the age of 25. Member for the University of Cambridge, 1806–7. Sat for Camelford, 1807–9

when on the death of his half-brother he succeeded to the title and to the Lords. Lord President of the Council, 1830–4, 1835–41. In this office he advanced the cause of state assistance to national education. His speech of 5 July 1839 in answer to the Archbishop of Canterbury was subsequently published. Lord President of the Council again, 1846–52. Lansdowne had considerable influence as an adviser to the monarchy, particularly after the death of the Duke of Wellington. His home was a meeting place for politicians and men of letters and science, and he was a great patron of art and literature. See Hayward, A., *Lord Lansdowne* (1872).

Laurie, Simon Somerville (1829–1909). Educationist. Born Edinburgh, son of a chaplain to Edinburgh Royal Infirmary. Educated Edinburgh High School, 1839–44 and University of Edinburgh, 1844–49, graduating MA. Secretary and visitor of schools, education committee to the Church of Scotland, 1855–1905, where he was influential in raising the professional status of teachers by better preparation: he was closely involved in the development of the day training college movement. Secretary, Royal Commission on Endowed Schools in Scotland, 1872. Laurie was appointed to the Bell Chair in Theory, History and Art of Education at Edinburgh University in 1876 at the same time that **J.M.D. Meiklejohn** took up a similar position at St Andrews. These were the first professorships of education in any British university. Laurie was a firm advocate of the scientific study of education. He also championed the movement for the admission of women to universities. See his *On Primary Instruction in Relation to Education* (1867, 6th edn., 1898); *The Training of Teachers and Methods of Instruction* (1901); *Studies in the History of Educational Opinion from the Renaissance* (1903), and Knox, H.M., 'Simon Somerville Laurie', *British Journal of Educational Studies*, 10 (2), 1962.

Lawrence, Dame Maude Agnes (1864–1933). School inspector and administrator. Daughter of 1st Baron Lawrence, Viceroy of India, 1864–8 and first chairman, London School Board, 1870–3. Educated privately and at Bedford College, London. Manager of London School Board schools for over 20 years. Co-opted member of the Board, 1900 and elected member, Westminster, 1901–4. Member, committees for domestic subjects and school accommodation and chairman, special schools sub-committee. Continued as non-elected member, London County Council Education Committee, 1904–5. When the Women Inspectorate was set up by **Morant** in 1905, Maude Lawrence was chosen as the Chief Woman Inspector. Although possessing no formal teaching qualifications or experience, she effectively built up a corps of inspectors with expertise in a number of educational areas. At first, the six women were confined to dealing with very young children and girls in elementary schools, mainly in domestic subjects. By 1912, the number had grown to 36, of whom a third were graduates and many operated in secondary schools, technical colleges and training colleges, using their special subjects. Director of Women's Establishments, Treasury, 1920–4. Dame, 1926. She was not an advocate of the removal of the marriage bar for women, equal pay or equal opportunities for promotion. See her evidence, Royal Commission on the Civil Service, 1930, Q. 14928–34.

Leach, Arthur Francis (1851–1915). Historian and Charity Commissioner. Born London. Educated at Winchester and New College, Oxford. First class in classics, 1873. Fellow of All Souls, 1874–81. Barrister, Middle Temple, 1874; Assistant Charity Commissioner (Endowed Schools Department), 1884–1901; Administrative Examiner, Board of Education, 1901–3; Senior Examiner, 1903; Assistant Secretary, 1904–6. In 1906 Leach was appointed Second Charity Commissioner, a post he held until his death. Leach's work for endowed schools led him to historical research and to his conclusions that Edward VI was the despoiler rather than the founder of schools, and that King's School, Canterbury was the oldest English school. He also wrote histories of a number of individual schools, contributed the educational material to 19 volumes of the *Victoria History of the Counties of England*, and produced a collection of documents on medieval English history which is still in use today. See his several writings including *English Schools at the Reformation* (1896); *Educational Charters and Docu-*

ments (1911); *Schools of Medieval England* (1915), and Tate, W.E., *A.F. Leach* (1963).

Leathes, Sir Stanley Mordaunt (1861–1938). Historian and administrator. Born London, son of professor of Hebrew, King's College, London. Educated at Eton, King's scholar, 1873–80, and Trinity College, Cambridge, where he gained first class in part one, classical tripos, and Chancellor's medallist, 1884. Fellow, Trinity College, 1886 and lecturer in history, 1892–1903. A joint editor with Lord Acton and contributor to the *Cambridge Modern History* (1901–12). Secretary, Civil Service Commission, 1903–7, Commissioner, 1907–10 and First Commissioner, 1910–27. CB, 1911; KCB, 1919. Leathes was chairman of a number of government commissions, including the Prime Minister's Committee on the Position of Modern Languages in Great Britain, 1916–18. The Report drew attention to the disadvantage under which modern languages laboured in schools because of their comparatively late appearance in the curriculum. See *The Teaching of English at Universities* (1913) and *The People of England: a social history for schools* (3 vols., 1915–23).

Lee, James Prince (1804–69). Headmaster and cleric. Born London. Educated at St Paul's School and Trinity College, Cambridge. BA, 1828; fellow of his college, 1829; ordained, 1830; MA, 1831. A most distinguished classical scholar. Master at Rugby School, 1830–8 where he earned the approval of **Thomas Arnold**. Headmaster of King Edward's School, Birmingham, 1838–48. Here his reputation was established as a fine teacher; Benson, Lightfoot and Westcott were amongst his pupils. He also took a keen interest in other educational institutions in Birmingham, especially the establishment of the school of art. Bishop of Manchester, 1848–69. In this office he continued his interest in national education, in particular its promotion by legislative means. He also encouraged church extension. He supported the establishment of the Manchester Free Library and spoke at its opening in August 1852. His own magnificent library, which included collections of Greek Testament literature, art and history, was bequeathed to Owens College, Manchester. See Fellows, E., *Sayings and Doings of the Lord Bishop of Manchester* (1852); Newsome, D., *Godliness and Good Learning* (1961).

Lethaby, William Richard (1857–1931). Architect, author and educationist. Born Barnstaple, Devon. Attended local school of art before entering an architect's office in the same town. Chief clerk to Norman Shaw, an important figure in the Arts and Crafts movement, 1880. In 1891, he began his own practice, being part-architect for New Scotland Yard and many country houses. As a member of the Society for the Protection of Ancient Buildings, Lethaby came in contact with Philip Webb and **William Morris** whose theories and work greatly influenced him. Lethaby promoted design education, believing that the form should be determined by the material used; his own work in metalwork, stained glass and furniture provided excellent examples of his philosophy. Art Inspector, Technical Education Board, London County Council, 1892–4, principal, Central School of Arts and Crafts, London County Council, 1894–1911 and first professor of Ornament and Design, College of Art, South Kensington, 1900. Surveyor to the Dean and Chapter, Westminster Abbey, 1906–28. His books include *Architecture, Mysticism and Myth* (1892); *Medieval Art* (1904, revised edn., 1912); *Home and Country Arts* (1923); *Philip Webb and his Work* (1935), and Rubens, G., *William Richard Lethaby* (1986).

Lindsay, Alexander Dunlop, 1st Baron Lindsay of Birker (1879–1952). Educationist. Born Glasgow, son of the Revd T.M. Lindsay, the historian of the Reformation. Educated Glasgow Academy and Glasgow University, obtaining a second class honours in classics, 1899, and University College, Oxford, where he gained firsts in classical moderations and *literae humaniores*, 1902. Clark fellow in philosophy, Glasgow University, 1902–4. Shaw fellow in philosophy, Edinburgh University, 1904–6. Fellow and tutor in classics, Balliol, 1906–22. He had studied philosophy under **Henry Jones** at Glasgow; this influence can be seen in his inaugural address as professor of Moral Philosophy, Glasgow University, 1922, the title of which was 'Idealism'. Lindsay involved himself with many causes: he was one of the first Workers' Educational Association lecturers, an adviser to the Labour Party and Trades Union Congress on education, and in 1938 was Labour candidate for Oxford, standing against Quintin Hogg as a protest at the Munich agreement. Master of Balliol College, Oxford, 1922–49, where he attempted to introduce university reforms for a Science Greats, which would have combined philosophy and science. Lindsay's view that social awareness was the essence of a successful university education took substance with the creation of the new University of North Staffordshire (now the University of Keele) which was established in 1949. Lindsay was appointed its first principal in 1951.

A four-year undergraduate course was introduced which included a foundation course in which science and art students became acquainted with each others' disciplines. Lindsay's best-known book was his translation of Plato's *Republic* (1907). His strong belief in democratic forms of government was asserted in *The Essentials of Democracy* (1929) and *The Modern Democratic State* (1943). See also Scott, D., *A.D. Lindsay. A Biography* (1971).

Lingen, Sir Ralph Robert Wheeler, Baron Lingen (1819–1905). Civil Servant. Born Birmingham. Educated at Bridgnorth Grammar School and Trinity College, Oxford. A friend of **Benjamin Jowett** and **Frederick Temple**, Lingen was a notable scholar – first class in classics, 1840, fellow of Balliol from 1841, DCL 1881. Student at Lincoln's Inn from 1844 and called to the bar, 1847. Entered the Education office and in 1849 at the age of 30 succeeded **Kay-Shuttleworth** as its secretary. In 1869 Lingen was promoted to Permanent Secretary of the Treasury, the highest post in the Home Civil Service. Alderman of the first London County Council, 1889–92, and chairman of its finance committee. Both at Education and the Treasury Lingen was noted for his desire to minimize public expenditure. This fitted well with the tenets of Gladstonian Liberalism but brought him considerable animosity particularly over the issue of the Revised Code. His dictatorial manner also aroused the antagonism of the Welsh (in 1847 he was one of the three commissioners of inquiry into Welsh education), and of teachers in general. 'It is from Mr Lingen, that all the sharp snubbing replies proceed.' CB, 1869; KCB, 1878; Baron, 1885. Martin, A.P., *Life and Letters of Robert Lowe* (2 vols., 1893); Bishop, A.S., 'Ralph Lingen: Secretary to the Education Department 1849–1870', *British Journal of Educational Studies*, 16 (2), 1968.

Livingstone, Sir Richard Winn (1880–1960). Educationist. Born Liverpool, son of a vicar. Educated at Winchester and New College, Oxford. Obtained first class in classical moderations, 1901 and *literae humaniores*, 1903. Fellow, tutor and librarian, Corpus Christi College, Oxford, 1905–24, during which time he served as an assistant master at Eton, 1917–18. An enthusiastic advocate of the place of humanities in education, Livingstone was a member of the Prime Minister's Committee on the Classics, 1920 and joint editor of the *Classical Review*. Vice-Chancellor, Queen's University, Belfast, 1924–33. President, Corpus Christi College, Oxford, 1933–

50. Vice-Chancellor, Oxford University, 1944–7. Knight, 1931. Besides writing on his own subject, as seen in *A Defence of Classical Education* (1916) and *The Legacy of Greece* (1921), Livingstone developed an interest in adult education, which he expressed in a wartime book, *The Future in Education* (1941). In it, he advocated part-time continuing education rather than a raising of the school-leaving age, with resident adult colleges being established on the Danish model.

Lockwood, Sir John Francis (1903–65). University administrator. Born Preston, Lancashire, son of a stockbroker. Educated Preston Grammar School and Corpus Christi College, Oxford, with first class in classical moderations and second in *literae humaniores*, 1926. Assistant lecturer in Latin, Manchester University, 1927, then lecturer in Greek, University College, London, 1930–40, reader, 1940–5, professor of Latin, 1945–51. Master, Birkbeck College, University of London, 1951 until his death in 1965. Vice-Chancellor, University of London, 1955–8. Lockwood's administrative ability was impressive and he played a leading part in the University, and national and international educational committees. He was chairman, Secondary School Examinations Council, 1958–64. A report produced by him, known as the Lockwood Report, in 1964 recommended that a Schools Council for Curriculum and Examinations should be established. The government adopted Lockwood's recommendation and the new body came into being in 1964. Knight, 1962. See his *The Tradition of Scholarship* (1946).

Londonderry, Vane-Tempest-Stewart, Charles Stewart, 6th Marquess of Londonderry (1852–1915). Statesman. Born London. Educated at Eton, the National University of Ireland and Christ Church, Oxford. MP for the county of Down, 1878–84, when he succeeded to the Lords on his father's death. Viceroy of Ireland, 1886–9, and in 1893 presided over the meeting at which the political alliance between the Conservatives and Unionists was formed. Chairman of the London School Board, 1895–7. In 1902 became the President of the Board of Education in Balfour's government and successfully administered the Education Act of that year. From 1903 to 1905 was also Lord President of the Council. Lord Lieutenant of Durham, a great coal-owner and improving landlord. Created KG in 1888. See Hyde, H.M., *The Londonderrys* (1979).

Lovett, William (1800–77). Chartist and radical reformer. Born in Newlyn, Cornwall into a strict Methodist family, receiving only a rudimentary education. Apprenticed to a ropemaker but in 1821 moved to London where he became a cabinet maker and joined the London Mechanics' Institute group. In 1829 he became secretary of the British Association for Promoting Co-operative Knowledge, but rejected Owenite ideas by 1836. Opposed the newspaper stamp duty. Between 1834–6 organized a group known as the Social Reformers who met in his coffee shop with attached library and reading rooms. This was the model for his next venture, the London Working Men's Association, which also had a library and regular lectures and discussions. Imprisoned 1839–40 for seditious libel in Warwick Gaol where he wrote *Chartism. A New Organization of the People* (1840). Fell out with O'Connor and other leaders who dubbed his moderate approach 'Knowledge Chartism'. From the 1840s Lovett became more active in education – as a teacher at several schools, as a textbook writer, and as a lecturer in various reforming causes. See his *Elementary Anatomy and Physiology, for Schools and Private Instruction* ... (1851); *Life and Struggles of William Lovett in his pursuit of Bread, Knowledge and Freedom* (1876), and Beckerlegge, J., *William Lovett* (1948); Hollis, P. (ed.), *Pressure from Without* (1974).

Lowe, Robert, 1st Viscount Sherbrooke (1811–92). Politician. Born at Bingham, Nottinghamshire where his father was the rector.

Educated at Winchester and at University College, Oxford. BA, 1833, first class in classics, second class in mathematics. MA, 1836. Fellow of Magdalen College, 1835–6. Worked as a private tutor in Oxford. Called to the bar at Lincoln's Inn, 1842. In 1842 travelled to Sydney, Australia where he practised law and sat on the New South Wales legislative council. Prominent in educational and financial politics. On his return to England in 1850 Lowe became a leader writer for *The Times*. MP for Kidderminster, 1852–9; Calne, 1859–68;

University of London, 1868–80. Created Viscount Sherbrooke, 1880. After posts at the Board of Control and the Board of Trade, in 1859 he accepted office in Palmerston's Liberal government as Vice-President of the Committee of Council on Education. Lowe rejected the major conclusion of the Newcastle Report, that county boards should be established for elementary education. Instead in 1862 he introduced the Revised Code whereby government grants to elementary schools were based principally upon pupils' performances upon an annual examination in reading, writing and arithmetic. This system of 'payment by results' continued, with modifications, for some 35 years. In 1864 Lowe resigned his office when a resolution condemning the mutilation of inspectors' reports was approved in the House of Commons by 101 votes to 93, though the resolution was later rescinded. After the Reform Act of 1867 Lowe became more convinced of the need 'to teach our future masters their letters', and was a member of the Cabinet responsible for the 1870 Act. Chancellor of the Exchequer, 1868–73; Home Secretary, 1873–4. LL.D, Edinburgh, 1867; DCL, Oxford, 1870; GCB, 1885. Lowe was long cast as the villain of nineteenth-century education. Attempts at rehabilitation have ensured that both he and the Revised Code have remained highly controversial. An albino, with very poor eyesight, Lowe was a combative figure, a master of epigram and sarcasm. See his *Primary and Classical Education* (1867); *Middle-Class Education. Endowment or Free Trade* (1868), and Martin, A.P., *Life and Letters of the Right Honourable Robert Lowe* (2 vols., 1893); Knight, R., *Illiberal Liberal. Robert Lowe in New South Wales, 1842–1850* (1966); Sylvester, D.W., *Robert Lowe and Education* (1974).

Lubbock, Sir John, 4th Bt. and 1st Baron Avebury (1834–1913). Scientist and banker. Son of 3rd Bt., a banker who was treasurer to the Royal Society. Born London. Showed mathematical ability at an early age. Educated at private school, Abingdon and Eton, 1845–9, which he left at 15 to enter his father's bank. Successful as a banker, Lubbock was able to devote himself to scientific pursuits, encouraged by his father's friend, **Charles Darwin**. Succeeded to the baronetcy, 1865 and created Baron, 1900. Elected Liberal MP, Maidstone, 1870–80, London University, 1880–1900. An ardent reformer, he was responsible for the Bank Holidays Act 1871, establishing a public holiday in August, the Preservation of Ancient Monuments Act, 1882 and the Early Closing Act, 1904. He was also Chairman of the London County Council, 1890–2. He took a keen interest in the advancement of education, holding the posts of Vice-Chancellor, London University, 1872–80, Chairman, Society for the Extension of University Teaching, 1894–1902, Principal, Working Men's College, 1883–98 and Rector, St Andrews University, 1908. Besides his many scientific publications, Lubbock wished to raise the level of culture among the working classes, reaching a wide audience with such books as *The Pleasures of Life* (1889), *Hundred Best Books* (1891) and *Peace and Happiness* (1909). See also Hutchinson, H.G., *Life of Sir John Lubbock, Lord Avebury* (2 vols., 1914).

Ludlow, John Malcolm Forbes (1821–1911). Christian Socialist. Born at Nimach, India. Educated in Paris at the *Collège Bourbon*, graduated *Bachelier ès lettres* in 1837 and moved to London in 1838. Called to the bar in 1843. At first despaired of English society but was attracted by **F.D. Maurice** and **Charles Kingsley** to the Christian Socialist cause. Joint editor with Maurice of *Politics for the People*, a weekly journal, in 1848. In 1850 founded and edited another weekly paper, the *Christian Socialist*. Became increasingly interested in co-operative ideas and working-class adult education. Worked hard for the foundation of the Working Men's College established in 1854 in Great Ormond Street, London. Ludlow lectured on French, English, law and the history of India. Contributed to various periodicals and wrote books on a wide range of subjects including India and the USA. Chief Registrar of Friendly Societies, 1875–91. Died without heirs and made a number of bequests to the Working Men's College, Society for the Promotion of Christian Knowledge and the British Museum. See his writings especially *Progress of the Working Classes* (1867), and Masterman, N.C., *J.M. Ludlow: the builder of Christian Socialism* (1963); Murray, A.D. (ed.), *John Ludlow: the autobiography of a Christian Socialist* (Cass, 1981).

Lyttelton, Edward (1855–1942). Schoolmaster, divine and cricketer. Born at Hagley, Worcestershire, the seventh of the eight sons of the **4th Baron Lyttelton**. Educated at Eton and Trinity College, Cambridge, second class honours in classics, 1878. Lyttelton's early prowess was as a cricketer. He captained the Eton eleven in 1874, and in 1878 was the only English batsman to make a century against the Australians. Assistant master at Wellington, 1880–2; at Eton, 1882–90; master of Haileybury, 1890–1905; headmaster of Eton, 1905–16. His earlier ordination (deacon 1884, priest 1886) now enabled him to take clerical appointments in London, Norfolk and from 1920–9, as Dean of Whitelands Training College, London. Honorary canon of Norwich from 1931 where he was in constant demand as a preacher and speaker. He wrote widely on education, moral, sporting and religious matters. See for example his *Cricket* (1889); *The Cornerstone of Education* (1914); *Memories and Hopes* (1925), and Alington, C.A., *Edward Lyttelton. An appreciation* (1943).

Lyttelton, George William, 4th Baron Lyttelton of Frankley (1817–76). Educational reformer. Born London, son of 3rd Lord Lyttel-

ton. Educated at Eton and Trinity College, Cambridge, BA and MA, 1838. Succeeded to the title, 1840 and by marriage was **W.E. Gladstone's** brother-in-law. Principal, Queen's College, Birmingham, 1845, was one of the founders of Saltley Training College and campaigned for night classes for working people. Under-Secretary of State, Colonies, in Peel's last government, January–July, 1846. With Edward Gibbon Wakefield and J.R. Godley established the province of Canterbury in New Zealand in 1850, where the town of Lyttelton was named after him. Member of the Clarendon Commission, 1861–4 and the Taunton Commission, 1864–8. He told the National Association for the Promotion of Social Science in 1868 that 'the best use of Educational Endowments is to bring out and develop the best youthful minds that can be found, in all classes of society for the service of the State'. Following the 1869 Endowed Schools Act, Lyttelton became Chief Commissioner, Endowed Schools Commission the same year. He vigorously pursued a policy of making some 235 schemes for endowed schools, which roused opposition from governing bodies and other vested interests. When Disraeli became Prime Minister in 1874, the powers of the Commission were transferred to the Charity Commission and Lyttelton was dismissed. Subject to bouts of depression, Lyttelton committed suicide at his London home in 1876. FRS, 1840. Published, with Gladstone, a volume of Greek translations of English poets included Tennyson and Milton in 1839, and *Thoughts on National Education* (1853). See also Stansky, P., 'Lyttelton and Thring: A Study in Nineteenth Century Education', *Victorian Studies*, 5 (3), 1962, and Gordon, P., *Selection for Secondary Education* (Woburn Press, 1980).

McDougall, William (1871–1938). Psychologist. Born Chadderton, Lancashire. Attended a local private school, the Real-Gymnasium at Weimar, and Owens College, Manchester where in 1890 he graduated with first class honours in biology and geology. Proceeded to St John's College, Cambridge, and achieved a first class in natural sciences in 1894. Entered St Thomas's Hospital but abandoned the idea of a medical career and in 1897 was elected fellow of St John's where he began to study psychology. Member of the 1898 Cambridge Anthropological expedition to the Torres Straits which lie between New Guinea and Northern Australia. After posts at Göttingen and University College, London, in 1903 McDougall moved to Oxford as reader in Mental Philosophy. In 1901 he had been a founding member of the British Psychological Society, and opened a research laboratory at Oxford. *Introduction to Social Psychology*, a book which won international recognition, was published in 1908. During the First World War McDougall served as a major in the Royal Army Medical Corps and specialized in the treatment of nerve cases. Professor of Psychology at Harvard, 1920–7, and at Duke University, North Carolina from 1927. FRS, 1912; D.Sc., Manchester, 1919. In the USA McDougall developed a controversial reputation with his opposition to behaviourism, and his experiments relating to inheritance and psychical research. In addition to the *Introduction* (1908), see his *Body and Mind* (1911); *Psychology: the Study of Behaviour* (1912); *An Outline of Psychology* (1923), and Robinson, A.M.L., *William McDougall* (1943); Van Over, R., and Oteri, L. (eds.), *William McDougall: explorer of the mind* (1967).

MacHale, John (1791–1881). Cleric. Born at Tobbernavine, County Mayo, Ireland. Educated at a local school. Entered Maynooth College in 1807 and in 1814 after ordination became lecturer in theology there. Bishop of Maronia from 1825, Archbishop of Tuam from 1834. MacHale was the most popular man in Ireland after O'Connell, and opposed all things English. In 1820 he began publication of a series of letters against the united education of Catholics and Protestants. In 1831 he advocated denominational education to Lord Grey, and subsequently led the opposition to the national education scheme for elementary education and to the Queen's Colleges. He also opposed **J.H. Newman** who in 1854 arrived in Dublin as Rector of the Catholic university, on the grounds that an Englishman should not head an Irish foundation. Twice visited Rome and published several works in Irish and English. See O'Reilly, B., *John MacHale* (2 vols.,1890); Costello, N., *John MacHale* (1939).

Mackail, John William (1859–1945). Administrator and man of letters. Born Ascog, Isle of Bute, son of a Free Church minister. Educated Ayr Academy, Edinburgh University and Balliol College, Oxford, 1878–81, gaining first class honours in classical moderations and *literae humaniores* as well as four scholarships. Whilst still an undergraduate, he published a book of poems *Mensae Secundae* (1879). Elected fellow and lecturer at Balliol, 1882, but entered the Education Department as a Junior Examiner two years later. Senior Examiner, 1898–1903, Assistant Secretary, Board of Education, 1903–19. Mackail played a leading part after the passing of the 1902 Education Act in the development of a system of secondary education in England. Grants were extended to subjects other than the natural sciences and the majority of public schools applied for inspection by the Board. Mackail was instrumental in bringing about both changes. His official work allowed time to continue his literary activities. He was professor of Poetry, Oxford, 1906–11. Order of Merit, 1934. His corpus of writings include *Latin Literature* (1895), *Life of William Morris* (2 vols., 1899), verse translation of the *Odyssey* (3 vols., 1903, 1905 and 1910), and *Studies of English Poets* (1926). See also Bailey, C., 'John William Mackail', *Proceedings of the British Academy*, 31, 1945.

McKenna, Reginald (1863–1943). Politician. Born London, son of a civil servant. Educated at St Malo, Ebersdorf, King's College School, London, and Trinity Hall, Cambridge, taking a mathematics tripos, 1885, and called to the Bar, Middle Temple, 1887. Stood unsuccessfully as Liberal candidate for Clapham, 1892, but elected MP for North Monmouthshire, 1895, remaining there until 1918. Played prominent part in discussions on the 1902 Education Bill. Financial Secretary, Treasury, 1905–7. President, Board of Education, with seat in the Cabinet, 1907–8. First Lord of the Admiralty, 1908–11, Home Secretary, 1911–15, Chancellor of the Exchequer, 1915–16. Defeated in 1918 election and retired from political life. See McKenna, S., *Reginald McKenna, a Memoir* (1948).

Mackinder, Sir Halford John (1861–1947). Geographer. Born Gainsborough, Lincolnshire, son of surgeon. Educated at Gainsborough Grammar School, Epsom College and Christ Church, Oxford, 1880–4, where he gained first class honours in natural science and second class in modern history. Barrister, Inner Temple, 1886. An exact contemporary and friend of **Michael Sadler**, Mackinder became from 1885 an enthusiastic Extension lecturer, speaking on the 'new geography' of which he was a leading exponent. He collaborated with Sadler in writing *University Extension: Has it a Future?* (1890) which recommended that State grants should be given to Extension authorities. Mackinder's energy was boundless; he held three academic posts simultaneously – Principal of University College, Reading, 1892–1903, Reader in Geography, Oxford, 1887–1905 and Director, London School of Economics and Political Science, 1903–8. His book *Britain and the British Seas* (1902) was a highly-acclaimed geographical work. In *Democratic Ideals and Reality* (1919), he endeavoured to consider, in the light of historical events, how to adjust ideals of freedom to the realities of the world. Made the first ascent of Mount Kenya, East Africa, 1899. He was a friend of Alfred Milner and, together with other young Imperialists, formed a club in 1902 called the 'Co-efficients' in order to explore how each department of national life could be raised to its highest efficiency. Unsuccessfully contested Warwick and Leamington as a Liberal Imperialist, 1900 and Hawick Burghs as a Liberal Unionist, 1909. Elected MP, Camlachie division, Glasgow, 1910–22. Knight, 1920. PC, 1926. Chairman, Imperial Economic Conference, 1926–31. See Gilbert, E.W., *Sir Halford Mackinder* (1961); Parker, W.H., *Mackinder* (1982).

McMillan, Margaret (1860–1931). Educationist. Born New York. Educated at Inverness High School in Scotland. Studied music in Frankfurt and languages at Geneva and Lausanne, and in 1883 became a governess and lady's companion. She also trained for the stage and became interested in socialism, and in 1893 moved to Bradford where she became a member of the newly-founded Independent Labour Party, and a member of the Bradford School Board, 1894–1902. McMillan became particularly interested in the health of school children. In 1899 she participated in the first recorded medical inspection of children under government auspices at Usher Street Schools, Bradford under Dr Kerr. In 1902 returned to London and campaigned successfully for the idea of school clinics. The first was established in 1908 at Bow with financial aid from Joseph Fels, an American businessman. In 1910 a larger health centre was opened at Deptford. London County Council grants for dental treatment were received in 1911, and in 1912 for eye and ear inspections. With her sister **Rachel** Margaret McMillan also established camp schools and a nursery school. Labour member of the LCC, 1919–1922, and president of the Nursery Schools Association from 1923. CBE, 1917; CH, 1930. In the same year she opened the Rachel McMillan Training College for teachers in memory of her sister. Margaret McMillan was a powerful organizer, speaker and writer who made the cause of the health of school children her own. See her *Early Childhood* (1900); *Education through the Imagination* (1904); *The Child and the State* (1911); *The Nursery School* (1919), and Mansbridge, A., *Margaret McMillan, Prophet and Pioneer* (1932); Ballard, P.B., *Margaret McMillan. An appreciation* (1937); Cresswell, D., *Margaret McMillan* (1948); Lowndes, G.A.N., *Margaret McMillan* (1960); Bradburn, E., *Margaret McMillan* (1976).

McMillan, Rachel (1859–1917). Educationist. Born New York, educated at Inverness High School and at a Midlands boarding school. Her early life was spent in Scotland but on joining her sister **Margaret** in London Rachel threw herself into the Socialist cause and obtained employment in a hostel for working-class girls. Trained as a sanitary inspectress and after a short spell in Bradford worked as a teacher of hygiene in south-east London and Kent. From 1913 the Rachel McMillan Open Air Nursery School, which became the largest and most important in the country, gave practical expression to her ideas of pre-school education with a large garden area with shelters and other facilities. Though McMillan had a wide range of interests her main purpose was to help young children from slum areas. Her sister Margaret maintained that she was the fount of all their ideas and in 1930 established the Rachel McMillan Training College in her memory. See McMillan, M., *The Life of Rachel McMillan* (1927); Ballard, P.B., *Margaret McMillan. An Appreciation* (1937).

MacMunn, Norman (1877–1925). Progressive educationist. Educated Marcon's Hall, Oxford. English literature tripos, 1899. Taught languages, King Edward VI Grammar School, Stratford-upon-Avon before First World War where he developed a partnership method, between pupils, of learning French. MacMunn, inspired by **Homer Lane**'s example and Montessori's writings in 1919 opened in Tiptree Hall, Essex, a school for a small number of boys, many of whom were war orphans. Whereas **Lane**'s Little Commonwealth was intended to reform and educate delinquents, MacMunn's was for normal boys (no girls were admitted). Tiptree Hall was a self-governing community in which children were free to develop. Apart from mathematics in the morning, pupils were encouraged to formulate their own timetables. MacMunn had hoped that the government would support the school financially but as this did not happen, he was forced to accept fee-paying pupils. The methods used in the school were questioned and it closed in 1924. MacMunn moved to Italy with some pupils, but died there the following year. See *Our Education Aim: Manifesto of the Tiptree Hall Community* (nd), and *The Child's Path to Freedom* (1926).

McNair, Arnold Duncan, 1st Baron McNair (1885–1975). Lawyer and academic. Educated at Aldenham School and Gonville and Caius College, Cambridge. Law tripos, 1909, and president of the Union. Solicitor in the City of London, 1909–13, but subsequently joined Gray's Inn, becoming a Bencher, treasurer in 1947, and a King's Counsel. Fellow of Caius in 1913 and subsequently its senior tutor. He was reader in International Law at London University, 1926–7, and held professorships in India and at the Hague. Whewell Professor of International Law at Cambridge, 1935–7, and Vice-Chancellor of the University of Liverpool, 1937–45. British member of the Permanent Court of Arbitration at the Hague, 1945–65, president of the European Court of Human Rights, 1959–65, and served on many commissions and committees. He chaired the Committee on the Supply and Training of Teachers which reported in 1944, and the Burnham Committee on Teachers' Salaries, 1956–8. The McNair Report of 1944 made a number of proposals concerning the training and status of teachers. These included longer courses of training, a widening of the field of recruitment, an end to the 'pledge' and to the ban on married women teachers, the establishment of area training organizations and a central training council, and an increase in teachers' salaries. CBE, 1918; knighted in 1943; raised to the peerage, 1955. Honorary doctorates from several universities in England, Scotland and continental Europe. See his several writings including *The Legal Effects of War* (1920);

Dr Johnson and the Law (1948); *International Law Opinions* (3 vols., 1956); *Lord McNair: selected papers and bibliography* (1974).

Macnamara, Thomas James (1861–1931). Politician and teachers' union representative. Born Montreal barracks, son of a regular soldier. Returned to England when young.

Educated at St Thomas's School, Exeter, was a pupil teacher for five years and then attended Borough Road Training College on a Queen's Scholarship, 1880. Taught in schools; headteacher of a Bristol board school, 1884–92. Together with **J.H. Yoxall**, Macnamara headed a group within the National Union of Teachers from January 1887 called the 'Indefatigables' which attacked the indecisiveness of the ageing Executive of the Union. Elected to the Executive, 1890. Editor, *The Teacher*, the organ of the Union, 1892–1907, and President of the Union, 1896. Macnamara was a radical liberal in politics. He unsuccessfully contested Deptford in 1895, but was returned as MP for North Camberwell, 1900–24. Parliamentary Secretary, Local Government Board, 1907–8, Parliamentary and Financial Secretary, Admiralty, 1908–20, Minister of Labour, Lloyd George's cabinet, 1920–2. Defeated at Walsall, 1929. See his *School-Room Humour* (1905), and Tropp, A., *The School Teachers* (1957).

Magnus, Sir Philip (1842–1933). Promoter of technical education. Born London. Educated at University College School and University College, London. Graduated in 1863 with a first class degree in arts and in the next year added a first class in science. Studied at the University of Berlin. From 1866 was assistant minister at the Reform Synagogue in Portland Place, London, but supplemented his work by private coaching and lecturing at University College, and Stockwell Teachers' Training College. In 1874 appointed examiner in Mathematics and Physics by the College of Preceptors. Wrote textbooks, notably the *Lessons in Elementary Mechanics* (1875). Director and secretary of the City and Guilds of London

161

Malthus

Institute, 1880–8; superintendent and secretary of the Institute's Department of Technology, 1888–1913. Member of the London School Board, 1890–1. Fellow of London University and member of the Senate, 1898–1931; president of the Council of the College of Preceptors, 1908–33; MP for London University, 1906–22. He served on the Royal Commission on Technical Instruction, 1881–4, and was knighted in 1886. Magnus was a pioneer in the fields of technical education, the London polytechnics, examinations and the registration of teachers, and was known as the greatest living authority on industrial and technical education. See his writings, especially *Industrial Education* (1888); *Educational Aims and Efforts 1880–1910* (1910), and Foden, F., *Philip Magnus, Victorian Educational Pioneer* (1970).

Malthus, Thomas Robert (1766–1834). Political economist. Born near Dorking, Surrey. Educated by his father, and subsequently became a pupil of Richard Graves, the poet and novelist, and also of Gilbert Wakefield. Between 1779 and 1783 when Wakefield was classical master at Warrington Academy Malthus accompanied him there. Attended Jesus College, Cambridge, 1784–8 and was placed 9th wrangler in the mathematical tripos, having also won prizes for Greek and Latin. MA in 1791, fellow in 1793, and in 1797 became curate at Albury in Surrey. The *Essay on the Principle of Population* was published anonymously in 1798. Travelled extensively in Europe in the following year to collect information for the pamphlet war in which he was now engaged. Subsequently modified his theory that population would outrun food supply. In 1805 Malthus became professor of History and Political Economy at the new East India College at Haileybury and lived there for the rest of his life. Published pamphlets on rent and the Corn Laws, and *Political Economy* (1820). FRS, 1819; a royal associate of the Royal Society of Literature, 1824; fellow of the Statistical Society, 1834; a member of the French Institute and of the Royal Academy of Berlin. Malthus was a moderate man in all things. He supported the cause of national education and the work of the British and National Societies. See his writings and Bonar, J., *Malthus and his Work* (1885, repr. Cass 1966); Drysdale, C.R., *The Life and Writings of T.R. Malthus* (1892); Glass, D.V., *Introduction to Malthus* (1953); Ambirajan, S., *Malthus and Classical Economics* (1959); James, P., *'Population' Malthus* (1979); Petersen, W., *Malthus* (1979); Wrigley, E.A., and Souden, D. (eds.), *The Works of Thomas Robert Malthus* (8 vols., 1986).

162

Mander, Sir Frederick (1883–1964). Teachers' union leader. Born London and educated Higher Grade School, Luton, Westminster Training College and B.Sc. (external), London University. Headmaster, Luton, 1915–31. Elected, Executive, National Union of Teachers, 1922, Vice-President, 1926, President, 1927. Led the Lowestoft strike, 1923, when 163 teachers were out for 11 months. General Secretary, National Union of Teachers, 1931–47. Vigorously opposed the 15 per cent reduction in teachers' salaries imposed by the National Government in 1931. Campaigned for the 1944 Education Act; from 1941, Mander demanded equality of opportunity in schooling, the raising of the school-leaving age, the ending of the 11-plus examination, the abolition of fees in secondary education and the provision of nursery schools. Chairman, Bedfordshire County Council, 1952–62. Knight, 1938.

Mangnall, Richmal (1769–1820). Headmistress and writer. Probably born in Manchester. Educated at Crofton Hall near Wakefield. On the death of her parents she was adopted by her uncle John Kay, a Manchester solicitor. She began teaching in the boarding school run by a Mrs Wilson at Crofton Hall and by 1808 had succeeded her as headmistress and proprietor, a post she occupied until her death. The school provided an education for some 70 daughters of middle-class parents, a maximum to which Mangnall adhered. Her publications included a slim volume of poems (1805) and a 694 page school geography (1815). Her fame, however, rested upon the *Historical and Miscellaneous Questions* first published anonymously in 1798. A much enlarged edition was produced in 1800, a third in 1803, which included her name as author, and a fourth in 1805. The work was published with additions and alterations throughout the nineteenth century. See Briggs, W.G., 'Richmal Mangnall and her School at Crofton Old Hall', *University of Leeds Researches and Studies*, 15, 1957.

Mannheim, Karl (1893–1947). Sociologist and educationist. Born Budapest, son of a businessman. Educated at universities of Budapest, Berlin, Paris, Freiburg and Heidelberg, studying philosophy, philology and pedagogy. Taught in a Budapest grammar school early in the First World War. Secretary of group of radicals, which included Georg Lukacs, Bartok and Kodaly: moving spirit in Free School of Arts and Social Science, an adult education college. Briefly, lecturer, Budapest University in philosophy and sociology, after the October Revolution of 1918; lecturer, Heidelberg

University, in sociology, 1926–30 and professor of Sociology, Frankfurt-am-Main University, 1930–3. Mannheim, who was Jewish, left Germany for England when Hitler came to power. Lecturer in sociology, London School of Economics, 1933–45. Professor of Education, University of London Institute of Education, 1946, until his death a year later. Mannheim's main interests as a sociologist were in the fields of knowledge, culture and society, but the nature of education was also one of his concerns. As there was difficulty in establishing the validity of beliefs or knowledge by generally agreed criteria, he saw the main hope for the future in a 'socially unattached intelligentsia' separated from family and community. Although Mannheim agreed with Marx on the relation between class, ideology and knowledge, the solutions adopted were very different. Education for the masses should be planned to produce personal autonomy, but the highest good of society could only be achieved by educating for a certain amount of conformity. The contradictory nature of the ultimate objectives of Mannheim's new social order and the means whereby they may be achieved is apparent throughout his writings. See his *Ideology and Utopia: An Introduction to the Sociology of Knowledge* (1936); *Man and Society* (1940); *Diagnosis of our Time* (1943), and Stewart, W.A.C., *Karl Mannheim on Education and Social Thought* (1967); Kettler, D., *Karl Mannheim* (1984).

Manning, Henry Edward (1808–92). Cardinal. Born Totteridge, Hertfordshire, son of a London merchant and Tory MP. Educated Harrow, 1822–7 and Balliol College, Oxford, obtaining a first in classics, 1830. Colonial Office as a clerk, then fellow, Merton College, Oxford, 1832. Ordained December 1832 and curate and rector, Woollavington-cum-Graffham, Sussex, 1833–50. Closely involved in the setting up of diocesan boards under the National Society for Promoting the Education of the Poor and a firm believer in the clerical control of education. Received into the Catholic Church, April 1851 and priest, June 1851. Superior, St Mary of the Angels, Bayswater, London, 1857–65, working in the slums of Westminster and promoting education. Archbishop of Westminster, 1865, and stressed the importance of schooling. Manning established the Westminster Diocesan Fund for providing elementary education for Catholic children. He was also an enthusiast for reformatories. Issued a pastoral in 1869, warning clergy of the implications of the Elementary Education Bill, followed by a second pastoral in 1872 addressed to both clergy and laity. Both were reprinted in book form under the title *National Education and Parental Rights* (1872). He founded an abortive university in Kensington, 1874, but a seminary for the training of clergymen at Hammersmith, 1876, was very successful. Cardinal, 1875. Wrote articles, 1882–3, calling for the amendment of the 1870 Act in favour of voluntary schools. Played active part in the negotiations leading to the 1891 Education Act, which made possible the provision of free education. Member, Royal Commission on the Housing of the Working Classes, 1884–5 and on the Elementary Education Acts, 1886–8 (Cross Commission). See McClelland, V.A., *Cardinal Manning: his public life and influence 1865–92* (1962); Selby, D.E., *Towards a Common System of National Education. Cardinal Manning and Educational Reform 1882–1892* (1977) and Gray, R., *Cardinal Manning* (1985).

Mansbridge, Albert (1876–1952). Founder of the Workers' Educational Association (WEA). Born Gloucester. Educated at Battersea Grammar School. Began work at 15 as an office boy in the City, and later as a clerk with the Co-operative Wholesale Society (CWS). Worked full time in the CWS from 1899 and also taught in evening schools. In 1903 published an article entitled 'Democracy and Education' in the *University Extension Journal*, and together with Frances Jane Pringle, his wife, began 'An Association to Promote the Higher Education of Working Men'. **William Temple** was the first president, Mansbridge the secretary. The first branch was formed in Reading in 1904 and the title was changed to WEA in 1905. Under Mansbridge's guidance it spread throughout the country. Member of the Prime Minister's Committee on the Teaching of Foreign Languages, 1915–18, and of the Royal Commission on Oxford and Cambridge Universities, 1919–22. Member of the Board of Education Consultative Committee, 1906–12, 1924–39. President of the World Association for Adult Education and one of the founders of the National Central Library; he lectured to numerous audiences in this country and in the USA. Companion of Honour, 1931, and honorary doctorates from Cambridge, Manchester, Pittsburgh and Mount Allison. See his writings including *University Tutorial Classes* (1913); *An Adventure in Working-Class Education* (1920); *The Trodden Road* (1940), and Smith, H.P., *Labour and Learning* (1956).

Marriott, Sir John Arthur Ransome (1859–1945). Educationist and politician. Born Bowdon, Cheshire. Educated at Repton and New College, Oxford. Lecturer there in modern history, 1884–7, and at Worcester College, 1885–1920, where he was elected fellow in 1914. Marriott's main interest, however, was the Oxford University Extension Delegacy. He was its secretary from 1895 to 1920 and also one of its most popular lecturers. Marriott enjoyed lecturing to large audiences, particularly on broad political subjects, which he saw as an education in citizenship, and preferred this to the Workers' Educational Association's tutorial class approach. Conservative MP for Oxford City, 1917–22 and for York, 1923–9. Marriott played an important role in averting the threatened general strike of 1921, was knighted in 1924, and chairman of the House of Commons select committee on estimates, 1924–5. He was an inveterate writer of books, articles and reviews chiefly in the fields of history, politics and biography. His writings, like his lectures, were always clear, and works such as *Second Chambers* (1910) and *The Eastern Question* (1917) achieved considerable notice. See also *Economics and Ethics* (1923); *The Mechanism of the Modern State* (2 vols., 1927); *The Evolution of the British Empire and Commonwealth* (1939); *Memories of Four Score Years* (1946).

Martineau, Harriet (1802–76). Political economist, novelist and children's writer. Born Norwich into a prominent Unitarian family of Huguenot origin. Educated at home where she learned Latin from her brother and music from the Norwich organist. Attended Isaac Perry's school in Norwich, 1813–15. In 1819 visited a schoolmistress aunt in Bristol where she became a devout follower of Lant Carpenter, the Unitarian minister of Bristol. Martineau believed that women should be given a sound education and the opportunity to express themselves. Her first article was published in 1821 and *Devotional Exercises for the use of Young Persons* in 1823. Following the deaths of her father, brother and fiancé, she supported herself as a professional writer. Visited the USA, 1834–6 where her abolitionist views were confirmed, and Egypt and Palestine, 1846–7. In 1849 she became secretary of Bedford College for Women, London. Martineau's writings included children's stories, collected in the *Playfellow* (1841), works on political economy, notably *Illustrations of Political Economy* (1832–4) and a *History of England during the Thirty Years' Peace* (1849). She wrote several pieces for the Society for the Diffusion of Useful Knowledge, contributed to many periodicals including *Household Words* and the *Westminster Review*, and supplied leading articles to the *London Daily News* (1852–66). Martineau who suffered from deafness and ill-health for most of her life had a wide circle of friends including **Brougham, W.J. Fox, Malthus**, Milman and the Wordsworths. She was in the forefront of the dissemination of liberal ideas in Victorian England. See her *Household Education* (1849); *Autobiography* (3 vols., 1877), and Miller, F., *Harriet Martineau* (1884); Webb, R.K., *Harriet Martineau, a Radical Victorian* (1960); Pichanik, V.K., *Harriet Martineau, the Woman and her Work* (1980); Weiner, G. (ed.), *Harriet Martineau's Autobiography* (2 vols., 1983).

Marvin, Francis Sydney (1863–1943). School inspector and author. Born City of London and educated Merchant Taylors' School and St John's College, Oxford, first class honours in classical moderations and *literae humaniores*, second in modern history, 1887. Taught in elementary schools in Oxford and East London and also was a university extension lecturer. Appointed Assistant Inspector, 1890, and full HMI, 1892, the first ex-elementary teacher to attain such a position. Divisional Inspector and Inspector of Training Colleges, Yorkshire, 1903–13, and East Central Division, 1914, Staff Inspector, History, 1915. Marvin was a committed Positivist and a friend of **Frederick Harrison**. His marriage to **Edith Deverell**, who was also an Inspector, in 1904 took place with a Positivist ceremony. Professor of Modern History, University of Egypt, 1929–30. Publications include *The Living Past* (1913), *The Making of the Western Mind* (1923) and *The Nation at School* (1933).

Mason, Charlotte Maria Shaw (1842–1923). Educationist. Born Bangor, daughter of a Liverpool merchant. Educated at home and student, Home and Colonial Training College, London, 1860–1. Head of Davison Infant School, Worthing, 1861–73, qualifying as teacher, 1863. Vice-Principal, Bishop Otter Training College, Chichester, 1874–8, where she formulated her educational philosophy. During her stay in Bradford, 1880–91, she wrote *Home Education* (1886) for parents with children under nine years of age; it suggested a method of education based on natural law and

contained practical advice on establishing good habits and religious ideas. Lecture tours led to the formation of the Parents' National Education Union (PNEU), 1887, moving to Ambleside, Westmorland to start the House of Education, 1892, where some of her ideas were put into practice. Editor, *The Parents' Review* from 1890. *Parents and Children* (1897) and *Home and School Education* (1905) discussed the nature of the school curriculum for under 12s and other aspects of education. Correspondence courses were sent out from Ambleside to enrolled elementary and secondary schools containing appropriate work for pupils. Governesses were trained there in enlightened methods of teaching; later it became the Charlotte Mason College for intending primary school teachers. See also her *Some Studies in the Formation of Character* (1906); *An Essay towards a Philosophy of Education* (1924), and Cholmondeley, E., *The Story of Charlotte Mason* (1960); King, J., *Charlotte Mason Reviewed* (1981).

Mason, Sir Josiah (1795–1881). Philanthropist. Born Kidderminster. Started selling in streets at the age of eight. Engaged in a variety of trades; shoemaker, blacksmith, carpenter, carpet weaver. In June 1825 he bought a split ring business and in 1829 began the manufacture of steel pens, soon becoming the largest manufacturer in the world. His fortune was further increased by his partnership with Elkington in electroplating, and their copper and nickel smelting works. He endowed an orphanage for some 300 children, and almshouses at a cost of £260,000. He gave a further £180,000 to found a scientific college in Birmingham. Mason College opened in 1880 and by 1893 had 556 students. It was subsequently incorporated into Birmingham University. Mason was knighted in 1872. See Bunce, J.T., *Josiah Mason, a Biography* (1882); Taylor, L., *The Story of Josiah Mason* (1893).

Mason, Stewart Carlton (1906–1983). Educational administrator. Educated Uppingham School, Worcester College, Oxford, 1925–8, studying modern languages. Assistant master, Berkhamsted School, 1930–1, Harrow School, 1931–7, HMI, 1937–9 and 1944–7. Seconded to the Admiralty, 1939–44. Director of Education Leicestershire, 1947–71. Formulated the 'Leicestershire Plan' which, from 1957, reorganized the county's secondary education on comprehensive lines without contravening the statutory requirement to transfer pupils at the age of 11. Junior high schools were established, taking in all 11 to 14 year olds; those who intended to stay at school until at least 16 moved to senior high schools, which had an age range from 14 to 18 years. The plan was later modified. One of the six acceptable choices offered to local education authorities by the Department of Education and Science Circular 10/65. See his *The Leicestershire Experiment* (1957), and *In Our Experience: the changing schools of Leicestershire* (1970).

Masson, David (1822–1907). Journalist and academic. Born Aberdeen. Educated there at the grammar school, at Marischal College and at Edinburgh University. Joined the staff of W. and R. **Chambers** as a textbook writer. Professor of English Literature at University College, London, and professor of Rhetoric and English Literature at Edinburgh, 1865–95. A very popular lecturer, and as a result an honours degree course in English was established. Masson also worked for the admission of women to the University and one of the first residences was called Masson Hall. A journalist, he started *Macmillan's Magazine* in 1859; an historian of literature, see for example his *Life of Milton* (6 vols., 1859–94); editor of the *Register of the Privy Council of Scotland* from 1880 to 1899 during which period he produced 13 volumes covering the years 1578–1627; and Historiographer for Scotland from 1893, Masson exercised a considerable influence on Scottish intellectual life. See his *College-Education and Self-Education* (1854); *Memories of Two Cities* (1911).

Maurice, (John) Frederick Denison (1805–72). Theologian. Born at Normanston near Lowestoft. His father was a Unitarian preacher who took pupils, and Maurice was brought up in a puritan atmosphere against which he rebelled. He studied at Trinity College and Trinity Hall, Cambridge, 1823–6, but as a Dissenter was unable to graduate. Studied law in London, 1826–7. Contributed articles to a number of journals including the *Westminster Review*. Entered Exeter College, Oxford, 1830, joined the Anglican Church and took a degree in 1831. In 1834 was ordained curate of Bubbenhall near Leamington. Became chaplain to Guy's Hospital, London in 1836 where he lectured to the students on Moral Philosophy, and to Lincoln's Inn, 1846–60. Professor of Literature at King's College, London from 1840 and professor of Theology, 1846–53. Professor of Moral Philosophy at Cambridge, 1866–72. Maurice made a variety of contributions to education. In addition to his professorships he was an editor of the *Educational Magazine* founded in 1839. In 1848 he was the prime mover in the foundation of Queen's College for ladies. He chaired its committee and himself taught there. By this date Maurice had become the leader of the Christian Socialist movement, a group which included **Thomas Hughes** and **Charles Kingsley**. In 1854 he launched the Working Men's College of which he became principal. Maurice's life and writings, for example the *Theological Essays* (1853), were controversial in the extreme. Though personally unassuming and seeking to promote cohesion in society, he provoked numerous theological disputes and was forced to resign his theological chair in 1853. See his works and Maurice, J.F. (ed.), *Life of F.D. Maurice* (1884); Wood, H.G., *Frederick Denison Maurice* (1950); Brose, O.J., *F.D. Maurice, rebellious conformist* (1971); MacClain, F.M., *Maurice: man and moralist* (1972).

Mayo, Revd Charles (1792–1846). Teacher. Born London and educated Merchant Taylors' School and St John's College, Oxford, reading law, BA, 1817 and doctorate, 1822. Headmaster, Bridgnorth Grammar School, 1817–19, ordained priest, 1818. Resigned post to join Pestalozzi at Yverdon, Switzerland, teaching English and classics to English boys, 1819–22. Determined to spread Pestalozzi's message in England, Mayo opened a boarding school for upper class boys at Epsom, 1822–6 and then at Cheam, 1826–46, where he was assisted by his sister **Elizabeth** and Charles Reiner, a former pupil of Pestalozzi. Mayo gave a lecture on Pestalozzi at the Royal Institution in 1828 where he stated that the two main principles in teaching were first, that learning begins with the child's own experience and second, that the teacher must study the individual needs of the child as he/she develops. See his *Memoir of Pestalozzi* (1831) and *Analysis of History Ancient and Modern* (1835), and Mayo, C.H., *A Genealogical Account of the Mayo and Elton Families* (1882).

Mayo, Elizabeth (1793–1865). Teacher and writer. Worked with her brother, **Revd Charles Mayo** at Cheam, 1822–34. Author of *Lessons* *on Objects* (1829) which claimed that by arranging and classifying objects and discovering their qualities, the child would be stimulated to learn. This method was universally used in elementary schools for the rest of the nineteenth century and often became exercises in rote-learning. There were 16 editions of the book by 1859. Elizabeth Mayo became supervisor in the schools and colleges of the Home and Colonial Society, 1834, the first woman in England to be appointed to a post in teacher training. The Society published her *Model Lessons for Infant Schools* (1838) and *Religious Instruction for Young Children* (1845). See also *Practical Remarks on Infant Education* (1837) with Mayo, C.

Meiklejohn, John Miller Dow (1836–1902). Educationist. Born Edinburgh, 1836, son of a schoolmaster. Educated at father's private school and Edinburgh University, MA, 1858. Schoolmaster at private schools in Westmorland and London and was a lecturer and journalist. War correspondent, Danish–German war, 1864, when arrested as a spy. Assistant Commissioner, Scottish Endowed Schools Commission, 1874–6. The passing of the 1872 Education (Scotland) Act released funds left by **Dr Andrew Bell** for the establishment of elementary schools in Scotland. Accordingly, in 1876, the trustees of the fund made grants to two universities to create the first two chairs in education in the United Kingdom – **S.S. Laurie** at Edinburgh and Meiklejohn at St Andrews. Meiklejohn's interesting inaugural address was delivered on 1 April 1876. He was a prolific writer of school textbooks, mainly on English and geography and helped to raise the standard of such books. Author of *An Old Educational Reformer, Dr Andrew Bell* (1881) and editor, *Life and Letters of William Ballantyne Hodgson* (1883). Unsuccessful parliamentary candidate, Liberal, Glasgow, Tradeston division, 1886.

Miall, Edward (1809–81). Politician. Born Portsmouth. Educated at St Saviour's Grammar School, London. In 1827 became an usher in a school in Essex and subsequently in Suffolk. In 1829 began training for the Congregational ministry, becoming a minister at Ware in 1831 and at Leicester in 1834. Miall spent the rest of his life working for the disestablishment of the Anglican church. In 1841 he founded the *Nonconformist*, a weekly journal which he edited. He supported the Anti-Corn Law League and the principle of widespread male suffrage. In 1843 he successfully opposed the education clauses of the Factory Bill, on the grounds that they would increase the Anglican control over schools. Entered Parliament in 1852 as MP for Rochdale. Lost his seat in 1857, but sat for Bradford, 1869–74. In 1858 he was appointed as the Dissenters' representative on the Newcastle Commission which inquired into popular education. Though he signed the general report Miall and Goldwin Smith also produced a minority report. In 1870 he opposed the Education Bill of his Bradford colleague **W.E. Forster** for being too favourable to the Anglican cause. By this date, however, Miall had accepted the need for state education. See Miall, A., *Life of Edward Miall* (1884).

Mill, James (1773–1836). Philosopher. Born near Montrose where he attended the Academy. In 1790 entered Edinburgh University where he studied philosophy, Greek, Latin and French. Licensed to preach in 1798 and did some tutoring. In 1802 settled in London and began a literary career, editing and writing for various periodicals. His *History of British India* was published in 1817, and led to his appointment in 1819 as assistant examiner in the East India Company Office. By 1832 he was head of the office and financially secure. In 1808 Mill began his acquaintance with **Bentham** whose friend and disciple he became. Mill also educated his own nine children including **John Stuart** whose account of his father is contained in his *Autobiography*. Mill was a strong supporter of the British and Foreign School Society and took a leading part in the West London Lancasterian Institution and Chrestomathic school schemes. He was also a founder of London University (University College) and a member of its first Council in 1825. His leadership of the utilitarian and radical causes was advanced by the founding of the *Westminster Review* in 1824. Mill was a man of profound thought and great learning. See his several writings including the *Encyclopaedia Britannica* article on 'Education', and Bain, A., *James Mill: a Biography* (1882); Cavenagh, F.A. (ed.), *James and John Stuart Mill on Education* (1931); Burston, W.H. (ed.), *James Mill on Education* (1969); Burston, W.H., *James Mill on Philosophy and Education* (1973); Mazlish, J., *James and John Stuart Mill* (1975).

Mill, John Stuart (1806–73). Philosopher. Born London, eldest son of **James Mill**. Taught by his father, Greek from the age of three, Latin from eight, logic at 12 and political economy at 13. Read very widely indeed. Lived in France 1820–1 and acquired a great interest in the country. In 1823 appointed a junior clerk in the India Office (rose rapidly and in 1858 retired as head of the department). Was groomed as the future leader of the utilitarian cause but in 1826 underwent an intellectual crisis brought on by overwork. Thereafter developed more concern for the development of the emotions. In 1830 there began Mill's long association with Harriet Taylor whom he married in 1851, two years after her husband's death. Mill was MP for Westminster, 1865–8 and advocated the cause of the extension of the franchise to women, and the prosecution of Governor Eyre for his handling of the Jamaican revolt. Rector of St Andrews University, 1866. Mill exerted a profound influence on nineteenth-century thought by such works as *On Liberty* (1859); *Representative Government* (1861) and *The Subjection of Women* (1869). See his *Autobiography* (1873), and Bain, A., *John Stuart Mill* (1882); Packe, M. St J., *The Life of John Stuart Mill* (1954); Garforth, F.W., *John Stuart Mill's theory of education* (1979); Garforth, F.W., *Educative Democracy: John Stuart Mill on Education in Society* (1980).

Moberly, George (1803–85). Schoolmaster and cleric. Son of a Russian merchant. Educated at Winchester and Balliol College, Oxford, 1822–5, gaining first class in *literae humaniores*. MA, 1828, DCL, 1836. Fellow, Balliol College, 1826 and a very gifted and popular tutor; amongst his students were **Manning** and Tait. In 1835, he was appointed headmaster of his old school, Winchester, remaining there until 1866. He held traditional views on education, favouring fagging and made few innovations in the school. A High Churchman, Moberly was appointed Bishop of Salisbury by **Gladstone** in 1868, holding the post for the rest of his life. See his *Remarks on the proposed admission of Dissenters into the University of Oxford* (1834); *Sermons at Winchester College* (1844, second series, 1848); *Letters to Sir W. Heathcote on Public Schools* (1861), and How, F.D., *Six Great Schoolmasters* (1904); Moberly, C.A.E., *George Moberly* (1912).

Morant, Sir Robert Laurie (1863–1920). Civil servant. Born London, son of decorative artist. Educated Winchester, 1876–81 and New College, Oxford, 1881–5, first class honours in theology. Considered entering the ministry, but became deputy headmaster, Temple Grove School, East Sheen, a preparatory school, 1885–6. Tutor to Crown Prince of Siam, 1887–94 and took part in organizing the country's education system as Examiner. Returned to England, 1894 and in April 1895, resident at Toynbee Hall, Whitechapel, as tutor. Appointed Assistant Director, Office of Special Inquiries,

January 1895, with **Michael Sadler**. In one of his articles, on the organization of education in Switzerland (1898), he set out his opinions on the deficiencies of the English system, especially noting the need for strong central direction. Private secretary, **Sir John Gorst**, Vice-President, Committee of Council on Education, 1899–1902, assistant private secretary, **8th Duke of Devonshire**, Lord President, 1902, Acting Secretary, Board of Education, 1902, Permanent Secretary, 1903–11. Played major part in the stages leading up to and the implementation of the 1902 Education Act. Morant was the main mover behind the scenes which led to the resignation of his former chief, Michael Sadler, from the office of Director of the Office of Special Inquiries in 1903. His vision of national education encompassed an authority for the 'guidance of brains' which would deal with the educational arrangements of all grades of schools and children. Morant's plan for elementary education has been described as 'education for followership', in contrast with the secondary sector 'education for leadership'. The school, according to Morant, was to form and strengthen character and to develop intelligence and to fit boys and girls practically and intellectually for the work of life. These aims were spelt out in the Elementary School Code of 1904. In the same year, the Regula-tions for Secondary Schools were issued which made detailed recommendations on the curriculum, with more emphasis on the humanities than hitherto. Regulations for training colleges and technical colleges followed in 1904 and in his last year in office, 1911, he completed his plan with a handbook on grants to universities. A ruthless and determined administrator, Morant's achievements were nevertheless impressive. He had the task after the 1902 Education Act of bringing together the Board of Education and the new local education authorities created by the Act into a working partnership. The municipal secondary schools also flourished and with his encouragement, the School Medical Service was established in 1907. Following the issue and public disclosure of the document on local education authority inspectors, written by the

Board's Chief Inspector for Elementary Schools, **Edmond Holmes**, Morant, as the officer responsible for its authorization, was obliged to leave the Board of Education and became Chairman, National Health Insurance Commission, 1911–19. Permanent Secretary, Ministry of Health, 1919–20. Member, Royal Commission on London University, 1911. CB, 1902, Knight, 1907. See Allen, B.M., *Sir Robert Morant* (1934); Eaglesham, E.J.R., *The Foundations of 20th Century Education in England* (1967); Lowe, R., 'Robert Morant and the Secondary School Regulations of 1904', *Journal of Educational Administration and History*, 16 (1), 1984.

More, Hannah (1745–1833). Playwright and religious and educational writer. Born Stapleton near Bristol, the fourth of five daughters. Her father, master of the free school at Fishponds, taught her Latin and maths. Became a pupil and then a teacher at her sisters' school in Bristol where she learned Italian and Spanish. In 1774 visited London where she became a member of the 'blue stockings' circle and a friend of Elizabeth Montagu. Knew Dr Johnson and Garrick and wrote successful plays including *A Search after Happiness* and *The Fatal Falsehood*. In 1787 More first met William Wilberforce. Their subsequent friendship helped to turn her mind to serious matters. In 1790 she exposed hypocrisy in *An Estimate of the Religion of the Fashionable World* and wrote a series of moral tracts for the poor, notably *Cheap Repository Tracts* (1795–8), which led to the foundation of the Religious Tract Society. In 1789 Hannah and her sister Martha visited Cheddar with Wilberforce and were dismayed at the ignorance of its inhabitants. The sisters established Sunday schools in the area, and held evening meetings for the parents. More's emphasis was on the Bible and catechism, reading but not writing. She became friendly with members of the Clapham Sect and her later writings reflect the high moral and religious purposes and sense of responsibility for the poor which characterized the Evangelical movement. Her conservative approach was shown in her *Strictures on the Modern System of Female Education* (1799). See her several writings and Thompson, H., *Life of Hannah More* (1838); Hopkins, M.A., *Hannah More and her Circle* (1947); Fox, L.P., *Hannah More, Evangelical Educationalist* (1949); Jones, M.G., *Hannah More* (1952); McLeish, J., *Evangelical Religion and Popular Education* (1969).

Morell, John Daniel (1816–91). School inspector. Born Little Baddow, Essex, son of Congregational minister. Educated at his father's school and Homerton College, London, for the education of dissenting ministers, 1834–8. Because of ill-health, did not enter ministry, but studied logic, moral philosophy and classics at Glasgow University. BA, 1840, MA, 1841, and LL.D, 1860, and University of Bonn, Germany, 1841, where he was taught by Fichte. Ordained minister at Gosport, 1842–5, but left ministry, devoting himself thereafter to philosophical rather than theological studies. Published *Historical and Critical View of the Speculative Philosophy of Europe in the Nineteenth Century* (2 vols., 1846) and later other works on aspects of metaphysics and *The Philosophy of Religion* (1849). Appointed HMI, 1848, and for some time the only inspector for dissenting schools. Editor of *The School Magazine*, a journal containing practical help for teachers, and wrote books on grammar. Morell was particularly interested in the teaching of music in schools. His Annual Reports make lively reading. Theobald, R.M., *Memorials of John Daniel Morell* (1891).

Morley, Henry (1822–94). Teacher and author. Born London. Educated at a Moravian school at Neuwied on the Rhine, which practised progressive methods, and Stockwell, London, 1833–8, King's College London, 1838–43, where he studied medicine. Partner in a practice, Madeley, Shropshire, 1844–8. Inspired by the revolutions then occurring in Europe in 1848, Morley opened a school in Manchester which offered individual instruction to children, a commercial education and practical lessons in chemistry. The school was a failure, and Morley moved to Wallasey, near Liverpool, beginning another school. He abolished corporal punishment, carpeted the floor and gave the children a homely environment and offered a wide-ranging curriculum. Morley disliked orthodox religion and encouraged his pupils to study the Bible in the light of scientific knowledge. The school only lasted two years, 1848–50, when Morley abandoned the experiment because of debt. Worked with **Dickens** in London. Staff of *Household Words* and its successor, *All the Year Round* (1851–65). Editor, the *Examiner*, 1861–7. Professor of English Language and Literature, University College, London, 1865–90. See his *Sunrise in Italy* (1848); *A Defence of Ignorance* (1851); *Morley's Universal Library* (63 vols., 1886–90, and Solly, H.S., *The Life of Henry Morley, LL.D.* (1898); McCann, W.P., and Stewart, W.A.C., *The Educational Innovators, 1750–1880* (1967).

Morrell, Derek Holtby (1921–68). Civil servant. Educated Harrow County School and Keble College, Oxford. From 1947, when he joined the Ministry of Education, he was one of the prime movers in the Architects Development Group in the Architects and Buildings Branch, becoming joint head of the Branch. Involved in fostering the Curriculum Study Group which led to the creation of the Schools Council for Curriculum and Examinations in 1964. As its first joint secretary, 1964–6, Morrell encouraged public discussion of curriculum issues. Assistant Under-Secretary, Children's Department, Home Office, 1966–8. Played key part in framing the Children and Young Persons Act, 1969. See his article, 'The Freedom of the Teacher in Relation to Research and Development Work in the Area of the Curriculum and Examinations', *Educational Research*, 5, 1963, and *The Schools Council* (1966).

Morris, Henry (1889–1961). Educational administrator. Born Southport. Educated at the local elementary school, left at 14 and worked on the local paper the *Southport Visitor*. Studied at the Harris Institute at Preston, at St David's, Lampeter, 1910–12, Exeter College, Oxford, 1912–14 and King's College, Cambridge, 1919–20, where he obtained a second class degree in moral sciences. Served in the Kent Education Office and, after moving to Cambridgeshire in 1921, became County Education Secretary (Chief Education Officer) in 1922 at the age of 33. This office he held until 1954. In 1924 he wrote a memorandum on *The Village College* which proposed in rural areas a grouping of all the educational and social agencies into one village college. He suggested ten such centres for Cambridgeshire, and the first was opened in 1930 by the Prince of Wales at Sawston. It included a school, a separate hall, an adult wing, a mechanics' workshop, library and playing fields for use by the school and the community, and a Warden's house. Morris spent much time in fund-raising, and two further colleges at Bottisham and Linton were opened in 1937. Impington, 1939, designed by Walter Gropius and Maxwell Fry, was a milestone in British educational architecture. Morris firmly believed 'that architecture is part of the essence of education'. CBE, 1942; ARIBA, 1954. Village colleges were established in other counties, for example, Hope Valley in Derbyshire opened by Morris himself in 1958. See Fisher, N., 'Henry Morris', *Education*, 29 Octr. 1954; Ree, H., *Educator extraordinary: the life and achievement of Henry Morris* (1973); Ree, H. (ed.), *The Henry Morris Collection* (1984).

177

Morris

Morris, William (1834–96). Artist, craftsman and poet. Born Walthamstow, London. Educated privately, at Marlborough College and at Exeter College, Oxford, where he took a pass degree. His early interest was in architecture but friendship with the pre-Raphaelites especially Burne-Jones and Rossetti led Morris to poetry and painting. In 1856 he was one of the founders of the *Oxford and Cambridge Magazine*. In 1861 the firm of Morris, Marshall, Faulkner and Company was formed to promote quality furnishings and interior design. The medieval craftsman was Morris's inspiration and the decoration of churches an important part of the business. In 1877 he founded a Society for the Protection of Ancient Buildings. In 1884 having left the Social Democratic Federation Morris became leader of the Socialist League, from which he withdrew in 1890. In that year he began the Kelmscott Press in Hammersmith to revive the art of medieval printing. Fifty-three books were printed in the period 1891–8, including the famous Chaucer edition of 1896. Morris was an honorary fellow of Exeter College from 1883 but resisted nominations both for the professorship of Poetry at Oxford in 1877 and the Laureateship itself in 1894. Morris's flight to nostalgic medievalism in the face of modern production methods may appear to have been futile but his energy and creativity in such diverse fields as art, architecture, craftsmanship, interior design, furnishings, poetry and prose writings exercised a considerable influence on later Victorian taste. See his *Collected Works* (24 vols., 1910–15) edited by Morris, M., and Mackail, J.W., *The Life of William Morris* (1899); Morris, M., *William Morris* (1936); Arnot, R.P., *William Morris, The Man and the Myth* (1964); Grennan, M.R., *William Morris: medievalist and revolutionary* (1970); Marshall, R., *William Morris and his earthly paradises* (1979).

Morris, William Richard, first Viscount Nuffield (1877–1963). Industrialist and philanthropist. Born Worcester. Elementary schooling. At the age of 16 he opened a bicycle shop, and progressed to motor cycle and motor car manufacture. Morris Motors Ltd. was incorporated in 1919. By 1926 when a new company was formed his 4,000 workforce was turning out 1,000 cars a week. His first gift to the University of Oxford, the endowment of a chair in Spanish, took place in this year, and between 1927–30 he made further big donations for medicine in London and Oxford. Morris was made a baronet in 1929, raised to the peerage in 1934 as Baron Nuffield, and to a viscountcy in 1938. In the 1930s his gifts were extended to the

178

Empire. In 1937 Nuffield College was founded at Oxford for the study of social, economic and political problems. The Nuffield Foundation, established in 1943, was intended to advance health and social well-being. Its large income has contributed to many research projects including those of curriculum reform. During his lifetime Morris gave away some £30 million. He received seven honorary doctorates, four honorary fellowships of Oxford colleges, and was honorary freeman of seven towns. See Andrews, P.W.S., and Brunner, E., *The Life of Lord Nuffield* (1955); Jackson, R., *The Nuffield Story* (1964); Overy, R.J., *William Morris* (1976).

Moseley, Revd Henry (1801–72). School inspector. Born Newcastle-under-Lyme, Staffordshire, son of a schoolmaster. Educated at Newcastle, Portsmouth Naval School, Abbeville and St John's College, Cambridge. 7th wrangler, 1826. Ordained priest and curate, West Monkton, Somerset, 1827–31. Professor of Natural and Experimental Philosophy and Astronomy, King's College, London, 1831–44. HMI, 1844–55. His report for 1847 on a small Dorset rural school at King's Somborne, conducted by the **Revd Richard Dawes**, received wide publicity. Moseley particularly praised the methods employed in science lessons – of observation, experiment and problem-solving. FRS, 1839. Vicar of Olveston, Gloucestershire, 1854–72. See his *A Treatise on Mechanics applied to the Arts* (1834); *Lectures on Astronomy* (1839); *The Mechanical Principles of Engineering and Architecture* (1843); *Astro-theology* (1851) and *Faith in the Work of the Teacher* (1854).

Mundella, Anthony John (1825–97). Politician. Born in Leicester, son of an Italian political refugee and educated at St Nicholas's National School, Leicester, leaving at the age of nine. He was apprenticed to a hosiery manufacturer and became manager, 1844. Partner in a Nottingham hosiery firm, 1848, making sufficient money to be able to devote the rest of his life to politics. His two main interests were factory legislation and popular education. Mundella studied the German system of instruction and thereafter advanced the cause of technical education in England; a Royal Commission on this subject, chaired by **Bernhard Samuelson**, was set up in 1881 with Mundella's enthusiastic support. Liberal MP, Sheffield, 1868–85 and Sheffield, Brightside, 1885–97. As Vice-President of the Committee of Council on Education, 1880–5, he was, together with **Lord Spencer**, responsible for the Education Act 1880, which introduced universal compulsory elementary education in England.

The 1882 Code, known as the 'Mundella Code', encouraged more enlightened teaching methods in schools and allowed for a wider variety of specific and optional subjects in the curriculum. He was President of the Board of Trade in the last two Gladstone ministries, 1886 and 1892–4. See Armytage, W.H.G., *A.J. Mundella* (1951).

Neill, Alexander Sutherland (1883–1973). Teacher and child psychologist. Born in Angus and educated at the Kingsmuir village school run by his father. Left school at 14 to become a clerk but subsequently took a degree in English at Edinburgh University and qualified as a teacher. Taught at King Alfred School, Hampstead and in 1921 at Dresden in an international school. In 1924 founded his own school at Lyme Regis, which subsequently moved to Leiston, Suffolk where it became famous as Summerhill School. Here he put into practice his iconoclastic views on education. The children were given considerable freedom; to govern themselves, to be at ease with the staff, to attend lessons only if they wished to do so. His numerous books and lectures made him the best known British progressive educationist of the twentieth century. He received honorary degrees from the Universities of Newcastle and Exeter. Neill carried on working at Summerhill until his death. See his many writings, for example *A Dominie's Log* (1916); *The Problem Parent* (1932); *Is Scotland Educated?* (1936); *That Dreadful School* (1937); *Summerhill* (1962); *Neill! Neill! Orange Peel* (1973), and Hemmings, R., *Fifty years of freedom* (1972); Croall, J., *Neill of Summerhill* (1983).

Nettleship, Richard Lewis (1846–92). Philosopher. Born Kettering, Northamptonshire, son of a solicitor. Educated at Uppingham and Balliol College, Oxford, gaining first class classical moderations, 1867 and second class, *literae humaniores*, 1869; MA, 1872. Fellow of Balliol from 1869. Greatly influenced by the philosophy of **T.H. Green**, with whom he collaborated in the translation of Lotze's *Logik* and *Metaphysik*, published in 1884. Nettleship's major undertaking was as editor of the *Works of T.H. Green* (3 vols., 1885–8); the third volume contains an extensive Memoir of Green. Apart from an essay on 'The Theory of Education in Plato's *Republic*' (1880), Nettleship's writings were few but his teaching impressed many contemporaries and undergraduates. Died at the age of 46 whilst climbing Mont Blanc. See Bradley, A.C. and Benson, G.R., *Philosophical Lectures and Remains of Richard Lewis Nettleship* (2 vols., 1897).

Newbolt, Sir Henry John (1862–1938). Poet and man of letters. Born Bilston, Staffordshire, son of a vicar. Educated at Clifton and Corpus Christi College, Oxford, gaining first class in classical moderations, 1882 and second class in *literae humaniores*, 1885. Practised as barrister, 1887–99, then devoted himself to writing. His best known volume of poems is perhaps *Admirals All* (1897), but he also wrote the final two volumes of the official *History of the Great War: Naval Operations*. Newbolt served on many official bodies, among which was the Prime Minister's Committee on the Position of English in the Educational System of England, appointed in 1919. Many leading literary figures served on the Committee, including Sir Arthur Quiller-Couch, Caroline Spurgeon and **J. Dover Wilson**. Newbolt was its chairman, and the findings of the Committee, known as the Newbolt Report, were published in 1921. The Report was forward-looking, advocating the centrality of English in schools and the doctrine that 'every teacher is a teacher of English'. See his *My World as in my Time* (1932), and Newbolt, M. (ed.), *The Later Life and Letters of Sir Henry Newbolt* (1942).

Newcastle, Pelham-Clinton, Henry Pelham Fiennes, 5th Duke of Newcastle (1811–64). Politician. Born London, educated at Eton and Christ Church, Oxford where he graduated in 1832 and was created DCL in 1863. Represented South Nottinghamshire, 1832–46 and was a Lord of the Treasury in Peel's first government, 1834–5, First Commissioner of Woods and Forests, 1841–6, and briefly Chief Secretary to the Lord Lieutenant of Ireland, 1846. MP for Falkirk burghs, 1846–51, when he succeeded to the title (he had previously been styled as the Earl of Lincoln) and to a seat in the Lords. Secretary of State for the Colonies, 1852–4, Secretary of State, War, 1854–5, Colonial Secretary, 1859–64. In 1860 accompanied the Prince of Wales to the USA and Canada. Newcastle was much criticized for the conduct of the Crimean War. Between 1858 and 1861 he was chairman of the Royal Commission appointed to inquire into Elementary Education, generally known as the Newcastle Commission. The Report showed that despite the considerable quantity of elementary instruction (only 120,305 children were considered to be entirely without schooling) there were doubts about its quality. The Commissioners' major proposal, the establishment of county and borough education boards with the power to assist schools from the rates, was not implemented. See Martineau, H., *Biographical Sketches* (1876); Brown, C., *Notting-*

hamshire Worthies (1882); Munsell, F.D., *The Unfortunate Duke* (1986).

Newman, Sir George (1870–1948). Pioneer in public health. Born Leominster, son of editor of the *Friend*, the Quaker journal. Educated at Bootham School, York, King's College, London and Edinburgh University. MB, 1892, MD, 1895. Diploma in Public Health, Cambridge University, 1895. Lecturer in Public Health, St Bartholomew's Hospital, London and demonstrator of comparative pathology and bacteriology, King's College, London, 1895–7, County Medical Officer, Bedfordshire, 1897–1907 and from 1900, also for Finsbury, London, then one of the poorest parts in the metropolis. In 1906 his influential report *Infant Mortality* pioneered the much improved public health and child welfare services. When the Board of Education established a school medical service, largely at the promptings of **Robert Morant**, Newman was appointed as the first Chief Medical Officer. He thereafter vigorously pursued a scheme to provide for the medical inspection of school children, administered by local education authorities. Newman was an advocate of open-air schools for delicate children and of physical education to promote good health. He served for a number of years as chairman of trustees, Dartford Physical Training College. In 1919 Newman became Chief Medical Officer, Ministry of Health, where Morant was Permanent Secretary, though still retaining his post at the Board of Education; he retired in 1935. Responsible for the report on postgraduate medical education (1921) which led to the setting up of the Postgraduate Medical School, University of London, and was the prime mover in the campaign to establish the London School of Hygiene and Tropical Medicine. Besides his series of Annual Reports to the ministers of Education and Health, Newman wrote *The Building of a Nation's Health* (1939), as well as several monographs on medical pioneers. Knight, 1911, KCB, 1918, GBE, 1935.

Newman, John Henry (1801–90). Theologian. Born London, educated at a private school in Ealing run by Dr Nicholas, and entered Trinity College, Oxford in 1817, graduating in 1820. In 1822 was elected to a fellowship of Oriel College. Ordained, 1824, in 1825 became vice-principal of St Alban Hall, in 1826 a tutor of Oriel and in 1828 vicar of St Mary's. His sermons there and the *Tracts for the Times*, particularly Tract 90, written by Newman himself in 1841, marked a further stage in the development of the Oxford movement. In 1843 Newman resigned his living at St Mary's and in 1846 was ordained a priest in the Roman Catholic church and awarded the degree of DD. In 1847 he returned to England from Rome and set up the Oratory in Birmingham. From 1854–8 he was Rector of the new Catholic University in Dublin. There he wrote the *Idea of a University Education*. In 1859 he established in Birmingham a school for sons of the Catholics of the upper classes. In 1877 Newman was elected an honorary fellow of Trinity College, Oxford and in 1879 was created a Cardinal. See his many writings especially the *Apologia pro Vita Sua* (1864), and Mozley, A., *Letters and Correspondence of J.H. Newman* (2 vols., 1891); Ward, W., *The Life of Newman* (2 vols., 1912); Trevor, M., *Newman* (1962); Vargish, T., *Newman: the contemplation of mind* (1970); Lash, N., *Newman on development* (1976); Chadwick, O., *Newman* (1983).

Newsom, Sir John Hubert (1910–71). Educational administrator. Educated at Imperial Service College and Queen's College, Oxford. Various posts in social and community service. Lecturer in philosophy, King's College, London then first director, Community Service Association, 1931–8. Joined staff of the Board of Education, National Fitness Council, 1938–9. Assistant Education Officer, Hertfordshire County Council, 1939–40. Chief Education Officer, 1940–57. Together with C.H. Aslin, then County Architect, Newsom pioneered in Britain the systematic study of school needs and their translation into good modern design. Chairman, Central Advisory Council on the education of average and below average children which produced the interesting report *Half our Future* (1963). Deputy chairman, Central Advisory Council, Children and their Primary Schools (chairman, Lady Plowden), 1963–7, and chairman, Public Schools Commission, 1965–8. Knight, 1964. See his *Willingly to School* (1944); *The Education of Girls* (1948); *The Child at School* (1950), and Maclure, S., *Educational Development and School Building: Aspects of Public Policy 1945 to 1973* (1984).

Norris, John Pilkington (1823–91). School inspector. Born Chester, son of a physician. Educated Rugby under Arnold and Trinity College, Cambridge, classics tripos. BA, 1846, MA, 1849, BD, 1875 and DD, 1881. Fellow, Trinity College, 1848, ordained priest, 1850. Appointed HMI, 1849 at the early age of 26, serving with great conscientiousness in Staffordshire, Shropshire, Cheshire, Kent and Surrey. Resigned in 1864. Curate, Lewknor, Oxfordshire, 1864, canon of Bristol, 1864–91 and perpetual curate, Hatchford, Surrey, 1864–70. Norris became Inspector of Church training colleges, 1871–6, then vicar, St Mary Redcliffe, Bristol, 1877–82, archdeacon of Bristol, 1881–91 and Dean of Chichester, 1891. Author of many works on religion, including *A Catechism for Young Children* (1874), and published a *Report on the Iron and Coal Masters' Prize Scheme for the Encouragement of Education* (1854) and *The Education of the People* (1869).

Northcote, Sir Stafford Henry, 1st Earl of Iddesleigh (1818–87). Politician. Born London. Educated by the Revd Roberts at Mitcham and Brighton, and subsequently at Eton and Balliol College, Oxford. BA, 1839; MA, 1840; DCL, 1863. Called to the bar, 1840, but in 1842 became private secretary to **William Gladstone.** One of the secretaries to the Great Exhibition, 1850–1. Co-author of the Northcote–Trevelyan Report, 1853 which recommended admission to the Civil Service by examination. MP for Dudley, 1855–7; Stamford, 1858–66; North Devon, 1866–85. President of the Board of Trade, 1866–7; Secretary for India, 1867–8; Chancellor of the Exchequer, 1874–80; First Lord of the Treasury, 1885–6. Created earl in 1885; Foreign Secretary, 1886–7. Northcote served on the Public Schools' Commission (Clarendon) and the Endowed Schools' Commission (Taunton) in the 1860s. He was also prominent in the reformatory and industrial schools movement, and in 1855 established a reformatory school near his home at Pynes in Devon. Rector of Edinburgh University from 1883. See his *Lectures and Essays* (1887) edited by his wife, and Lang, A., *Life, Letters and Diaries of Stafford Northcote* (2 vols., 1890), Clark, E.A.G., 'Sir Stafford Northcote's "Omnibus": The Genesis of the Industrial Schools Act, 1857', *Journal of Educational Administration and History*, 14 (1), 1982.

Norton *see* **Adderley.**

Norwood, Sir Cyril (1875–1956). Educationist. Born at Whalley, Lancashire, son of a schoolteacher. Educated at Merchant Taylors' School, London and St John's College, Oxford, where he obtained first class in classical moderations, 1896 and *literae humaniores*, 1898. Entered the Admiralty, 1899, but two years later became master at Leeds Grammar School. Headmaster, Bristol Grammar School, 1906–16. Master, Marlborough College, 1916–26 and headmaster, Harrow School, 1926–34. President, St John's College,

THE
ENGLISH TRADITION
OF EDUCATION

BY

CYRIL NORWOOD, M.A., D.Lit.

HEADMASTER OF HARROW SCHOOL

LONDON
JOHN MURRAY, ALBEMARLE STREET, W.

Oxford, 1934–46. Knight, 1938. Norwood wrote a number of influential books including *The Higher Education of Boys in England* (1909) with A.H. Hope, *The English Tradition of Education* (1929) and *The Curriculum in Secondary Schools* (1936). Chairman, Secondary School Examinations Council, 1921–46. Best known as chairman of a committee of this Council on Curriculum and Examinations in Secondary Schools, 1941–3. The Norwood Report, the outcome of the Committee's deliberations, reflects Norwood's strong opinions on the nature of secondary schooling. Like the earlier Spens Report (1938), it supported the notion of a tripartite division of secondary education into grammar, technical and modern schools, each with its own type of curriculum corresponding to the 'needs' of pupils. The Report also recommended the replacement of the existing group examination, the School Certificate Examination, by a single subject examination. In 1951 the General Certificate of Education examination was established in place of the School Certificate. See Petch, J.A., *Fifty Years Examining* (1953).

Nuffield, Viscount *see* **Morris, William Richard.**

Nunn, Sir Thomas Percy (1870–1944). Educationist. Born Bristol, son of a proprietary school headmaster. The school, which was

transferred to Weston-super-Mare in 1873, provided Nunn's education and from the age of 16 he helped with the teaching there. He took over responsibility for running the school on his father's death in 1890. B.Sc., University of London, 1890 and BA, 1895. Resigned his post and taught at grammar schools in Halifax and London becoming mathematics and physics master, William Ellis School. In 1903, appointed to demonstrate methods of teaching science and mathematics at the newly-founded London Day Training College. A brilliant teacher, two years later he became Vice-Principal and in 1922 succeeded **Sir John Adams** as Principal; he retired from the post in

1936. From 1913, he was also professor of Education, University of London. As early as 1908, Nunn had advocated that teacher training in London should be recognized as of university rank: the institution should act as a clearing house of educational ideas and provide for the further education of practising teachers. Nunn's vision was realized in 1932 when the London Day Training College became the London University Institute of Education. His own interests were very wide; he was a philosopher, mathematician, scientist and a musician. Besides publishing a number of mathematical and scientific textbooks for schools before the First World War, Nunn kept abreast of the latest developments in science and mathematics and published *Relativity and Gravitation: An Elementary Treatise upon Einstein's Theory* in 1923. He is best remembered for his book *Education: Its Data and First Principles*, first published in 1920 with a third edition in 1935. Its central thesis was 'that nothing good enters into the human world except in and through the free activities of individual men and women and that educational practice must be shaped to accord with that truth'. Nunn's book was a powerful influence on those teachers wishing to introduce progressive methods in the primary school with its chapters on 'Play' and 'Freedom in Education'. See Tibble, J.W., 'Sir Percy Nunn', *British Journal of Educational Studies*, 10 (1), 1961.

Owen, Hugh (1804–81). Educationist. Born at Llangeinwen, Anglesey. Educated at the school in Caernarvon run by Evan Richardson, the famous Calvinistic Methodist minister. In 1825

went to London where after clerkships to a barrister and solicitor he entered the Civil Service. In 1853 he became chief clerk to the Poor Law Commission and subsequently to the Local Government Board. He retired in 1872. In 1839 Owen helped to fund a British school in Islington, and in 1843 he published a *Letter to the Welsh People*, on the need for day schools. In the same year he secured the appointment of an agent of the British and Foreign School Society to work in North Wales, and subsequently another for the South. In 1846 Owen became secretary of the Cambrian Educational Society. In the following year the Cambrian Association for the Education of the Deaf and Dumb was established. In 1856 he was one of the chief supporters of the normal college for teachers, opened at Bangor in 1858, and also promoted the women's college at Swansea. In 1879 he led the North Wales Scholarship Association Scheme to connect elementary and higher grade schools. His lasting memorial, however, is the University College of Wales at Aberystwyth. Owen first mooted the idea in 1854, became a secretary of the committee formed in 1863, was secretary of the college, 1871–7, and conducted a fund-raising campaign across Wales to ease the debts of the college which had opened in 1872. Took the initiative in establishing the Aberdare Committee, helped to reform the Eisteddfod, member of the London School Board from 1872 and was knighted for his services to Welsh education in 1881. See Davies, W.E., *Sir Hugh Owen* (1885), Davies, B.L., *Hugh Owen* (1977).

Owen, Owen (1850–1920). School inspector. Born Llaniestyn, Caernarvonshire and educated at Botwnnog Grammar School and Jesus College, Oxford, taking a degree in classics. Headmaster of private school in Oswestry, Shropshire, 1878, which developed into Oswestry High School, 1883, at which many future Welsh leading figures were educated. Whilst in Oswestry, Owen led a campaign for disestablishment and from 1890–3, was co-secretary of joint conferences for devising county schemes for establishing inter-mediate schools under the Welsh Intermediate Education Act (1889). A Central Welsh Board was set up in 1896 to administer the schools, and in the following year Owen was appointed the first Chief Inspector to the Board. He was an effective inspector, remaining in the post until his retirement in 1915.

Owen, Robert (1771–1858). Socialist. Born Newtown, Mont-gomeryshire. Attended a day school and read widely and acted as usher. Aged ten he was employed in a draper's shop in Stamford, and subsequently in London and Manchester. Manager of a cotton mill at the age of 19, in 1799 he married the daughter of David Dale, the owner of New Lanark mills in Scotland. In 1800 he settled there as manager and part owner. There he established schools for all children under the age of 12 and gave particular emphasis to the infant school. **James Buchanan**, its first teacher, exemplified Owen's ideals of kindness, activity and co-operation. In 1819 an infant school was established in Westminster to which Buchanan was transferred. New Lanark received many prominent visitors and Owen became famous. He travelled widely and in 1825–7 established the community of New Harmony in the USA. In England Owen turned to a variety of schemes – journals, congresses, and lectures – to promote his ideas of co-operation, secularism, socialism and spiritualism. His interest in education continued to the end. He attended the Educational Conference of 1857 and the National Association for the Promotion of Social Science conferences of 1857 and 1858. See his *A New View of Society* (1813–16); *Autobiography* (2 vols., 1857–8), and Podmore, F., *Robert Owen* (2 vols., 1906); Davies, A.T., *Robert Owen* (1948); Cole, G.D.H., *The Life of Robert Owen* (1925, repr. Cass 1965); Silver, H. (ed.), *Robert Owen on Education* (1969); Pollard, S. and Salt, J. (eds.), *Robert Owen, prophet of the poor* (1971).

Pakington, Sir John Somerset, 1st Baron Hampton (1799–1880). Politician. Born near Worcester. Educated at Eton and Oriel

College, Oxford where he matriculated but did not graduate. Conservative MP for Droitwich, 1837–74, when he was raised to the peerage. Colonial Secretary, 1852; First Lord of the Admiralty, 1858–9 and 1866–7, Secretary of State, War, 1867–8. First Civil Service Commissioner, 1875–80. In the 1850s and 1860s Pakington was the leading parliamentary champion of national education. He introduced education bills in 1855 and 1857, secured the representation of education in the Commons in 1856, was the father of the Newcastle Commission of 1858–61, and chairman of the Select Committee on Education, 1865–6. He played a role in the National Society and the Church Education Society, effected the union of the contending education parties in Manchester in 1856, and took an active part in educational movements in Worcestershire and Birmingham. Chairman of the Board of Visitors at Sandhurst and Woolwich and a governor of Wellington College. See his *National*

Education (1856), and Aldrich, R., *Sir John Pakington and National Education* (1979); Aldrich, R., 'Sir John Pakington and the Newcastle Commission', *History of Education*, 8 (1), 1979.

Palgrave, Francis Turner (1824–97). Author and civil servant. Born Great Yarmouth, son of Sir Francis Palgrave, historian and antiquary. Educated at Charterhouse, 1838–43 and Balliol College, Oxford, 1843, first class in classics, 1847. Assistant private secretary to **Gladstone**, then Secretary of State for War and the Colonies. He was appointed as Second Examiner in the Education Department in 1849, Vice-Principal, Kneller Hall Training College, 1850–5, Examiner, Education Department, 1855–71, Senior Examiner, 1871–3 and Assistant Secretary, 1873–84. Palgrave's work at the Department did not occupy the whole of his energies. He produced numerous books, the best known of which is *The Golden Treasury*, published in 1861 (a further volume appeared in 1896). He was art critic for the *Saturday Review*, wrote an autobiography, under a pseudonym, *The Passionate Pilgrim* (1858), *Essays on Art* (1866) and many anthologies of poems as well as children's stories. After his retirement from the Department he was professor of Poetry at Oxford, 1885–95, succeeding **Matthew Arnold**. See Palgrave, G.F., *Francis Turner Palgrave* (1899).

Pankhurst, Emmeline (1858–1928). Campaigner for women's rights. Born in Manchester, the eldest of ten children of a prosperous Manchester calico printer. Educated in Manchester and Paris. In 1879 Emmeline Goulden married Dr Richard Pankhurst, a barrister and radical reformer, who died in 1898. Together they worked for the causes of women's suffrage and property rights, and joined the Independent Labour Party in 1893. In 1903 together with her daughter Christabel, Pankhurst formed the Women's Social and Political Union. From 1908 more militant methods were adopted to secure the franchise, and Pankhurst endured imprisonment and hunger strikes. The campaign was suspended during the war years, 1914–18. In 1925 she returned to London after having lived for some time in Canada, and joined the Conservative party in the following year as prospective parliamentary candidate for Whitechapel. Pankhurst was an unsuccessful ILP candidate for the Manchester School Board in 1894 but was elected in 1900. She opposed the practice of higher salaries for male teachers, and deplored the abolition of school boards with the consequent loss of female representation. Pankhurst was, however, co-opted on to the new Manchester local education authority established under the 1902 Act, and was the only woman on its Technical Instruction Committee. See her autobiography *My Own Story* (1914), and Pankhurst, S., *The Life of Emmeline Pankhurst* (1935).

Paton, John Brown (1830–1911). Religionist and philanthropist. Born Galston, Ayrshire into a devout Congregationalist family. Educated Loudon parish school and from 1838 by his maternal uncle, a Congregational minister. Determined to be a minister himself, Paton attended Spring Hill College, Birmingham, later Mansfield College, 1847–54, graduating BA, 1849 and MA, 1854 in classics and philosophy. Minister, Wicker, Sheffield, 1854–63. Principal, Congregational Institute, Nottingham, 1863–98. DD, Glasgow University, 1882. Active in promoting educational enterprises, Paton was a strong supporter of the founding of University College, Nottingham in 1880. He was responsible for the creation of the National Home Reading Union (NHRU) in 1887. This was based on a pattern developed at Chautauqua in the USA where summer holiday courses of instruction had grown up into a national system of organized courses of home reading. The aim was to guide people to reading which appealed to the imagination or higher feelings. Those who held office in the Union included **A.H.D. Acland**, **Michael Sadler** and **John Percival**. Paton instituted the Recreative Evening School Association in 1893, the forerunner of the continuation school. See his *Secondary Education for the Industrial Classes of England* (1895), and Marchant, J., *J.B. Paton* (1909); Paton, J.L., *John Brown Paton* (1914).

Paton, John Lewis (1863–1946). Schoolteacher. Born Brightside, Sheffield, son of a Congregational minister. Educated Germany, Nottingham, Shrewsbury and St John's College, Cambridge, first class honours, classical tripos, and fellow, St John's, 1887. Joined the staff of The Leys School the same year, moving to Rugby in 1888; headmaster, University College School, London, 1898–1903, high master, Manchester Grammar School, 1903–24. An inspiring teacher, Paton enhanced the reputation of the schools with which he was associated. He organized classes for working-class men in Rugby and assisted in the activities of boys' clubs in London and Manchester. He was a firm believer in the values of a grammar school education. He also advocated the provision of places for children of all classes at these schools. After retirement, Paton became first president of the Memorial University College, now the

Memorial University, at St John's, Newfoundland, 1924–33. See his *English Public Schools* (1905), and Barnard, H.C., 'A Great Headmaster: John Lewis Paton', *British Journal of Educational Studies*, 11 (1), 1962.

Pattison, Mark (1813–84). Scholar and critic. Born Hornby, Yorkshire. Educated by his father, the rector of Haukswell, and at Oriel College, Oxford where he graduated BA in 1836, MA, 1840. Fellow of Lincoln College from 1839. Ordained deacon, 1841; priest, 1843. In 1843 appointed to a college tutorship. Became public examiner in 1848, 1853 and 1870, and in 1861 Rector of Lincoln College till his death. In 1878 he declined the Vice-Chancellorship of Oxford University, but acted as pro-Vice-Chancellor in 1861 and curator of the Bodleian Library in 1869. As a tutor, lecturer, author and scholar, Pattison exercised considerable influence. He paid several visits to German universities, in 1858 was for three months Berlin correspondent of *The Times*, and in 1859 was one of the Assistant Commissioners appointed under the Newcastle Commission to collect information upon continental education. Although his projected history of learning was never completed he published widely and collected the largest private library in Oxford, some 14,000 volumes. In 1868 Pattison read a paper on university reform to the National Association for the Promotion of Social Science in Birmingham, and in 1876 presided over the Education section in Liverpool. See his several writings including *Suggestions on Academical Organisation* (1868); *Memoirs* (ed. E.F. Pattison, 1885), and Tollemache, L.A., *Recollections of Pattison* (1885); Green, V.H.H., *Oxford Common Room. A Study of Lincoln College and Mark Pattison* (1957); Sparrow, J., *Mark Pattison and the Idea of a University* (1967).

Payne, Joseph (1808–76). Educationist. Born Bury St Edmunds, Suffolk. Elementary schooling only but whilst a boy earned a living by teaching and writing for the press. By 1828 was teaching in London. In 1830 wrote a pamphlet entitled *A compendious exposition of Professor Jacotot's celebrated system of education*. This brought him to public notice and he established the Denmark Hill Grammar School with some 70 boys. In 1831 he published *Universal Instruction*. His teaching was based on the theory of 'lessoning not lecturing'. In 1845 Payne moved to Leatherhead in Surrey where he established the Mansion House School for boys, which he continued successfully until 1863. In 1865 he gave evidence to the Taunton

Commission on teaching methods and curriculum. He also advocated the registration of teachers. In the 1860s Payne devoted himself to lecturing and writing. He was prominent in the Philological Society, and in the National Association for the Promotion of Social Science. He also became involved in the work of the College of Preceptors and urged it to undertake the training of secondary school teachers. In 1872 the College elected Payne to the position of professor of Education, the first professorship in the subject in England. Payne threw himself into the work of lecturing and promoting the college with great energy. He also advanced the cause of the education of women and was chairman of the central committee of the Women's Education Union. Payne toured educational establishments in Germany in 1874 and wrote an account of their work. His lifelong concerns were the improvement of teaching methods and the enhancement of the teacher's status. See Payne, J.F. (ed.), *The Works of Joseph Payne* (2 vols., 1883); Chapman, J.V., *Professional Roots* (1985).

Pearse, Patrick Henry (1879–1916). Educationist, poet and revolutionary. Born Dublin. Educated in a private school, at the Christian Brothers School in Westland Row and at the Royal University. BA and called to the Irish bar. Pearse was very interested in Irish language and culture. He was a member of the Gaelic League and editor of its journal. In 1908 he founded a bilingual school, St Enda's, to advance the idea of a free Gaelic Ireland. He also lectured in Irish at the Catholic University in Dublin and published stories and poetry in Irish and English. In Easter Week, 1916, Pearse was commander in chief of the republican forces and president of the provisional government. Court martialled, found guilty, and shot in Kilmainham jail. See his writings and Edwards, R.E., *Patrick Pearse: the triumph of failure* (1979); Buachalla, S. (ed.), *A significant Irish educationalist: the educational writings of P.H. Pearse* (1980).

Pease, Joseph Albert, first Baron Gainford (1860–1943). Politician and industrialist. Born Darlington, the younger son of Sir Joseph Whitwell Pease, MP for South Durham, and grandson of Joseph Pease, the first Quaker MP, who had held the same seat. Educated at Tottenham Grove House, a Quaker school, and at Trinity College, Cambridge. Began work in the family coal and iron business, becoming mayor of Darlington in 1889, and Liberal MP for the Tyneside division of Northumberland, 1892–1900. Subsequently represented Saffron Walden, 1901–10, and Rotherham, 1910–17. In that year he was raised to the peerage and thereafter supported the Liberal cause in the Lords. Pease became a junior lord of the Treasury in 1905 and in 1908 was promoted to Chief Whip and to the Privy Council. Chancellor of the Duchy of Lancaster, 1910–11, and President of the Board of Education, 1911–15. His period of office was notable for developments in teacher training, school medical services and for laying the foundations of the Department of Scientific and Industrial Research. Chairman of the British Broadcasting Company, 1922, president of the Federation of British Industries, 1927, and of the National Confederation of Employers' Organizations, 1932. See his *A National System of Education* (1913), and Sherington, G., *English Education, Social Change and War, 1911–20* (1981).

Pelham, Sir Edward Henry (1876–1949). Educational administrator. Son of Professor H.F. Pelham, President of Trinity College, Oxford. Educated at Harrow and Balliol College, Oxford, first class honours in mathematics and second class in modern history, 1899. Entered Board of Education, 1901. Private secretary to **Sir W.R. Anson**, Parliamentary Secretary, 1903–5, and to **Augustine Birrell**, President of the Board, 1906–7. Assistant Secretary, 1914–20. Principal Assistant Secretary, 1920–9, Deputy Secretary, 1929–31, Permanent Secretary, Board of Education, 1931–7. CB, 1921. Created knight, 1933.

Penrose, Dame Emily (1858–1942). Scholar and administrator. Born London, eldest daughter of Francis Cranmer Penrose, the archaeologist and architect. Educated at a private school in Wimbledon, in France, Germany and Greece, and at Somerville College, Oxford. First class in *literae humaniores*, 1892, the first woman to be so placed. Lectured at the British Museum and South Kensington museums, and became Principal of Bedford College, London in 1893, and its professor of Ancient History in the following year. Principal of Royal Holloway College, 1898–1907, and in 1900 both colleges were constituted as schools of the University of London. Principal of Somerville College, Oxford, 1907–26. In 1920 Oxford University admitted women to degrees and to full membership. Penrose was a distinguished teacher and academic, a painter, and a mountaineer, but she was best known for her skills in finance and administration. She served on the Senate of London University, 1900–7, on the Advisory Committee on University Grants,

1911–19, on the Royal Commissions on University Education in Wales, 1916, and on the Universities of Oxford and Cambridge, 1919, and was a University of Oxford Commissioner, 1923. OBE, 1918; DBE, 1927. Honorary degrees from Oxford and Sheffield. See Tuke, M.J., *A History of Bedford College for Women, 1849–1937* (1939).

Percival, John (1834–1918). Schoolmaster and bishop. Born Brough Sowerby, Westmorland. Educated at Appleby Grammar

School and Queen's College, Oxford. Double first class in classics and mathematics. Elected a fellow of his college. Master at Rugby School, 1860–2 and first headmaster of Clifton College, 1862–79. In a few years Clifton under his leadership became recognized as a premier public school. Like **Thomas Arnold**, whose views he largely shared, Percival used the chapel pulpit to communicate his scale of values to the whole school. Prebend of Exeter Cathedral, 1871–82, and canon of Bristol, 1882–7. In 1879 Percival left Clifton to become president of Trinity College, Oxford. There he espoused the causes of the higher education of women (he was a promoter and first president of the council of Somerville College) and of the University Extension movement. In 1887 Percival became headmaster of Rugby School but as always his energy and commitment placed a strain on his health. In 1895 he became Bishop of Hereford. Percival was a man of great seriousness, with a belief in righteousness and the need for new developments in education. He frequently pushed himself and others to the limits. He found Oxford too conservative and comfortable. Though he died there he was buried in Clifton chapel, the scene of his greatest influence. See his *Some helps for school life* (1880), and Oakley, E.M., *Bishop Percival* (1919); Temple, W., *Life of Bishop Percival* (1921).

Percy, Eustace Sutherland Campbell, Baron Percy of Newcastle (1887–1958). Politician. Born London, son of Earl Percy, later 7th

Duke of Northumberland. Educated Eton and Christ Church, Oxford, gaining first class honours in modern history, 1907. Entered diplomatic service, 1909: served at Washington Embassy, 1910–14, and resigned in 1919. Stood as unsuccessful Conservative candidate for Hull, 1919, but elected for Hastings, 1921 where he was MP until 1937. Rose rapidly to become President of the Board of Education, 1924–9, where his interests in raising the school leaving age and technical education became manifest. Minister without Portfolio, 1935 and resigned the following year in protest at Britain's failure to react to growing German militarism. Rector, King's College, Newcastle upon Tyne, 1937–52 and Vice-Chancellor by rotation. Chairman, 1944, of a Special Committee set up by the Minister of Education 'to consider the needs of higher technological education in England and Wales and the respective contributions made thereto by universities and technical colleges'. The recommendations published in the Percy Report the following year were far-reaching, and were important in casting the mould for post-war technical education. Chairman, Royal Commission on Mental Health, 1954–7. See his *Education at the Crossroads* (1930); *Democracy on Trial* (1931); *The Study of History* (1935) and an autobiography, *Some Memories* (1958).

Pillans, James (1778–1864). Scottish educational reformer. Born Edinburgh, son of a printer. Educated Edinburgh High School and Edinburgh University, MA, 1801. Acted as tutor in Ayrshire, Northumberland and at Eton. Elected Rector, Edinburgh High School, 1810, introducing the monitorial system into the classical schools of Scotland, and taught Greek and Latin. Professor, Humanity and Law, Edinburgh University, 1820, holding the post until 1863: advocated the elementary teaching of classics at the university, lecturing on 'universal grammar'. In his spare time Pillans visited many continental countries to learn about their educational systems; he frequently toured Scottish schools and held enlightened views on popular education. See his *Letters on the*

Principles of Elementary Teaching, etc. (1828); *Three Lectures on the Proper Objects and Methods of Instruction* (1836); *A Word for the Universities of Scotland* (1848); *The Rationale of Discipline* (1852); *Contributions to the Cause of Education* (1856), and *Educational Papers* (1862) as well as many works on classical authors.

Pipe, Hannah Elizabeth (1831–1906). Headmistress. Born Manchester. Educated there at an elementary school run by the Quaker, Charles Cumber, and at the Chorlton High School under **W.B. Hodgson**. In 1848 began taking in pupils herself. By 1852 she had established a large school for girls in Manchester near to Owens College. In 1856 Miss Pipe and her mother moved to London and established a boarding school for girls at Clapham Park. Most pupils came from wealthy Wesleyan families in the north of the country. The curriculum was broad and in addition to English, history, geography and religious knowledge (all taught by Pipe herself) there were lessons in foreign languages and sciences and considerable emphasis upon polite accomplishments. Pipe sought to encourage a cultured private household atmosphere and was wary of marks, examinations and prizes. In later years some of her girls proceeded to Newnham and Girton. She herself retired in 1890. See Stoddart, A.M., *Life and Letters of Hannah E. Pipe* (1908).

Pitman, Sir James (1901–85). Inventor of the Initial Teaching Alphabet. Born London and grandson of Sir Isaac Pitman who invented Pitman's shorthand. Educated Eton and Christ Church, Oxford, second class honours degree in modern history, 1922. He played rugby for Oxford against Cambridge, 1921 and for England against Scotland, 1922. Chairman, Sir Isaac Pitman and Sons Ltd., 1934–66. Director, Bank of England, 1941–3 and Director, Organisation and Methods at the Treasury, 1943–5. Conservative MP, Bolton, 1945–64. Vice-President, British and Foreign School Society, and prominent supporter of the National Union of Teachers. He was the inventor of the Initial Teaching Alphabet (ita), a simplified format to aid learning of reading which enjoyed a vogue particularly in primary schools, during the 1960s. Knight, 1961. See his *Alphabets and reading. The Initial Teaching Alphabet* (1969) with St John, J.

Place, Francis (1771–1854). Social reformer. Born London. Attended several schools in the Fleet Street area and was apprenticed aged 14 to a breeches maker. Read widely and in 1794 became secretary to his trade club and joined the London Corresponding Society. Chaired its committee, 1795. From 1799 he opened a tailor's shop in Charing Cross and made considerable profits. He became friendly with **Bentham, James Mill** and **Robert Owen**. Supported **Joseph Lancaster,** helped to organize the West London Lancasterian Association, and became a committee member of the British and Foreign School Society. Place established a library at his Charing Cross shop and carried on informal publishing. In 1824 he secured the repeal of the anti-combination laws, and worked for the passage of parliamentary reform in 1832. In 1838 he drafted the People's Charter. He wrote several pamphlets and 71 volumes of his manuscripts were deposited in the British Museum. See Wallas, G., *The Life of Francis Place* (1898); Rowe, D.J. (ed.), *London radicalism, 1830–1843. A selection from the papers of Francis Place* (1970); Thale, M. (ed.), *The Autobiography of Francis Place* (1972).

Playfair, Lyon, 1st Baron Playfair of St Andrews (1818–98). Politician and scientist. Born at Chunar, Bengal, son of chief inspector-

general of hospitals, Bengal. Educated at St Andrews Parish School and St Andrews University, 1832–5, studied medicine, Glasgow University, 1835–7 and then chemistry, graduating PhD at Geissen, where he worked with Liebig, in 1840. He carried out important investigations, such as on the gases of the blast furnace, in conjunction with Bunsen. Chemical manager of a calico works at Clitheroe, Lancashire, 1841. Professor, School of Mines, London 1845–53. When the Science and Art Department was formed in 1853, Playfair becme its first Secretary for Science and two years later, joint Secretary for the united Department with **Henry Cole**. Professor of Chemistry, Edinburgh University, 1858–69. Liberal MP, Edinburgh and St Andrews Universities, 1868–85, and Leeds South, 1885–92. Postmaster-General, 1873–4 and Chairman of Ways and Means and Deputy Speaker, House of Commons, 1880–3. In 1886, he was appointed

Vice-President of the Committee of Council on Education. Sat on a number of Commissions, including that for the Great Exhibition of 1851 and the Cattle Plague, 1863. Responsible for setting up the Select Committee on Scientific Instruction, 1868 and chairman of a Committee on the selection of civil servants, 1875. FRS, 1848, KCB, 1883, and created Baron, 1892. See his *Subjects of Social Welfare* (1889), and Reid, T.W., *Memoirs and Correspondence of Lyon Playfair* (1899) (reprinted, 1976).

Pounds, John (1766–1839). Teacher. Born Portsmouth. Apprenticed at the age of 12 to a shipwright, in 1781 he fell into a dry dock and was crippled for life. In 1803 he began work as a shoemaker, and in 1818 took charge of his five-year-old nephew. Other children came to his shop, numbering about 40 at a time, and he taught them without fee. The children were instructed in the 3Rs and in a range of other activities. Pounds' teaching and philanthropy were recognized after his death and he was hailed as the founder of ragged schools. See Harwood, P., *The Poor Shoe-mender* (1839); Hawkes, H., *Recollections of John Pounds* (1884); Jayne, R.E., *The Story of John Pounds* (1925).

Priestley, Joseph (1733–1804). Theologian and scientist. Born near Leeds. Educated at Batley Grammar School, by Dissenting ministers, and at Daventry Academy from 1751. In 1755 he became a Presbyterian minister at Needham Market in Suffolk. In 1758 he moved to Nantwich as minister and also gave private tuition. In 1761 he became tutor in languages and *belles lettres* at Warrington Academy. He met Franklin in London and published a *History of Electricity* (1767) and an *Essay on Government* (1768) which contained the phrase 'the greatest happiness of the greatest number'. LL.D, 1765 from the University of Edinburgh, and FRS, 1766. In 1767 became minister at Chapel Hill, Leeds, where he continued to study chemistry. From 1772 he was librarian to the 2nd Earl of Shelburne and supervisor of his sons' education. He received foreign honours, being elected to the French Academy of Sciences in 1772 and to the St Petersburg Academy in 1780. In England he was involved in much controversy in defence of Unitarianism, and through his reply to Burke's *Reflections*. His Birmingham house was ransacked by the mob in 1791. In 1794 he emigrated to America, but declined offers of a chemistry chair and the principalship of the University of Pennsylvania. He died at Northumberland, Pennsylvania. His writings were numerous and covered many fields but

Priestley is chiefly remembered as a chemist and as one of the discoverers of oxygen. See his *Works* (ed. Rutt, J.T., 26 vols., 1817–32) which includes his *Autobiographical Memoir* (2 vols.,1806–7), and various selections from his writings, for example those edited by Brown, I.V., (1962) and Passmore, J.A., (1965), and Gibbs, F.W., *Joseph Priestley* (1965).

Pullinger, Frank (1866–1920). School inspector. Educated Manchester Grammar School and Corpus Christi College, Oxford, gaining first class honours in natural science, 1887, and London University, B.Sc. Oxford University Extension lecturer, 1891–2. Education Secretary, Devon County Council, 1891–4. HMI, 1894–1904. Chief Inspector, Technological Branch, 1904–20. CB, 1912. Pullinger, keen to expand further and technical education in England, wrote a report in 1909 pointing out the deficiencies in provision due to the Board's failure to identify and define the aims of technical education. **Morant** and **Chambers** at the Board, working with Pullinger, produced as a result a Circular in 1911, announcing a revision in grant regulations for this sector. In junior technical schools, examinations in single subjects were to be replaced by a system of course work. Thus a balance between technical and literary studies would be achieved. Continuation schools were also to be established. See Sherington, G., *English Education, Social Change and War, 1911–20* (1981).

Quick, Robert Herbert (1831–91). Schoolmaster and writer. Born London 1831, son of a City merchant. Educated at Harrow and Trinity College, Cambridge, graduating in the mathematics tripos, 1854. Ordained, 1855, and after working in two London parishes spent two years in Germany. Returning to England in 1858, he was assistant master, Lancaster Grammar School, then Guildford Grammar School, Hurstpierpoint, Cranleigh, Harrow, and head of preparatory schools in Guildford and London. In 1881, Quick gave the first series of lectures on the history of education to students at the Teachers' Training Syndicate, established by the University of Cambridge two years previously. He was a strong advocate of training for secondary school teachers and of the establishment of university chairs in education. Vicar of Sedbergh, 1883–7. He is best remembered for his perspicacious and often amusing comments on many aspects of education which are contained in his book *Essays on Educational Reformers* (1868, 2nd edn., 1890), which was also published abroad. See also his *Some Thoughts Concerning Edu-*

cation (1880), and Storr, F. (ed.), *Life and Remains of the Revd R.H. Quick* (1899).

Raikes, Robert (1735–1811). Promoter of Sunday schools. Born at Gloucester, son of the printer, Robert Raikes, the founder of the *Gloucester Journal*. Educated at St Mary le Crypt School and at Gloucester Cathedral College School. At the age of 20 he succeeded with his mother to the paper's ownership on his father's death. Advocated humanitarian causes, including the alleviation of the condition of prisoners. His concern for vagrant children led him to take up the idea of Sunday schools. Critics declared that his main motive was to restore peace to the Sabbath rather than any particular concern for the well-being of the children themselves. In 1780, together with the Revd Thomas Stock, Raikes established a Sunday school, and in 1783 inserted an account of the work in the *Gloucester Journal*. This led to considerable correspondence and one of Raikes' replies to a Colonel Townley of Sheffield was published in the *Gentleman's Magazine* in 1784. Sunday schools spread rapidly and the Sunday School Union was established in 1803. Raikes attracted considerable attention – consulted by bishops and Nonconformists, granted an interview with Queen Charlotte in 1787 – and was accorded a centenary celebration at Gloucester in 1880. He did not invent Sunday schools but did popularize them. See Webster, G., *Memoir of Robert Raikes* (1873); Booth, F., *Robert Raikes of Gloucester* (1980).

Rathbone, Eleanor Florence (1872–1946). Social reformer. Born London, the ninth of ten children of William Rathbone, Liberal MP for Liverpool. Educated at Kensington High School and Somerville College, Oxford where she graduated in 1896 with second class honours. Social work in Liverpool was documented in *How the Casual Labourer Lives* (1909), and *The Conditions of Widows under the Poor Law in Liverpool* (1913). She became a campaigner for women's suffrage and for family allowances, advocated in her books *The Disinherited Family* (1924) and *The Case for Family Allowances* (1940), a reform achieved in 1945. Member of Liverpool city council from 1909, and independent MP for the Combined English Universities, 1929–46, the only woman to be elected to Parliament without party backing. She was a firm advocate of university representation, a supporter of women's rights in Britain and in India, and tireless in her efforts on behalf of war refugees. A Fellow of the Royal Statistical Society, honorary degrees were conferred on her by the universities of Durham (1930), Liverpool (1931) and Oxford (1938). See her writings and Stocks, M.D., *Eleanor Rathbone, a biography* (1949).

Rayleigh, Baron *see* **Strutt.**

Redcliffe-Maud, John Primatt Redcliffe, Baron Redcliffe-Maud (1906–82). Civil servant and academic. Educated at Eton and New College, Oxford, where he achieved firsts in moderations and greats, and at the University of Harvard where he studied politics. Research fellow of University College, Oxford from 1929 and fellow and dean, 1932–9. The first full-time university tutor in politics, and university lecturer in politics, 1938–9. Master of Birkbeck College, London, 1939–43. Maud had served as a city councillor in Oxford, 1930–6, and in 1941–4 became Deputy Secretary and later Second Secretary at the Ministry of Food. In 1944 he became Second Secretary at the Ministry of Reconstruction, in 1945 Secretary to the office of the Lord President of the Council, and between 1945 and 1952 Permanent Secretary to the Ministry of Education. The chief issues in this period were the raising of the school-leaving age, the implementation of secondary education for all and the training of large numbers of teachers. Permanent Secretary to the Ministry of Fuel and Power, 1952–8, High Commissioner and subsequently Ambassador to South Africa, 1958–63, and Master of University College, Oxford, 1963–76. Maud chaired the Royal Commission on Local Government, 1966–9, but its radical report was not implemented in full. He held honorary fellowships and doctorates from several universities. KCB, 1946; GCB, 1955; life peerage 1976. See his *Local Government in Modern England* (1932); *The Prospect for Education* (1946); *Support for the Arts* (1976); *Experiences of an Optimist* (1981).

Reddie, Cecil (1858–1932). Schoolmaster. Born Fulham, London. Educated at Godolphin School, at a day school at Birkenhead, and at Fettes College. Entered Edinburgh University in 1878, B.Sc., 1882, and for the next two years studied advanced chemistry at Göttingen where he was awarded a Ph.D. in 1884. Science master at Fettes, 1885–7, and at Clifton College, 1887–8. As a member of the Fellowship of the New Life he decided to found a new school, and in 1888 expressed his ideas in *Today* in a series of articles called 'Modern Mis-education'. In 1889 Reddie began his new school at Abbotsholme on a 133-acre site in Derbyshire. He remained as headmaster for 37 years. His New School Movement was an attempt to reform the education then provided in boys' public schools. At Abbotsholme boys were encouraged in co-operation rather than in competition, and organized games were limited to two afternoons a week. There was practical outdoor work on the estate. Education in sex, health and hygiene was provided. Artistic, musical and poetic talents were fostered. All boys were, however, given the opportunity to exercise leadership, for Reddie believed that he was educating a 'Directing Class'. Reddie's ideas as exemplified at Abbotsholme attracted much interest both in Britain and abroad. A bachelor and benevolent despot, however, he clung on for too long. In 1927 the school reached its nadir with only two boys on the roll and Reddie was forced to retire. See Reddie's writings, especially *John Bull: his Origin and Character* (1901), and Ward, B.M., *Reddie of Abbotsholme* (1934); Giesbers, J.H.G.I., *Cecil Reddie and Abbotsholme* (1970).

Reed, Sir Charles (1819–81). Chairman, London School Board. Son of philanthropist and independent minister, Andrew Reed.

Born Sonning, Berkshire and educated at Madras House, Hackney, Hackney Grammar School and Silcoates, near Wakefield. Apprentice, woollen manufacturers, Leeds, 1836 and partner of a firm of printers in London in 1842 and set up his own typefounding factory in City of London 19 years later. Reed's lifelong interest in education took many forms. Elected as member of the Common Council for Farringdon, 1855, he was an enthusiastic advocate of the development of the Guildhall Library, publishing a pamphlet that year entitled *Plea for a Free Public Library and Museum in the City of London*, and took a keen interest in the City of London School. Liberal MP, Hackney, 1868–74, playing a leading part in the debates on Forster's Education Bill, urging bible teaching without sectarian instruction. MP, St Ives, Cornwall, 1880–1. When the London School Board was established in 1870, Reed was elected in

November as representative for Hackney, and Vice-Chairman of the Board in the following month. In 1873, he succeeded Lord Lawrence as Chairman, remaining in that post until his death in 1881. FSA, 1849, Knight, 1874. See Reed, C.E.B., *Memoir of Sir Charles Reed* (1883).

Reichel, Sir Harry Rudolf (1856–1931). Academic and educationist. Born Belfast, son of a professor of Latin, Queen's College, Belfast. Educated at Christ's Hospital, London, 1866–72 and Balliol College, Oxford, obtaining first class in classical moderations, 1876, mathematical moderations, 1877, *literae humaniores*, 1879 and modern history, 1880. Fellow of All Souls, 1880–94 and Jesus College. First principal, University College of North Wales at Bangor, 1884–1927. Influenced by **John Viriamu Jones**, who had been appointed to the newly-formed University College of South Wales in the previous year. Reichel worked with him to achieve a national University of Wales. Vice-Chancellor, 1896–7 and on four subsequent occasions. A man of wide interests, he encouraged the establishment of a music department at the college and was closely associated with the International Training School for Teachers in Sloyd woodwork at Naas, Norway, from 1896. Member, Moseley Education Commission to USA, 1903 and of the Consultative Committee of the Board of Education from 1907. Chairman, Royal Commission on University Education in New Zealand, 1925. Knight, 1907. See Lloyd, Sir J.E. (ed.), *Sir Harry Reichel* (1934).

Reith, John Charles Walsham, 1st Baron Reith of Stonehaven (1889–1971). Pioneer of broadcasting. Born Stonehaven, fifth son of a minister of the Free Church of Scotland. Educated Glasgow Academy, Gresham's School, Holt and Royal Technical College, Glasgow, 1906–8. Served engineering apprenticeship, Glasgow, 1908–13, moving to a London firm in the latter year. Severely wounded in France as major in the Royal Engineers, 1915. In charge of contracts for munitions for Great Britain, 1916–17 and then to Department of Civil-Engineer-in-Chief, Admiralty, 1918. General manager of a factory of William Beardmore at Coatbridge, 1920. Appointed first general manager of the British Broadcasting Company, 1922, Reith quickly realized the importance of broadcasting as a national public service, independent of government. Reith aimed at the highest standards of presentation with particular emphasis on cultural, religious and educational programmes. The extensive broadcasting service for schools and other institutions developed as a result. The annual Reith Lectures, given by distinguished individuals, were established by the BBC in 1947. First Director-General, British Broadcasting Corporation, 1927–38. Chairman, Imperial Airways, 1938–9, first chairman, British Overseas Airways Corporation, 1939–40. National MP, Southampton, 1940. Minister of Information, 1940, Minister of Transport, 1940, first Minister of Works, 1940–2. Director of Combined Operations, Material Department, Admiralty, 1943–5. Knight, 1927. Created Baron, 1940. See his *Into the Wind* (1949); *Wearing Spurs* (1946), and Boyle, A., *Only the Wind Will Listen. Reith of the BBC* (1972); Stuart, C. (ed.), *The Reith Diaries* (1975).

Rennie, Belle (1875?–1966). Pioneer of progressive education. Rennie was a member and later secretary of the New Ideals in Education group which held a conference at East Runton in Norfolk in 1914. Inspired by the educational ideas and practice of Montessori, Rennie and her friends founded Gypsy Hill Training College to train teachers for nursery and infant schools. The college continued as an independent institution under Miss Rennie's leadership until 1946 when it was taken over by the Surrey County Council, though Rennie remained on the governing body. Her other great interest was the Dalton Plan. She visited Dalton High School, Massachusetts where Helen Parkhurst's plan of work assignments was in operation. Rennie became secretary of the Dalton Association, and popularized the idea in England from 1920 so that by 1926 it was claimed that over 2,000 schools in Britain were using it. By the 1930s, however, the novelty had worn off and its principles were being absorbed into normal classroom practice. See Kimmins, C.W., and Rennie, Belle, *The Triumph of the Dalton Plan* (1932).

Richard, Henry (1812–1888). Politician and peace campaigner. Born in Cardiganshire. Educated at Llangeitho grammar school, and in 1826 apprenticed for three years to a draper in Carmarthen. Studied at Highbury College, 1830–4 and in 1835 was ordained as pastor of Marlborough Congregational Chapel in the Old Kent Road, London. Left the ministry in 1850. From 1848 to 1885, Richard was secretary to the International Peace Society and played an important role in peace conferences. In 1856 he was instrumental in securing the inclusion of an arbitration clause in the Treaty of Paris. Settlement of international disputes by arbitration was his particular remedy and he was known as 'The Apostle of Peace'.

Richardson

From 1868 until his death he was Liberal MP for Merthyr and earned the title of 'The member for Wales'. In 1843, Richard was a founder member of the Congregational Board of Education. In 1844, he toured South Wales to encourage fund raising for schools. He was also instrumental in establishing a normal college at Brecon in 1846 which moved to Swansea in 1853. Richard was a firm champion of the voluntary principle and opposed **Forster's** 1870 bill on the grounds that religious education should not be supported out of public funds. Was a member of the Aberdare Committee, 1880–1, which investigated intermediate and higher education in Wales, and of the Cross Commission, 1886. Supported the foundation of University College, Cardiff and became its first vice-president in 1883. See Miall, C.S., *Henry Richard MP* (1889); George, M.V., 'Henry Richard and Welsh Education', *Education for Development*, 10 (1), 1985.

Richardson, Marion (1892–1946). Teacher of art. Born into a large family, her skill at drawing was soon apparent, and from the age of

16 Richardson studied at the Birmingham School of Arts and Crafts. Art mistress at the Dudley High School for Girls, 1913–30. She encouraged her pupils to paint representations of mental images. The accurate drawing required for School Certificate examinations was enlivened by the use of imaginative lighting, and the grouping of objects. This approach was encouraged by Margaret Bulley and Roger Fry, and exhibitions of her pupils' work were held in London and Manchester. From 1918 she also taught handicraft and embroidery classes in the Birmingham Prison, and in 1926 Richardson visited schools and prisons in Russia. In 1924 she was appointed part-time lecturer in art at the London Day Training College, but her influence was greatest during the years 1930–42 when she was District Art Inspector for the London County Council. Programmes of lectures, courses and practical classes were arranged, and 1,500 teachers applied for the 150 places on the first three

courses. In 1934 she toured Canada, and the exhibition of children's work held in County Hall in London in 1938 was visited by 26,000 people. See her series on *Writing and Writing Patterns* (1935); *Art and the Child* (1946), and Tomlinson, R.R., *Children as Artists* (1947); Macdonald, S., *The History and Philosophy of Art Education* (1970).

Rigg, Revd Arthur (1812–80). Pioneer of technical education. Born Carlisle, moving at the age of eight to the Isle of Man, where he was privately educated. His interest in mathematics and science started from this time. Graduated from Cambridge University, 1835 as 27th wrangler, and immediately ordained. Senior Mathematical and Philosophical master, Royal Institution, Liverpool, 1835–9, during which time he was also curate at two Liverpool churches. Principal, Chester Diocesan Teachers' Training College, 1839–69. Rigg was one of the earliest advocates of technical training for pupils, to be pursued along with the traditional subjects of the curriculum. He built, attached to the Training College, a model school to serve as a Practising and Demonstration School, and a Commercial and Agricultural School, which later became the Science School. By 1854, the 'Industrial, Trade and Scientific School' was offering courses for part-timers over the age of 13 and employers of labour and their families. In 1860 students were being prepared for the Indian Civil Service, as well as university science scholarships. Opposition from the Diocesan Board and others who questioned Rigg's unorthodox approaches to education, which stemmed from the views of Fellenberg and Pestalozzi, coupled with the waning popularity of the College, led ultimately to Rigg's resignation in 1869. For the remainder of his life, he devoted himself to the dissemination of technical knowledge by lectures and writing textbooks. See *The Harmony of the Bible with Experimental Physical Sciences* (1869); *An Easy Introduction to Chemistry* (1873); with Hooker, W., *A Practical Treatise on the Steam Engine* (1878), and Astbury, S., *A History of Chester Diocesan Training College* (1946); Foden, F.E., 'The Rev Arthur Rigg: Pioneer of Workshop Practice', *Vocational Aspects of Secondary and Further Education*, (11) 23, 1959; Layton, D., *Science for the People* (1973); Bradbury, J.L., *Chester College and the Training of Teachers 1839–1975* (1975).

Rigg, James Harrison (1821–1909). Wesleyan minister and educationist. Born Newcastle upon Tyne, son of a Methodist minister. Educated at Kingswood School, near Bristol, 1830–5, and junior teacher there, 1835–9. Taught in Leeds, London and Biggleswade, Bedfordshire, 1839–45. Entered Methodist ministry, 1845, ordained, 1849. Widely read and prolific author on theological matters especially critical of the Broad Church teachings of **F.D. Maurice**, **Kingsley** and **Jowett**. Principal, Westminster Training College, a Wesleyan foundation, 1868, holding the post until 1903. After the 1870 Education Act, Rigg strongly opposed secularism, corresponding with **Gladstone** and **W.E. Forster** on the topic, though he later modified this view. Member, London School Board, Westminster, 1871–6. Promoted a syllabus for religious instruction with the assistance of two other members, **T.H. Huxley** and W.H. Smith. Member, Royal Commission on Elementary Education (Cross Commission), 1886–8, where he pronounced in favour of school board management rather than the voluntary system. See his *National Education in its Social Conditions and Aspects* (1873); *Wesleyan Reminiscences Sixty Years Ago* (1904), and Telford, J., *Life of J.H. Rigg* (1909).

Robbins, Lionel Charles, Baron (1898–1984). Economist. Born Sipson, Middlesex, son of a farmer. Educated Southall County Grammar School, University College, London and London School of Economics, 1920–3, gaining a first class honours degree. Here, his teachers included Hugh Dalton and **Graham Wallas**. Lecturer, New College, Oxford, 1924, lecturer, London School of Economics, 1925–7, fellow and lecturer, New College, Oxford, 1927–9, and at the age of 30, professor of Economics, London School of Economics, 1929, retiring in 1961. Director, economic section of the War Cabinet, 1941–5. Chairman, *Financial Times*, 1961–70. Played leading part in developing the social sciences in the University of London, as well as making many distinguished contributions to economics in his writings. Chairman, Prime Minister's Committee on Higher Education, 1961–3. The Robbins Report, published in 1963, assumed as an axiom that courses in this sector 'should be available for all those who are qualified by ability and attainment to pursue them and wished to do so'. The creation of a number of new universities and the establishment of Colleges of Advanced Technology followed. FBA, 1942, CB, 1944. Companion of Honour, 1968. Baron (life peer), 1959. See his *Autobiography of an Economist* (1971) and *Higher Education Revisited* (1980).

Robinson, Canon Hugh George (1819–82). Cleric and educationist. Born Stratford-upon-Avon. Educated King Williams College, Isle of Man and Clare College, Cambridge, BA, 1842. Barrister, Middle

Temple, 1846. Ordained priest, 1847 and curate in Cheshire, Lancashire and Yorkshire, 1848–52. Principal, York and Ripon Diocesan Training College, 1854–64. Rector, Bolton Abbey, Yorkshire, 1864–74. The Liberal government appointed an Endowed Schools Commission in 1869 to investigate schools and reform their charitable endowments. The **4th Baron Lyttelton** was the Chief Commissioner, **Henry Roby** was the Secretary and **Arthur Hobhouse** and Canon Robinson were the other two Commissioners. Robinson, a near neighbour and friend of **W.E. Forster**, carried out the work with great thoroughness, but unlike his colleagues, opposed the sweeping treatment of endowments. When the Commission was dismantled by Disraeli in 1874, Robinson was the only one who was asked to continue as a Charity Commissioner, 1874–82. See his *The first book of the Excursion by William Wordsworth* (1862) and *Man in the Image of God and other Sermons* (1876).

Robson, Edward Robert (1835–1917). School board architect. Born Durham and educated in private schools. Pupil of John Dobson, Newcastle upon Tyne and later, Giles Gilbert Scott. Built New Gallery, Regent Street, the People's Palace, museums, churches. He was employed for six years as architect in charge of Durham Cathedral, and as surveyor to Liverpool Corporation for seven years. FRIBA. Worked as surveyor then as chief architect to the London School Board, 1871–84. Robson was a pioneer of elementary school architecture planning large buildings which contained specialist facilities. He advocated the provision of more separate classrooms than had hitherto been the case: 'experience has shown that the separation or isolation of classes in separate rooms has an important bearing on results.' He also introduced the Queen Anne style into school architecture in place of the previously-favoured Gothic. Left the London School Board, accused of negligence, but in 1890, became an important architectural consultant to the Education Department. See his *School Architecture* (1874, reprinted 1972), and Seaborne, M., and Lowe, R., *The English School, Its Architecture and Organization, 1870–1970* (1977).

Roby, Henry John (1830–1915). Educational reformer and classical scholar. Born Tamworth, Staffordshire, son of a solicitor. Educated at Bridgnorth School and St John's College, Cambridge. Senior classic, 1853, fellow, St John's College, 1854, lecturer 1855–61, when he relinquished this post on marriage. Played a leading part in attempts to reform the use of college endowments. Founder and first secretary of the Cambridge Local Examinations. Second master, Dulwich College, 1861–5 and author of *An Elementary Latin Grammar* (1862). In 1864, Roby was appointed Secretary, Schools Inquiry Commission, a Royal Commission, chaired by **Lord Taunton,** to inquire into all the endowed schools of England and Wales except the nine 'public' schools investigated by the Clarendon Commission. Roby also occupied the chair of Jurisprudence at University College, London, 1866–8, but decided to devote himself henceforth to the reform of the endowed schools. When the Endowed Schools Commission was set up in 1869, Roby was its first secretary and a member, 1872–4 when the Conservative government brought the Commission to an end. Entered business as partner in a firm of sewing-cotton manufacturing for the next 20 years. Liberal MP, Eccles, Lancashire, 1890–5. See his *Roman Private Law* (1902) and *Grammar of the Latin Language from Plautus to Suetonius* (1871–4, 7th edn. 1904).

Rooper, Thomas Godolphin (1847–1903). School inspector. Born Abbots Ripton, Huntingdonshire. Educated Harrow, 1862–6 and Balliol College, Oxford, gaining second class in both classical moderations, 1868, and *literae humaniores*, 1870. At Oxford, Rooper came under the influence of **T.H. Green,** whose philosophical beliefs later permeated his own writings. Private tutor to the future 11th Duke of Bedford, 1871–7. He was appointed HMI in 1877, serving until his death in 1903 in Northumberland, Bradford, Southampton, and the Isle of Wight. Rooper's devotion to the advancement of elementary education was reflected in his wide range of interests: these included efforts to improve the teaching of geography in schools and methods of instruction in infant classes. He strongly supported manual training and extolled the virtues of school gardens for rural schools. Rooper involved himself with the Parents' National Education Union, established by his friend **Charlotte Mason,** and gave much time to the promotion of the Hartley University College, Southampton. His most important publication was *School and Home Life* (1896). For a brief biography, see Tatton, R.G. (ed.), *Selected Writings of Thomas Godolphin Rooper* (1907); Leinster-Mackay, D., 'T.G. Rooper: a Case of Early Promise?' in *Cross-Pollinators of English Education: Case Studies of Three Victorian School Inspectors* (1986).

Roscoe, Sir Henry Enfield (1833–1915). Chemist and educator. Born London. Educated at the High School of the Liverpool Institute and University College, London, where he graduated in chemistry. From 1852 worked in Heidelberg, where he obtained his doctorate in 1854 with Bunsen on the measurement of the chemical action of light. In 1857 on returning to England Roscoe was elected to the chair of Chemistry at Owens College, Manchester. His work in this post advanced the ideal of a centre of scientific education at the heart of a great industrial area. Roscoe was a founder and first president of the Society of Chemical Industry, 1880. He was president of the Chemical Society, 1881–3, and of the British Association at Manchester in 1887. He served on the Royal Commission on Technical Instruction, 1881–4 which led to the Technical Instruction Act of 1889. He played a significant part in the development of the new universities both in Manchester and in London, whose Vice-Chancellor he became in 1896. He was knighted in 1884, elected Liberal MP for Manchester South in 1885, and became a privy councillor in 1909. Roscoe's greatest contribution to chemistry was the preparation of pure vanadium, but he also advanced the cause of science in education and in social reform, particularly in such areas as working conditions, sewage disposal, hygiene and health. See his various scientific writings ranging from *Lessons in Elementary Chemistry* (1866) to *A New View of the Origin of Dalton's Atomic Theory* (1896); *The Life and Experiences of Sir Henry Enfield Roscoe written by himself* (1906), and Thorpe, T.E., *The Right Honourable Sir H.E. Roscoe* (1916).

Ruskin, John (1819–1900). Author and critic. Born London. Educated at home by his parents and at Christ Church, Oxford. His mother took lodgings nearby and his father came at weekends. Winner of the Newdigate Prize for Poetry. BA, 1842; MA, 1843; DCL, 1893; LL.D Cambridge, 1867. Ruskin achieved recognition with the first volume of *Modern Painters* (1843) which championed the work of J.M.W. Turner. *The Seven Lamps of Architecture* (1848) and *The Stones of Venice* (1851–3) established him as the greatest critic of his time, and as a moral guide who exposed the ugliness and squalor of industrial Britain. Honorary fellow of Corpus Christi College from 1871 and the first Slade Professor of Fine Art at the University of Oxford, 1869–79, 1883–4. Ruskin lectured on art at the Working Men's College in London, 1854–8, and in the years 1855–70 lectured throughout the country on art, politics, science, history, to learned societies, working men's clubs and institutes, as well as at Eton, Woolwich and the Royal Institution. He spent much of the fortune inherited from his father in social experiments and gifts to colleges and schools. He instituted the May Queen festival at Whitelands College, 1882. The John Ruskin School was opened in 1899, as was Ruskin Hall which subsequently became Ruskin College, Oxford. He wrote over one hundred works, many of which, especially *Fors Clavigera* (1871–84) and *Praeterita* (1886–8), contain autobiographical sections. See Collingwood, W.G., *The Life of John Ruskin* (1900); Evans, J., *John Ruskin* (1954); Quennell, P., *John Ruskin* (1956); Abse, J., *John Ruskin: the passionate moralist* (1980); Landow, G.P., *Ruskin* (1985).

Russell, Bertrand Arthur William, 3rd Earl Russell (1872–1970). Philosopher, reformer and educationist. Born Trelleck, Monmouthshire, son of Viscount Amberley. Orphaned at the age of two, Russell remained in the care of his grandmother, widow of the first Earl Russell, until the age of 18 and received his education from governesses and tutors at Pembroke Lodge in Richmond Park. Entered Trinity College, Cambridge, 1890, became a member of the Apostles. 7th Wrangler, mathematics tripos, 1893 and first class honours, moral science tripos, 1894. Elected fellow, Trinity College, 1895. Russell's publications in mathematics and philosophy were numerous, including *Principia Mathematica* with **A.N. Whitehead** (1910–13), *Introduction to Mathematical Philosophy* (1919) and a *History of Western Philosophy* (1945). However, he became increasingly known as a writer on social and political issues, such as *The Practice and Theory of Bolshevism* (1920, republished 1949), *Religion and Science* (1935) and *Common Sense and Nuclear Warfare* (1959). Russell's academic career was damaged when his lectureship at Trinity was withdrawn in 1915. This followed from Russell's authorship of a leaflet written for the No-Conscription Fellowship and resulted in a fine. He was subsequently imprisoned in 1918. Although he was reinstated by his college after the war, he resigned in 1920. A marriage to his second wife, **Dora**, followed the next year. She shared many of his radical views and in 1927, they established Beacon Hill School at Telegraph House, near Petersfield, Hampshire. A progressive school which attracted individualistic teachers and pupils, it carried into practice Russell's view that children should not be obliged to follow a strictly academic curriculum. Together with Dora, he wrote *The Prospects of Indus-*

trial Civilization (1923) and later he published *On Education* (1926) and *Education and the Social Order* (1932). Although Dora and Russell were divorced in 1935, the school continued until after the outbreak of the Second World War. See his own *Autobiography* (3 vols., 1967, 1968 and 1969) and Wood, A., *Bertrand Russell – The Passionate Sceptic* (1957); Clark, R.W., *The Life of Bertrand Russell* (1975).

Russell, Dora (1894–1986). Feminist. Born London, daughter of a senior civil servant. Educated at private school, Sutton High School and Girton College, Cambridge, gaining first class honours in modern languages, 1914. Fellow of Girton, 1918. She met **Bertrand Russell** the following year, touring China with him and marrying in 1921. Together they opened a boarding school at Telegraph House on the West Sussex Downs at Beacon Hill in 1927. It was run on the principle that freedom, if understood early enough, would result in a natural evolution to maturity and self-discipline. Democracy, too, could only spring from practising it early. Although one of the earlier progressive schools, it was not as permissive as that of, for example, **A.S. Neill**'s Summerhill. The Russells continued with the school until their divorce in 1935. Thereafter Dora continued with the venture alone until 1943. Besides her writings with her husband, she wrote *The Right to be Happy* (1927), which suggested that the source of human happiness lay with human beings themselves, and in *In Defence of Children* (1932) she argued that children's rights should be respected. Her first book, *Hypatia or Women and Knowledge* (1925), arguing for sexual freedom for women, was heavily attacked. See her autobiography *The Tamarisk Tree* (3 vols., 1975, 1980 and 1985).

Russell, Lord John, 1st Earl Russell (1792–1878). Statesman. Born London. Educated at a private school at Sunbury, Westminster School, and by tutors at Woburn Abbey and Sandwich. Studied at Edinburgh University, 1809–12. Entered Parliament in 1813 as MP for Tavistock, and subsequently sat for Huntingdonshire, South Devon, Stroud and the City of London. Russell was a champion of parliamentary reform, and the repeal of the Test and Corporation Acts, 1828, and the Reform Act of 1832 brought him to the front of Whig politics. Home Secretary,1835–9; Colonial Secretary, 1839–41; Prime Minister, 1846–52; Foreign Secretary, 1852–5 and 1859–65; Prime Minister, 1865–6. Created Earl Russell and KG in 1862. He was a strong supporter of national education. In 1839 he was

responsible for the establishment of the Committee of the Privy Council on Education and for the inauguration of government inspection of schools. His government of 1846 instituted the pupil-teacher system. Subsequently in the Commons and in the Lords he introduced further proposals for the diffusion of popular education. He was president of the British and Foreign School Society, and, with other Scottish-educated politicians like **Brougham**, prominent in the Society for the Diffusion of Useful Knowledge, and the new University of London. In later years he returned to his writings which were chiefly historical, for example his *Life and Times of Fox* (3 vols., 1859–67). He was president of the Royal Historical Society, 1872, and Rector of Aberdeen University, 1863–78. See his *Speeches and Despatches* (1870); *Recollections and Suggestions* (1875) and Reid, S.J., *Lord John Russell* (1906); Tilby, A.W., *Lord John Russell* (1930); Prest, J.M., *Lord John Russell* (1972); Alexander, J.L., 'Lord John Russell and the Origins of the Committee of Council on Education', *The Historical Journal*, 20 (2), 1977.

Russell, John Scott (1808–82). Engineer and advocate of scientific and technical education. Born at Parkhead near Glasgow. His early education was gained from his father, a parish school teacher turned minister. Entered Glasgow University at the age of 13 and graduated MA in 1825. Taught mathematics at a new university preparatory school in Edinburgh. Taught at the Leith Mechanics' Institution from 1829 and from 1830 lectured on mathematics and natural philosophy to medical students. In 1832 temporarily occupied the chair of Natural Philosophy at Edinburgh. Russell was a keen engineer and designed a steam-driven road carriage and four iron ships. Presented annual papers to the British Association, 1834–44. In 1837 was awarded the gold medal of the Royal Society of Edinburgh and became a Fellow and member of its Council. In 1838 narrowly failed to become professor of Mathematics at Edinburgh University. In 1844 moved to London as editor of *The Railway*

Chronicle. In 1847–9 helped to organize exhibitions for the Royal Society of Arts and was one of the Commissioners for the Great Exhibition of 1851. A founder member of the Institute of Mechanical Engineers and the Institute of Naval Architects, his major treatise *The Fleet of the Future: Iron or Wood?* was published in 1861. In *Systematic Technical Education for the English People* (1869) he advocated a Minister for Public Instruction, a central technical university in London, 15 technical colleges in industrial centres and 1000 trade schools, with teachers supplied through a technical teacher training scheme. Russell was a product of the Scottish enlightenment, a teacher, a man of ideas, an inventor, an engineer, and an ardent advocate of technical education. He was less successful as a businessman, as a self-appointed peacemaker between France and Prussia in 1870, and in his scheme for a New Social Alliance between enlightened peers and leaders of working men. See Emmerson, G.S., *John Scott Russell, A Great Victorian Engineer and Naval Architect* (1977).

Russell, Sir Lionel (1903–83). Educational administrator. Born Bristol. Educated at Clifton College and Christ's College, Cambridge, 1922–5, first class in mathematics. Lecturer, University of Lund, Sweden, 1925–31. Taught English at Charterhouse, 1932–5. Assistant Director of Education, Liverpool, 1935–8. Assistant Education Officer, Birmingham, 1938–46 and Director, 1946–68. Member, University Grants Committee, 1954–63 and the Council for National Academic Awards, 1967–70. President, Association of Chief Education Officers, 1955–7. Knight, 1962. A sound, practical administrator, and a private adviser to Education ministers. Chairman, Committee of Inquiry appointed in 1969 to review the provision of non-vocational adult education in England and Wales. Its report, issued in 1973 and entitled *Adult Education: A Plan for Development*, recommended an expansion of the service, with central government funds to assist local authority financing of adult education. The recommendations were not implemented by the then Secretary of State for Education and Science, Margaret Thatcher.

Ryder, Dudley Francis Stuart, 3rd Earl of Harrowby (1831–1900). Politician. Heir of Dudley Ryder, 2nd Earl, and styled during his lifetime as Viscount Sandon. Educated at Harrow and Christ Church, Oxford, 1849–53. BA, 1853. Elected MP, Lichfield, 1856–9, as a supporter of Palmerston and private secretary to **Henry**

Labouchere (later Lord Taunton) at the Colonial Office, 1856–8. Became a Conservative, MP for Liverpool, 1868–82, in which latter year he succeeded to the earldom. Member of the first London School Board and Chairman of its Statistical Committee. In March 1874, he became Vice-President of the Committee of Council on Education, a post he held for some four years. Sandon welcomed **Forster**'s Education Act of 1870 though as a churchman, favoured making more use of voluntary rather than school board accommodation. The 1876 Elementary Education Act, which provided for extending compulsory attendance – children under the age of ten were forbidden to enter full-time employment – was his greatest achievement in office. President, Board of Trade, 1878–80, with a seat in the Cabinet. Member of the Cross Commission on Elementary Education, 1886–8. President, British and Foreign Bible Society, 1888 and Chairman, Staffordshire County Council, in the same year. See Gordon, P., 'Lord Sandon and the Centenary of Compulsory Education', *History of Education Society Bulletin*, 18, Autumn 1976.

Sadler, Sir Michael Ernest (1861–1943). Educationist. Born Barnsley, Yorkshire, son of a doctor. Educated Rugby and Trinity College, Oxford, gaining first class honours in classical moderations and in *literae humaniores*, 1884. A great nephew of M.T. Sadler, the factory reformer, Sadler was drawn towards political and economic radicalism which found an outlet in 1885, when he succeeded his friend, **A.H.D. Acland** as Secretary of the Oxford University Extension Lectures Committee. During the next ten years, he delivered lectures throughout the country to working-class adult audiences and provided courses of lectures and lecturers, as well as libraries and summer school meetings. Sadler provided the model in Extension work which was emulated by other universities. He was also Steward, Christ Church, Oxford, during the same period, 1885–95. He was instrumental in the convening of a Conference on Secondary Education at Oxford in 1893 which led to the setting up of the Bryce Commission on Secondary Education in the following year. As Director, Office of Special Inquiries, 1895–1903, Sadler established a research body which produced a series of valuable volumes on all aspects of education in different parts of the world. His assistant, **R.L. Morant**, was later responsible, as Permanent Secretary to the Board of Education, for Sadler's resignation from the Office. Part-time professor of Education, Manchester University, 1903–11, during which time he was commissioned to investigate the secondary education needs of nine local education authorities. His interest in continuing education was expressed in a volume which he edited entitled *Continuation Schools in England and Elsewhere* (1907). See also *Moral Instruction and Training in Schools* (2 vols., 1908) and *Syllabus of a Course on the History of Education 1800–1911* (1911). Vice-Chancellor, Leeds University, 1911–23 and Master, University College, Oxford, 1923–34. Chairman, Commission for the University of Calcutta, 1917. Knight, 1919. See Sadleir, M., *Michael Ernest Sadler* (1949); Grier, L., *Achievement in Education. The Work of Michael Ernest Sadler* (1952).

Samuelson, Sir Bernhard (1820–95). Promoter of technical education. Born Hamburg, son of a merchant. Educated private school at Hull, East Yorkshire. From the age of 14, gained wide experience in industrial fields, eventually establishing a railway works at Tours and a reaping-machine factory at Orleans. His main achievement was the building of an ironworks at Middlesbrough, Yorkshire, in 1870, then the largest and most up-to-date plant of its kind. Liberal MP, Banbury, 1859, 1865–85, North Oxfordshire, 1885–95, FRS, 1881, Baronet, 1884. Samuelson was a strong advocate of technical instruction. Chairman, Select Committee on the provision of instruction in theoretical and applied science to the industrial classes, 1868. Member, Royal Commission on Scientific Instruction, 1870–5. Best known as Chairman, Royal Commission on Technical Instruction, 1881–4. The Samuelson Report, which drew comparisons between technical instruction given to the working classes in England and in other countries, outlined a programme for the development of technical education at all levels and recommended that local authorities be given power to set up secondary and technical schools. Member, Royal Commission on Elementary Education, 1886–8. See Betts, R.S., 'The Samuelson Commission of 1881–1884 and English Technical Education', *History of Education Society Bulletin*, 34, 1984.

Sanderson, Frederick William (1857–1922). Headmaster. Born Brancepeth, County Durham. Educated at the local village school and became a pupil teacher in the next village of Tudhoe. Theological student at the University of Durham and gained a first class BA in mathematics and physical science in 1877. Fellow of Durham from 1881. Open mathematical scholarship to Christ's College, Cambridge, eleventh wrangler in 1882. Lecturer at Girton College, 1882–5. In 1885 Sanderson was appointed to Dulwich College to

217

introduce physics and develop the subject of chemistry. In addition to fulfilling these duties he created an engineering side with applied science taught by means of actual machines and workshops. In 1892 Sanderson became headmaster of Oundle School in Northampton-shire, a fifteenth-century foundation which had only 92 boys. Sanderson believed in co-operative learning whereby each boy or group of boys was responsible for a particular part of an overall project. This method was applied to many subjects but particularly to the scientific and engineering studies which Sanderson intro-duced. Laboratories and workshops were established and the boys designed, built and tested engines and other machines. During the First World War the school workshops were used for munitions production. Sanderson's work ensured the future of Oundle; by 1920 there were 500 boys in the school. See his writings, for example *Science and Educational Reconstruction* (1918); *A Duty and Service of Schools* (1921), and Anon, *Sanderson of Oundle* (1923); Wells, H.G., *The Story of a Great Schoolmaster . . . Sanderson of Oundle* (1924); Palmer, R.J., 'The influence of F.W. Sanderson on the development of science and engineering at Dulwich College 1885–1892', *History of Education*, 6 (2), 1977; Palmer, R.J., 'The Origins, Development and Influence of the Religious Views of F.W. Sander-son, Headmaster of Oundle School 1892–1922' in McClelland, V.A. (ed.), *The Churches and Education* (1984).

Sandford, Francis Richard John, 1st Baron Sandford (1824–93). Administrator. Born Glasgow. Educated at Glasgow High School, the Grange School, Sunderland, the University of Glasgow and Balliol College, Oxford. BA, 1846; MA, 1858. In 1848 he entered the Education Office and apart from two short intervals, in 1862 as organizing secretary to the International Exhibition, and 1868–70 as Assistant Under-Secretary in the Colonial Office, remained there until 1884. From 1870, as Secretary, he was permanent head of the office in the crucial period which followed the Elementary Edu-cation Act of that year. He combined this post with that of secretary to the Committee of Council on Education in Scotland from 1873, and secretary to the Science and Art Department from 1874. In 1884 he became a Charity Commissioner, and in 1885 Under-Secretary for Scotland. He was a member of the Committee of Council on Education in Scotland from 1885 to 1892 and of the Cross Commission, 1886–8. Knighted in 1862; CB, 1871; KCB, 1879; PC, 1885; created a baron in 1891. See Armytage, W.H.G., 'F.R.J. Sandford', *Bulletin of the John Rylands Library*, 31, 1948; Bishop,

A.S., *The Rise of a Central Authority for English Education* (1971); Sutherland, G., *Policy-making in Elementary Education 1870–1895* (1973); Roper, H., *Administering the Elementary Education Acts, 1870–1885* (1976).

Sandon, see **Ryder**.

Schofield, Herbert (1882–1963). Principal of Loughborough College. Born Halifax and educated there at Holy Trinity Higher Grade School. At 14 entered his father's small engineering firm as an apprentice. Attended evening classes at Halifax Municipal Technical College, and subsequently studied at the Royal (later Imperial) College of Science in London where he obtained a B.Sc. in physics and worked as a demonstrator. From 1912 held the post of assistant director of further education at Dover and also taught physics at the Dover County School. In 1915 moved to Loughborough as principal of the Technical Institute. Developed pioneering work in the training of munitions workers. After the war the Institute developed into Loughborough College, a leading school of engineering training. In 1923 Schofield was awarded a Ph.D. by London University for his direction of research into internal combustion engines. By 1925 the college had also established a considerable reputation in athletics and in 1930 a teacher training department was added. Schofield was awarded the CBE in 1947 and retired in 1950. Two years later the college was split into four separate institutions and in 1966 Loughborough University of Technology was established. Schofield was an autocrat, but a man of vision who developed the concept of 'training on production'. See Harvey, J.M., *Herbert Schofield and Loughborough College* (1976); Cantor, L.M., and Matthews, G.F., *Loughborough: from College to University* (1977).

Schonell, Sir Fred Joyce (1900–69). Educationist. Born Perth, Western Australia. Educated at Perth Modern School and at the University of Western Australia. Studied at King's College, London and at the Institute of Education, London. Lecturer at Goldsmiths' College, 1931–42. Professor of Education at University College, Swansea from 1942, and at the University of Birmingham from 1946 where he was also head of the department of education. In 1950 Schonell returned to Australia as professor of Education and dean of the faculty, 1950–9 at the University of Queensland, whose Vice-Chancellor he became in 1960. Schonell's diagnostic work was done in the schools of London and Kent, and he had a profound influence on primary school methods. In particular he transformed the approaches to children with learning difficulties. His books, *Backwardness in Basic Subjects* (1942), *The Psychology and Teaching of Reading* (1945), and journals (he founded and edited the *Educational Review* at Birmingham and *The Slow Learning Child* in Queensland) spread these ideas throughout the Commonwealth. His *Happy Venture* reading books, *Essential Spelling Lists* and arithmetic books sold millions of copies. He was knighted in 1962.

Scott, Robert Pickett (1856–1931). Teacher and school inspector. Born London. Educated Central Foundation School, London, Christ's College, Cambridge, 1875–6, King's College, Cambridge, 1876–80. Members' prize (English essay), 1877. Assistant master, Central Foundation School, London, 1881–2, Vice-Principal, Hull and East Riding College, Yorkshire, 1881–4. Headmaster, George Green's School, Poplar, London, 1884–7 and headmaster, Parmiter's School, Victoria Park, London, 1887–1904. MA and LL.M, 1883, LL.D, 1889. Honorary secretary, Incorporated Association of Head Masters, 1890–1902, Chairman, Teachers' Registration Council, 1903–4. One of the three Staff Inspectors, Board of Education, appointed to the newly-formed Secondary Branch in 1904, serving until 1911. Assistant Secretary, Board of Education, Secondary Branch, 1911–20. Member, Consultative Committee, Board of Education, 1920–5. See his *What is Secondary Education?* (1899).

Selby-Bigge, Sir Lewis Amherst (1860–1951). Civil servant. Born Beckenham. Educated at Winchester and Christ Church, Oxford. Fellow and lecturer in philosophy, University College, Oxford, 1883. Barrister, Inner Temple, 1891. Assistant Charity Commissioner, 1894–1903. Senior Examiner and Acting Assistant Secretary, Board of Education, Whitehall, 1903–7, Principal Assistant Secretary, 1908–11, Permanent Secretary, 1911–25, succeeding **R.L. Morant**. He was one of the leading architects of the 1918 Education Act, which encouraged initiatives by local education authorities. Selby-Bigge also helped to establish the Burnham Committee in 1919, which provided machinery for negotiating teachers' salaries. Member, Departmental Committee and Statutory Commission for London University, 1927–8. Member, Committee on Growth of Education in India, 1928. See his *Hume's*

Treatise (1888), *British Moralists* (1897), *Hume's Enquiries* (1907) and *The Board of Education* (1927).

Shaftesbury, Anthony Ashley Cooper, 7th Earl of Shaftesbury (1801–85). Philanthropist. Born London. Educated at Harrow and Christ Church, Oxford. First class in classics, 1822; MA, 1832, DCL, 1841. MP for Woodstock, 1826–30; Dorchester, 1830–1; Dorset 1831–46; Bath, 1847–51. Styled Lord Ashley until 1851 when he succeeded to the title. He championed the causes of slaves, lunatics, factory workers, chimney sweeps, coal miners and others. This brought him into contact with the child victims of industrial society and spurred him to introduce a series of parliamentary bills to end these evils. His concern for working-class health and housing led Shaftesbury to become chairman of the Central Board of Health, 1848, to chair the sanitary commission on the Crimea, to lay the foundation stone of the Shaftesbury Park estate in Battersea, and build a model village on his own Dorset estate. Shaftesbury was strongly evangelical. He was president of the British and Foreign Bible Society, and a supporter of the London City Mission, the Church Missionary Society and the Young Men's Christian Association. He was chairman of the Ragged School union for nearly 40 years. See Hodder, E., *Life and Work of the Seventh Earl of Shaftesbury* (3 vols., 1886); Hammond, J.L. and B., *Lord Shaftesbury* (1923); Battiscombe, B., *Shaftesbury* (1974); Finlayson, G.B.A.M., *The Seventh Earl of Shaftesbury* (1981); Pollock, J., *Shaftesbury: The Poor Man's Earl* (1985).

Sharp, Sir Percival (1867–1953). Educational administrator. Educated at a public elementary school at Bishop Auckland, County Durham, and Homerton Training College. Taught in elementary schools and at the Hull School of Science, and served as an inspector at St Helens, Lancashire. Director of Education at St Helens, 1905–19, and at Sheffield, 1919–32. Secretary of the Association of Education Committees, 1925–44. Member of the Burnham Committee on Teachers' Salaries from its inception in 1919 until 1949. He also served on the Norwood Committee. He was knighted in 1938. Sharp contributed to the concept and status of the local education authority and of its chief officer, and was a shrewd and able administrator.

Sharpe, Thomas Wetherhed (1829–1905). School inspector. Son of vicar of Doncaster, educated Rossall and Trinity College, Cambridge, 12th wrangler and double first class, classical and mathematics tripos, 1852. Fellow and lecturer, Christ's College, Cambridge, 1852–7. Ordained priest, 1854. Assistant Inspector of Schools, 1857–62, HMI, 1862–76, Chief Inspector, 1876–90. From 1890–7, he was the first Senior Chief Inspector of Schools. Principal, Queen's College, Harley Street, London, 1898–1903. County alderman, Surrey. CB, 1894.

Shaw, George Bernard (1856–1950). Playwright. Born Dublin, son of a corn miller. Educated by a governess, by his uncle Revd William Carroll, and at the Wesley Connexional School, Dublin. In 1871 became a clerk in an estate agency. In 1876 moved to London and lived there with his mother and elder sister. Five novels were written, 1878–83, but he was more successful as a book reviewer for the *Pall Mall Gazette* and music critic for the *Star*. He joined the Fabian Society in 1884, became an effective writer and speaker in the socialist cause, and in 1889 edited *Fabian Essays in Socialism*. In the 1890s Shaw turned to the writing of plays although he met with little success until *The Devil's Disciple* was performed in 1897 in New York. Shaw served on the St Pancras Council in London, 1897–1903 and in 1904 published *The Common Sense of Municipal Trading*. In 1913 he was one of the founders of the *New Statesman*. His social doctrines, however, were now being expressed in a series of highly successful plays. *Pygmalion* was produced in 1914, *Back to Methuselah* in 1922 and *St Joan* in 1924. Some of Shaw's earlier works, for example *Mrs. Warren's Profession* (1893) and *Arms and the Man* (1894), now received their due recognition. By this time he was the world's most famous playwright, and was awarded the Nobel prize for literature in 1925. In his will Shaw left bequests to the British Museum, the Royal Academy of Dramatic Art, the National Gallery of Ireland and to establish a scheme for a British alphabet of at least forty letters. Shaw was a man who sought to provoke thought about a whole range of political, social, religious and cultural issues. This he did successfully for some 50 years. See his several writings collected in 35 volumes especially *The Intelligent Woman's Guide to Socialism and Capitalism* (1928); *The Black Girl in Search of God* (1932); *Everybody's Political What's What?* (1944), and Henderson, A., *Bernard Shaw: Playboy and Prophet* (1911); Rattray, R.F., *Bernard Shaw, a Chronicle* (1951); Ervine, St John, *Bernard Shaw, His Life, Work and Friends* (1956); Laurence, D.H., *Bernard Shaw: a bibliography* (2 vols., 1983).

Shirreff, Emily Anne Eliza (1814–97). Educationist. Second daughter of a Rear-Admiral and sister of **Maria Grey**. Educated at home and for a short period at a boarding school in Paris, she accompanied her father on his several postings. In 1834 she returned to England. In 1850 she published in conjunction with her sister *Thoughts on Self Culture, addressed to Women*, and in 1858 her first independent work, *Intellectual Education, and its Influence on the Character and Happiness of Women*. Shirreff became fully involved in the campaign for the education of women and girls. She was a member of the council of Girton College and for two terms in 1870 acted as principal of the establishment at Hitchin. In 1871 she helped Maria Grey to found the National Union for Improving the Education of Women of all Classes. Shirreff held the post of honorary secretary and was also joint editor of its journal until its cessation in 1883. She was a member of the council of the Girls' Public Day School Company, 1872–96 and vice-president, 1896–7. The Teachers' Training and Registration Society and the Maria Grey Training College were other particular interests. Shirreff's name, however, came to be particularly connected with the Froebelian movement. In 1875 she became president of the Froebel Society which she had helped to found in the previous year, and held that office until her death. She emphasized the importance of the proper training of Kindergarten teachers and advanced the cause in numerous speeches and publications. See for example her *The Kindergarten* (1876); *Friedrich Froebel* (1877); *The Kindergarten at Home* (1884), and Grey, M., *Memorials of Emily A.E. Shirreff, with a Sketch of her Life* (1897); Ellsworth, E.W., *Liberators of the Female Mind* (1979).

Sidgwick, Eleanor Mildred (1845–1936). Educationist. Born at Whittingehame, East Lothian, eldest surviving child of James and Blanche Balfour and sister of **Arthur Balfour** the future prime minister. Educated at home by her mother, she showed considerable interest in mathematics and science and collaborated with her brother-in-law **Lord Rayleigh** in some of her research. In 1876 she married **Henry Sidgwick**, lecturer and subsequently professor of Moral and Political Philosophy at Trinity College, Cambridge. He died in 1900 and there were no children. In 1880 Eleanor Sidgwick became sole treasurer of Newnham College, Cambridge, a post she held until 1919. She was vice-principal, 1880–2, and principal, 1892–1910. She contributed greatly to the development of the college and personally donated more than £30,000 to its

223

funds. In 1894 Sidgwick was one of three women appointed to serve on the Bryce Commission on Secondary Education, the first woman to serve on a royal commission. She was awarded honorary degrees by the universities of Manchester, Birmingham, St Andrews and Edinburgh. She was also a founder member of the Society for Psychical Research, established in 1882 by her husband, its president in 1908 and its 'president of honour' in 1932. See Sidgwick, E., *Mrs Henry Sidgwick* (1938).

Sidgwick, Henry (1838–1900). Philosopher. Born Skipton, Yorkshire, son of headmaster of Skipton Grammar School. Educated Blackheath, 1849–52, Rugby, 1852–5 and Trinity College, Cambridge, where he proved to be a brilliant classicist. Scholar, 1857 and fellow of his College, 1859. Decided to devote himself to philosophy, under the influence of **J.S. Mill**'s writings. Lecturer, moral philosophy from 1869, with the ambition of establishing a school of philosophy at Cambridge. Prominent in campaign for abolition of religious tests, giving up his fellowship in 1869. Praelector, Trinity College, Cambridge, 1875–83, and Knightsbridge Professor, 1883–1900. Actively involved in promotion of women's education, providing a house for students at Cambridge in 1869, with **Anne Jemima Clough** as superintendent from 1871. This led to the opening of Newnham Hall five years later. He married **A.J. Balfour**'s sister, **Eleanor**, the same year and she in turn became vice-principal of the College and later principal. In 1881, Sidgwick campaigned, with success, for the admission of women to university examinations, but resigned from the University Council in protest at their refusal to grant degrees to women. Author of many books, including *The Methods of Ethics* (1874, 6th edn., 1901) and *The Principles of Political Economy* (1883, 3rd edn., 1901). See also Sidgwick, A., and Sidgwick, E.M., *Henry Sidgwick, A Memoir* (1906).

Simon, (Dorothy) Shena, Lady Simon of Wythenshawe (1883–1972). Educationist and philanthropist. Born Croydon, Surrey. Educated privately, at Newnham College, Cambridge and the London School of Economics. In 1912 Shena Potter married Ernest Simon, later Lord Simon of Wythenshawe. Their partnership has been compared with that of the **Webbs**. Ernest's interests were particularly in business and politics, Shena's centred upon education. Lady Mayoress of Manchester, 1921. They made gifts to the city including Wythenshawe Hall and its 250 acres of parkland. She served on the Wythenshawe planning committee from 1926, chairman, 1931–3. Member of the Manchester City Council, 1924–33. Elected chairman of the Manchester Education Committee in 1932, and served as a co-opted member, 1934–70. Shena Simon resisted cuts in education wherever possible. Member of the Board of Education Consultative Committee, a member of the Spens Committee in 1938, of the Council of the University of Manchester, and prominent in the work of the Workers' Educational Association. In 1936 the Simons visited Russia and Shena, whilst regretting the underlying uniformity of the educational philosophy, admired the equality of educational opportunity it afforded. She was an early advocate of comprehensive secondary schooling in Britain. In 1960 her Manchester house Broomcroft and its beautiful grounds were bequeathed to the University. Freeman of Manchester from 1964 for her services to the city and to education, honorary fellow of the London School of Economics, 1965. See her *A Century of City Government* (1938); *The Four Freedoms in Secondary Education* (1944); *The Education Act, 1944, Provisions and Possibilities* (1945); *Three Schools or One* (1948), and Stocks, M., *Ernest Simon of Manchester* (1963); Tylecote, M., *The Work of Lady Simon of Wythenshawe for Education in Manchester* (1974).

Simpson, James (1781–1853). Author and advocate. Born Edinburgh. Called to the bar in 1801. Visited Waterloo immediately after the battle in 1815 and wrote a famous account of it. In 1823 with **George Combe** he helped to found the *Phrenological Journal* for which he wrote regularly until its demise in 1847. He was a founder of the Edinburgh modern infant school, and lectured on non-sectarian education in many towns in England and Scotland. In 1837 he appeared as a witness before the House of Commons Select Committee on Education. His testimony lasted seven days. Simpson's essay on raising the status of teachers was published in the *Educator* (1839), a collection of essays written for a prize offered by the Central Society of Education. See his several writings including *Necessity of Popular Education as a National Object* (1834); *The Philosophy of Education* (1836); *Lectures to the Working Classes* (1844), and Ely, R., *In Search of the Central Society of Education* (1982).

Simpson, James H. (1888–1959). Teacher. Born Rugby. Educated at Rugby School, Pembroke College, Cambridge where he studied classics and history, and at the Cambridge University Day Training

College. Taught at Charterhouse, Clifton, Gresham's School, Holt, and Rugby. Served as a junior inspector for the Board of Education from 1911. After war service in the Brigade of Guards, in 1919 was appointed head of Rendcomb in Gloucestershire, a school opened in 1920 as the brainchild of F. Noel Hamilton Wills (of the tobacco family). Rendcomb admitted boys both from elementary schools and fee-paying preparatory schools. Simpson had been influenced by **Edmond Holmes**, and by **Homer Lane**, founder of the Little Commonwealth. He was a member of the New Ideals in Education group and thus at Rendcomb grafted ideas from progressive educational philosophy, including a form of pupil self-government, on to the English public school tradition. In 1932 Simpson left Rendcomb to become principal of the teacher training college of St Mark and St John. Served on the Consultative Committee of the Board of Education, 1933–9, and also acted as chairman of the governing bodies of several London schools and as dean of the College of Preceptors. See his *An Adventure in Education* (1917); *Sane Schooling* (1936); *Schoolmaster's Harvest* (1954), and Osborne, C.H.C., James, J.C., and James, K.L., *A History of Rendcomb College* (1976).

Smiles, Samuel (1812–1904). Author and educator. Born Haddington, Scotland, son of a paper-maker. Educated Haddington Grammar School, followed by an apprenticeship to medical practitioners, 1826–9 and studied at Edinburgh University for a doctor's diploma, 1829–32. Published *Physical Education: or the Nurture and Management of Children* (1837). Editor, the *Leeds Times*, 1838–42. A supporter of the Liberal cause, Smiles was the first secretary of the Leeds Household Suffrage Association. Assistant secretary, Leeds to Thirsk railway project, 1845–54 and secretary, South Eastern railway in London, 1854–66. Smiles was able during this time to combine his activities of popular lecturing, authorship and expounding his views on ways of elevating the working classes and for bringing about social progress. A series of biographies, such as those of *George Stephenson* (1857) and *Boulton and Watt* (1868) illustrated how success could be achieved by individual effort. The series was very popular and was republished in 1874 in five volumes under the title *Lives of the Great Engineers*. His greatest success, however, was *Self-Help, with Illustrations of Character and Conduct* which appeared in 1859. Sales rose from 20,000 in the first year to 150,000 by 1889, and it was translated into many languages. Smiles continued to write biographies, though these were overshadowed by *Self-Help*. See Mackay, T. (ed.), *Autobiography of Samuel Smiles* (1905).

Smith, Arthur Lionel (1850–1924). Historian and supporter of adult education movement. Born London, son of civil engineer. Educated Christ's Hospital and Balliol College, Oxford, 1869. First class in classical moderations and *literae humaniores* and second class in modern history, 1874. Fellow and lecturer, Trinity College, Oxford, 1874–9. Lecturer and tutor in modern history, Balliol, 1879–1916. Smith was responsible, along with a few colleagues, for advancing the reputation of history as a subject at Oxford. Fellow, 1882–1916, Master of Balliol, 1916–24. Smith had been befriended by **T.H. Green** and **R.L. Nettleship** as an undergraduate and had absorbed their high ideals. He was one of the seven representatives of the University who formed a joint committee with the Workers' Educational Association (WEA) and produced the report, *Oxford and Working-Class Education* (1908). It recommended the setting up of a joint committee in Oxford, with equal numbers of WEA and Delegacy members, to organize tutorial classes: the report was accepted by Congregation the same year. Smith subsequently was closely identified with the movement for higher education of the working classes, especially the WEA summer schools held at Balliol from 1910. Chairman, Adult Education Reconstruction Committee established by the Ministry of Reconstruction, 1917–19. See Smith, M.P., *A.L. Smith, Master of Balliol: A Biography and some reminiscences by his wife* (1928).

Smith, Sir Hubert Llewellyn (1864–1945). Civil servant. Born Bristol, son of a grocer; both parents were Quakers. Educated Bristol Grammar School and Corpus Christi College, Oxford, gaining first class honours in mathematics, 1886. One of the founders there of a Social Science Club, which questioned orthodox economics, collected facts and disseminated members' views on social issues. Lecturer, Oxford Extension Delegacy, 1887–8 and Toynbee Trust, living for a number of years at Toynbee Hall in East London. Supported Ben Tillett in the dockers' strike, 1889. Secretary, National Association for the Promotion of Technical Education, 1889–93 and member Royal Commission on Secondary Education (Bryce Commission), 1894–5. A brilliant administrator, Smith occupied the posts of First Commissioner of Labour, Board of Trade, 1893–1903, Controller-General, Commercial, Labour and Statistical Department, 1903–7, Permanent Secretary, Board of Trade, 1907–19 and chief economic adviser to the government, 1919–27. See Acland, A.H.D., and Smith, H.L. (eds.), *Studies in Secondary Education* (1892), and Sutherland, G. (ed.), *Studies in the Growth of Nineteenth-Century Government* (1972).

Smith, Sir Swire (1842–1918). Promoter of technical education. Born Keighley, Yorkshire. Educated privately at Wesley College, Sheffield. Apprenticed to learn techniques of worsted manufacture and later owner of two mills. Became interested in technical education after hearing a lecture on the subject by **Samuel Smiles**. Began drawing class for apprentices in Keighley and a Mechanics' Institute and Trade School was established, of which he was secretary. Member, Royal Commission on Technical Instruction, 1881–4. Expressed the view that universities should promote technical education. Chairman, Keighley School Board and from 1889, member, West Riding Technical Instruction Committee. A free trade Radical, Smith was Liberal MP, Keighley, 1915–18. Knight, 1898. See his *Educational Comparisons, or remarks on industrial schools in England, Germany and Switzerland* (1873), and Argles, M., 'The Royal Commission on Technical Instruction, 1881–4', *Vocational Aspects of Secondary and Further Education* (9) 23, 1959.

Sneyd-Kynnersley, Edmund Mackenzie (1841–1933). School inspector. Born Bordesley Park, Worcestershire, son of a barrister. Educated Rugby and Balliol College, Oxford, 1860–4, gaining second class honours in classical moderations and in *literae humaniores*. Fereday fellow, St John's College, Oxford, 1865–79. Barrister, Inner Temple, 1869. Offered and accepted post of Inspector of Returns under the Elementary Education Act 1870 in May 1871, working in North Wales until 1874. Appointed HMI, second class, 1874, through his father who 'knew two of the Ministry, one of whom was in the Cabinet'. Served in Norfolk, 1874–7, Chester, 1877 (promoted to full HMI) and North Wales, to 1903, and Divisional Inspector, north-west division, 1903–6. For his lively autobiography, see *HMI. Some Passages in the Life of one of HM Inspectors of Schools* (1908) and a further volume *HMI's Notebook or Recreations of an Inspector of Schools* (1930).

Snow, Charles Percy, Baron Snow (1905–80). Writer. Educated at Alderman Newton's Grammar School, Leicester, at Leicester University College, and at Christ's College, Cambridge. First class

H.M.I.

SOME PASSAGES IN THE LIFE OF ONE
OF H.M. INSPECTORS OF SCHOOLS

BY

E. M. SNEYD-KYNNERSLEY

FORMERLY H.M.I. NORTH-WEST DIVISION

MACMILLAN AND CO., LIMITED
ST. MARTIN'S STREET, LONDON
1908

London external degree in chemistry, and a masters degree in physics. Research student at Christ's College where his particular interest was infra-red spectroscopy. Fellow of Christ's, 1930–50. His first novel, *The Search* (1934) was concerned with the strains and disappointments of scientific research. In 1939 Snow was a member of a group established by the Royal Society to report on the efficient deployment of the nation's scientific resources. This was absorbed into the Ministry of Labour whose Director of Personnel Snow became in 1942. Civil Service Commissioner with special responsibility for scientific recruitment, 1945–60. CBE, 1943. Knighted, 1957. Life peer, 1964. Parliamentary Under-Secretary to the Ministry of Technology, 1964–6. In his novels Snow wrote of the academic, scientific and political worlds which he knew so well. *The Masters* (1951) deals with the intrigue leading up to the appointment of a master of a Cambridge college. *Corridors of Power* (1964), about parliamentary and political life at Westminster, became a widely-used term, as did *The Two Cultures and the Scientific Revolution*, his Rede Lecture delivered in 1959. This work, revised in *The Two Cultures and a Second Look* (1964), provoked a famous controversy with F.R. Leavis. Snow has been compared with Trollope in his subject matter, and with Wells and Bennett for his place in English life, thought and culture. He held numerous honorary degrees from universities in Canada, England, Scotland, USA and USSR. See his writings and Thale, J., *C.P. Snow* (1964); Shusterman, D., *C.P. Snow* (1965); Halperin, J., *C.P. Snow, an oral biography* (1983).

Solly, Henry (1813–1903). Promoter of adult education. Born London. Educated at Mr Cogan's school in Walthamstow and at Dr Morell's school at Hove. In 1829 entered the new University of London in Gower Street to study classics and mathematics. Family requirements, however, forced him to leave, and he worked successively in a shipbrokers, in banking and in a private scientific laboratory. In 1840 Solly became a Unitarian minister at Yeovil where he espoused the cause of moral force Chartism. Further pastorates followed at Tavistock, Shepton Mallet, Cheltenham, Islington and Lancaster. He became interested in social questions – franchise extension, teetotalism, and above all working men's clubs. On 14 June 1862 Solly called the meeting in the rooms of the Law Amendment Society, Waterloo Place, London, at which the Working Men's Club and Institute Union was born. Acted as secretary, 1862–7, and as organizing and travelling secretary, 1871–

3. Clubs were to be politically and religiously neutral. A circulating library and reference lending library were established. *The Club and Institute Journal* was published monthly, and prizes were given for essays and examinations. Nevertheless the educational work of the Union was not very successful until the establishment of the Workers' Educational Association and Ruskin College. Solly also founded an Artisans Institute in London and a national Trades Guild of Learning. At his death the Union claimed more than 300,000 members. See his several writings including *What says Christianity to the present distress?* (1842); *Working Men's Social Clubs and Educational Institutes* (1867 but see the 1904 edition reprinted 1980 which includes biographical and other additions); *These Eighty Years* (1893), and Hall, B.T., *Our Sixty Years: the Story of the Working Men's Club and Institute Union* (1922).

Somerville, Mary (1780–1872). Mathematician and scientist. Born Mary Fairfax, at Jedburgh, Scotland. A keen observer of nature and determined scholar, her formal education was limited to a brief stay in a fashionable boarding school in Musselburgh. Her marriage to Captain Samuel Greig ended after three years with his death in 1807. In 1812 she married another of her cousins Dr William Somerville, an army doctor. She flourished in the company of Edinburgh intellectuals and pursued a wide range of studies including mathematics, astronomy, botany and geology. In 1816 she moved to London and there entered a brilliant circle including **Brougham**, Herschel, Lyell, Mackintosh and Melbourne. Her first published paper in the *Philosophical Transactions of the Royal Society* (1826) on 'The Magnetic Properties of the Violet Rays of the Solar System' attracted much attention. This was followed by *Mechanism of the Heavens* (1831), *On the Connection of the Physical Sciences* (1834), and *Physical Geography* (1848). Somerville was a supporter of the causes of higher education for women and of women's suffrage, causes which she advanced by the example of her scientific erudition and exposition. She was awarded a civil pension by Sir Robert Peel and honoured by scientific societies both in Britain and abroad. Somerville College, founded in 1879, and the Mary Somerville scholarship for women in mathematics at Oxford commemorate her name and influence. See Somerville, M. (ed.), *Personal Recollections from Early Life to Old Age of Mary Somerville* (1873); Browne, P., *Mrs Somerville and Mary Carpenter* (1887); Patterson, E.C., *Mary Somerville 1780–1872* (1979); Patterson, E.C., *Mary Somerville and the cultivation of science 1815–1840* (1983).

Spearman

Spearman, Charles Edward (1863–1945). Psychologist. Born London and educated Leamington College. Entered the Army, 1883, serving in Burma, resigning as captain, 1897, returning during the South African and the 1914–18 wars. During the latter period, he conducted psychological researches in the Forces. Favoured the experimental approach to psychology used in Germany rather than that of association favoured in England. Spearman studied in Germany, 1897–1907, with Wündt at Leipzig, Külpe at Wurzburg and Müller at Göttingen, gaining a doctorate at Leipzig. Reader in experimental psychology, University College, London, 1907–11 and also at the same institution, Grote professor of Philosophy of Mind and Logic, 1911–28 and professor of Psychology, 1928–31. Spearman's contribution to his subject contained in *The Nature of Intelligence and the Principles of Cognition* (1923) was the enunciation of eight laws of psychology, qualitative and quantitative, which could be applied to various fields. Spearman is best remembered for his identification of a single general factor of intelligence and of a number of specific abilities – 'g' and 's' factors – which could be elicited by applying mental (intelligence) tests. See his *The Abilities of Man* (1927) and with Jones, L.W., *Human Ability* (1950), a posthumous publication. He also wrote a two-volume book *Psychology Down the Ages* (1937). FRS, 1924. See his *A History of Psychology in Autobiography* (1930) unfinished (ed. Murchison, C.).

Spencer, Frederick Herbert (1872–1946). School inspector. Born Swindon, Wiltshire, son of a factory worker. Educated Great Western Railway School, Swindon, 1878–86, pupil teacher, 1886–92 and attended Borough Road Training College, Isleworth, 1892–4, Teacher, Nottingham Board School, 1894–5, elementary school, Plumstead, London, 1895–9, studying part time for LL.B. Appointed research assistant to the **Webbs** on local government project, 1899–1905, during which undertook part-time lecturing in economic theory. Head of Department, City of London College, 1906–12. Appointed HMI, Technical Branch, south-west Lancashire, 1912–19, Divisional Inspector, north-western division, 1919–22, Chief Inspector, London Education Committee, London County Council, 1923–34. See his *An Inspector's Testament* (1938); *Education for the People* (1941); *The Public School Question* (1944).

Spencer, Herbert (1820–1903). Philosopher. Born Derby. Attended a day school. His father was a teacher, and secretary of the Derby Philosophical Society. Between the ages of 13 and 16 lived with his uncle, the radical Thomas Spencer, near Bath. Began school teaching in Derby but from 1837 to 1841 worked in the engineers department constructing the London to Birmingham Railway. Worked alternately as a railway engineer and a journalist, becoming in 1848 sub-editor of the *Economist*. This gave him the freedom to publish such works as *Social Statics* (1851), a defence of *laissez-faire* economics, and several articles including 'Development Hypothesis' (1852) which predated **Darwin**'s work on evolution. In 1853 a legacy from his uncle enabled him to leave the *Economist* and to devote himself to writing. Subsequent works included the *Principles of Psychology* (1855), the *System of Synthetic Philosophy* (1862–93) and the *Principles of Ethics* (1879–93). Many of these works had educational implications but in 1861 he published *Education: intellectual, moral and physical* which maintained that Science was the knowledge of most worth, both intrinsically and as a mental discipline. This book was translated into many languages and had a considerable influence. Children were to be trained not by command but by giving them the freedom to experience the direct consequences of their actions. Spencer refused all honours including the Rectorship of St Andrews University, but his influence as a philosopher was worldwide. See his various works, and *Autobiography* (1904), and Duncan, D., *The Life and Letters of Herbert Spencer* (1908); Cavenagh, F.A. (ed.), *Herbert Spencer on Education* (1932); Low-Beer, A. (ed.), *Herbert Spencer* (1969); Kennedy, J.G., *Herbert Spencer* (1978); Wiltshire, D., *The Social and Political Thought of Herbert Spencer* (1978).

Spencer, John Poyntz, 5th Earl Spencer (1835–1910). Statesman. Born in London at Spencer House, St James's Place, and known as Viscount Althorp. Educated at Harrow, 1848–54 and Trinity College, Cambridge, 1854–7. In 1857, elected as one of the two MPs for South Northamptonshire where the family's country seat, Althorp Park, is situated, but on the death of his father in December that year, he thenceforth sat in the Lords. Groom of the Stole to the Prince Consort, 1859–61, and to the Prince of Wales, 1862–7. Knight of the Garter, 1865. Appointed Lord-Lieutenant of Ireland in Gladstone's first ministry, 1868–74 and Lord President of the Council in 1880, this time with a seat in the cabinet. Together with his Vice-President, **A.J. Mundella**, Spencer prepared an Education Bill in 1880 which established effective universal compulsory attendance for elementary school children. In May 1882, on the resignation of Lord Cowper as Lord-Lieutenant of Ireland, Spencer was appointed as his successor, remaining there until the defeat of the Liberals in June 1885. Lord President of the Council, February–July 1886. First Lord of the Admiralty, 1892–5. Leader of the Opposition in the House of Lords, 1902–5. See Gordon, P., *The Red Earl. The Papers of the Fifth Earl Spencer* (2 vols., 1981 and 1986).

Spens, Sir Will (1882–1962). Academic and administrator. Educated at Rugby School and King's College, Cambridge. First class in part one of the natural science tripos, 1903. Took a junior post in the Cavendish laboratory but turned to theology. Fellow of Corpus Christi College, 1907, tutor from 1912. Worked in the Foreign Office during the First World War, CBE 1918. Master of Corpus, 1927–52. During his mastership the academic standing of the college was raised by the recruitment of eminent fellows and by the admission of only honours undergraduates. Vice-Chancellor of Cambridge University, 1931–3. Appointed chairman of the Consultative Committee of the Board of Education in 1934. Gave his name to the Spens Report of 1938 which recommended the continuation of separate grammar, secondary modern and technical schools, parity of staffing and treatment between such schools, and the raising of the school-leaving age. The multilateral and comprehensive school ideals were thus specifically rejected. Knighted in 1939. Chairman of the board of governors of Rugby school, 1944–58. Regional commissioner for East Anglia during the Second World War. Spens was a man of deep Christian conviction, humility and simplicity. See his *Belief and Practice* (1915); *The Relationship between the Work of Secondary Schools and Universities* (1939).

Stainer, Sir John (1840–1901). Organist, composer and school inspector. Born in Southwark, South London, son of a schoolmaster. He received his early music lessons from his father. Blinded in his left eye in an accident at the age of five, it did not affect his musical progress. He was an accomplished organist when he was seven and a full chorister at St Paul's Cathedral at nine. Appointed organist at a London church in 1854 and after three years took up a similar post at St Michael's, Tenbury. Entering Christ Church, Oxford in 1859, he gained a B.Mus. the following year, a BA at St Edmund's Hall, 1864, D. Mus., 1865 and MA, 1866. Organist,

Magdalen College, Oxford, 1860 and for the University, 1861 and of St Paul's Cathedral, 1872–88. Professor of the organ, National Training School for Music, 1876 and Principal, 1881–2. Appointed Inspector of Music in training colleges, 1882, resigning in 1888 when blindness threatened. He was knighted in that year. Professor of Music, Oxford, 1889–99. Stainer's most famous composition is his oratorio *The Crucifixion* (1877), though he also wrote widely on musical theory and history. See Charlton, P., *John Stainer and the Musical Life of Victorian Britain* (1984).

Stanley, Arthur Penrhyn (1815–81). Cleric. Born Alderley, Cheshire. Educated at a private school at Seaforth and at Rugby School where he became devoted to **Thomas Arnold** whose *Life* he subsequently wrote. Balliol College, Oxford, Ireland scholar and Newdigate prizeman. First class classics, 1838; MA, 1840; DD, 1858. Fellow of University College, 1838–50; tutor, 1843. Ordained in 1839. Travelled widely in Europe in 1840–1 and thereafter spent much time in foreign travel. Secretary to the Oxford University Commission, 1850 and wrote most of the report issued in 1852. Canon of Canterbury, 1851–6; chaplain to the Prince Consort, 1854; professor of Ecclesiastical History at Oxford, 1857–63. Dean of Westminster Abbey, 1864–81. Here, as at Oxford, his sermons, personal example and writings exercised a considerable influence in favour of a broad theology and a comprehensive national church. He championed **Bishop Colenso** and preached in Scottish Presbyterian pulpits. His *Life and Correspondence of Dr Arnold* (2 vols., 1844) ensured his own and Arnold's reputation. See his works and Bradley, G.G., *Recollections of A.P. Stanley* (1883); Prothero, R.E., *The Life and Correspondence of Dean Stanley* (1893); Baillie, A.V., and Bolitho, H.H. (eds.), *A Victorian Dean* (1930); Woodward, F.J., *The Doctor's Disciples* (1954).

Stanley, Edward George Geoffrey Smith, 14th Earl of Derby (1799–1869). Statesman. Born at Knowsley Park, Lancashire. Educated at Eton and Christ Church, Oxford. Won the Chancellor's Latin verse prize, 1819, but did not take a degree. Entered Parliament as a Whig in 1822 for Stockbridge. Returned for Preston, 1826, for Windsor, 1831, and sat for North Lancashire, 1832–44 when he moved to the Lords. Succeeded to the earldom in 1851. In 1834 Stanley left the Whigs and in 1841 became Colonial Secretary in Peel's Conservative government. Prime Minister, 1852, 1858–9 and 1866–8. In 1831 as Chief Secretary for Ireland he was responsible for establishing a

Stanley

Board of Commissioners through whom parliamentary funds for education in Ireland would be channelled. The aim was to unite the children of the different Christian denominations. The schools would provide united literary and moral, but separate religious instruction. In 1852 Stanley succeeded the Duke of Wellington as Chancellor of the University of Oxford and was created a DCL. He was a scholar who produced translations of classical, French and German poetry. See his *Conversations on the Parables for the Use of Children* (1837); *Iliad* (a blank verse translation, 1864), and Saintsbury, G.E.B., *The Earl of Derby* (1892); Jones, W.D., *Lord Derby and Victorian Conservatism* (1956); Akenson, D.H., *The Irish Education Experiment* (1970).

Stanley, Edward Lyulph, 4th Baron Sheffield of Roscommon and 4th Baron Stanley of Alderley (1839–1925). Educationist and administrator. Born London. Educated at Eton and Balliol College, Oxford. First class in *literae humaniores* in 1861. Fellow of Balliol, 1862–9. Called to the bar at the Inner Temple, 1865, and became an assistant commissioner for the Friendly Societies Commission, 1872. Liberal member of Parliament for Oldham, 1880–5. Member of the Royal Commission on the Housing of the Poor, 1884, and in 1886 was appointed to the Cross Commission, established to inquire into the working of the Elementary Education Acts. Stanley was first signatory to the minority report of 1888. This deplored the pupil-teacher system, and opposed the majority proposal for use of ratepayers' money for the support of voluntary schools. In the following year he was a founder member of the National Education Association, a body which was heir to the principles of the former National Education League. Stanley's major contribution, however, was his work for education in London. He was a member of the London School Board, 1876–85, 1888–1904, and served from 1897 as vice-chairman. He advanced the cause of local public control of education and supported the extension into higher grade and evening schools. He championed

236

the London School Board against the Technical Education Board. There was no place for him, however, on the London County Council after 1904. Stanley's principle of 'a school place for every child and every child in its place, and that a good place' helped to put the work of the London School Board at the forefront of educational development. He was an active philanthropist and established a private fund to help pay the fees of poor scholars, including pupil teachers. See his *Oxford University Reform* (1869); *Our National Education* (1899), and Spalding, T.A., *The Work of the London School Board* (1900); Philpott, H.B., *London at School* (1904); Gautrey, T., *'Lux Mihi Laus': School Board Memories* (1937).

Stanley, Oliver Frederick George (1896–1950). Politician. Born London, younger son of Edward Lord Stanley, the 17th Earl of Derby. Educated at Eton. Served in the First World War, winning the MC and the Croix de Guerre. Called to the bar, 1919 at Gray's Inn, but became Conservative MP for Westmorland, 1924–45. Represented Bristol West, 1945–50. Parliamentary private secretary to the President of the Board of Education, 1924–9; Under-Secretary of State at the Home Office, 1931–3. Played a large part in the Children and Young Persons Act of 1932. Minister of Transport, 1933–4, Minister of Labour, 1934–5. President of the Board of Education, 1935–7. The major event of Stanley's tenure of the Presidency of the Board of Education was the Education Act of 1936 which provided for the eventual raising of the school-leaving age to 15, a provision postponed by the outbreak of the Second World War in 1939. President of the Board of Trade, 1937–40; Secretary of State, War, 1940; Secretary of State for the Colonies, 1942–5. Succeeded his father as Chancellor of the University of Liverpool in 1948. See Simon, B., *The Politics of Educational Reform, 1920–1940* (1974).

Stenhouse, Lawrence (1927–82). Educationist. Educated Manchester Grammar School, and St Andrews, where he read English, and Glasgow, M.Ed., 1951–6. Taught in a multilateral school in Glasgow, becoming particularly interested in the curriculum offered to the low attainers, and in Dunfermline. Staff tutor in psychology and secondary education, Durham University Institute of Education, 1957–63, and Head of Education Department, Jordanhill College of Education, Glasgow, 1963–7. Following the publication of *Culture and Education* (1967), an early application of the sociology of knowledge to the curriculum, Stenhouse

237

was appointed in the same year as Director, Humanities Curriculum Project (HCP), funded by the Nuffield Foundation and Schools Council, 1967. The Project, a humanities-based learning experience for the 'average' secondary school pupil, had a stimulating effect on curriculum thinking for this age group. Established the Centre for Applied Research in Education (CARE) at the University of East Anglia, 1972, which generated curriculum research and postgraduate courses at the University. Professor of Education, 1978. By the time of his death in 1982, the Centre had received international recognition. See his *Discipline and Education: a symposium* (editor) (1967); *Introduction to Curriculum Research and Development* (1975); *Curriculum Research and Development in Action* (1980); *Teaching About Race Relations* with Verma, G. (1982); *Authority, education and emancipation: a collection of papers* (1983), and Lawton, D., 'Lawrence Stenhouse: his contribution to curriculum development', *British Educational Research Journal*, (9) 1, 1983.

Stewart, Dugald (1753–1828). Philosopher. Born Edinburgh. Educated there at the High School, and at the University where he studied Greek, logic and natural philosophy. Also studied at Glasgow University, 1771–2. From 1772 taught mathematics at the University of Edinburgh and from 1778 added astronomy and moral sciences. In 1785 Stewart became professor of Moral Philosophy. His influence was considerable and Edinburgh, the centre of the Scottish Enlightenment, attracted many English students, particularly during the period of war with France when travel to the European continent was severely curtailed. Stewart also lectured on political economy. He retired from active teaching in 1809. Though much of his philosophy was derived from Thomas Reid, and his political economy from Adam Smith, Stewart's personal integrity and lecturing ability allowed him to influence the minds of a generation of thinkers and statesmen, particularly those connected with the *Edinburgh Review* and the Whig party. Thus his students included Francis Horner, Francis Jeffrey, Sydney Smith, **Brougham**, Palmerston and **Lord John Russell**. See Sir William Hamilton (ed.), *The Collected Works of Dugald Stewart* (11 vols., 1854–60), and Stewart, M., *Memoir of the late Dugald Stewart* (1838); Horn, D.B., *A Short History of the University of Edinburgh* (1967).

Stow, David (1793–1864). Educationist. Born Paisley. Educated at Paisley Grammar School and by 1811 was working in Glasgow. In 1816 Stow established a Sunday evening school for children in the poor Saltmarket district. Became an elder of **Dr Chalmers'** church. At Stow's invitation **Wilderspin** lectured at Edinburgh and Glasgow on infant schools. In 1824 Stow secured the establishment by the Glasgow Educational Society of a training school at Drygate. This developed into a teacher training college which in 1836 moved to new premises at Dundas Vale, Glasgow. The college received the support of **Kay-Shuttleworth** and a government grant, but the disruption of 1843 led to a further move and its redesignation as the Free Church Normal College. Stow remained its guiding spirit until his death. Students trained at Glasgow were sought by English schools and Stow's methods were widely adopted, particularly by the Wesleyans. Stow advocated the provision of playgrounds, coeducation at the elementary school level and infant schools, and opposed corporal punishment and prizes. See his writings especially *Physical and Moral Training* (1832); *The Training System* (1836); *National Education* (1847), and Fraser, W., *Memoir of David Stow* (1868); Insh, G.P., *The Life and Work of David Stow* (1938); Cruickshank, M., *A history of the training of teachers in Scotland* (1970).

Strutt, John William, 3rd Baron Rayleigh (1842–1919). Mathematician and physicist. Born Maldon, Essex. Educated at Eton, a private school at Wimbledon, at Harrow and then for four years in the care of Revd George Warner who took pupils at Torquay. His earlier schooling had been dogged by ill-health. Trinity College, Cambridge, senior wrangler, 1865. Studied chemical analysis. Fellow of Trinity, 1866; FRS, 1873. In 1873 he succeeded his father as Baron Rayleigh. His first scientific paper was printed in 1869, to be followed by a further 445 which are included in the six volumes of his collected works. In 1879 he became Cavendish professor of Experimental Physics at Cambridge. In 1884 resigned this post to become secretary of the Royal Society whose president he was in 1905. OM, 1902; joint Nobel prizewinner, 1904; Chancellor of Cambridge University from 1908. Chairman of the committee which in 1898 reported in favour of the establishment of a National Physical Laboratory, whose executive committee he subsequently chaired. Strutt was the leading organizer and expounder of his day of knowledge in the physical sciences. His inscription in Westminster Abbey reads 'An unerring leader in the advancement of natural knowledge'. See his *Scientific Papers* (6 vols., 1899–1920); *Treatise on the Theory of Sound* (1877), and Strutt, R.J., *John William Strutt* (1924, augmented edition 1968); Lindsay, R.B., *Lord Rayleigh – the man and his work* (1970).

Stuart, James (1843–1913). Pioneer of university extension. Born at Balgonie, Fifeshire, Scotland. Educated at the Madras College, St

Andrews, at home by a tutor, and at the University of St Andrews. BA, 1861, winner of the Ferguson scholarship for classics and mathematics. Proceeded to Trinity College, Cambridge, 3rd wrangler, 1866. In the same year wrote up part of the report of Lemprière Hammond, one of the sub-commissioners of the Taunton inquiry. Master at Wellington College, 1866–7. Fellow of Trinity, 1867 and assistant tutor from 1868, in which year he gave one of the first courses of inter-collegiate lectures at Cambridge. Between 1867 and 1875 he promoted the idea of university extension. This began with his lectures for the North of England Council for promoting the Higher Education of Women, on the subject of astronomy. In 1867–8 he also lectured to the Mechanics' Institute at Crewe, whilst at Rochdale a class was established to follow up the lectures. Stuart issued a short summary before each lecture, and follow-up questions. In 1871 the University of Cambridge established a Syndicate with Stuart as secretary to investigate the idea of University Extension, and in 1873 the experiment began with lecture courses at Derby, Leicester and Nottingham. In 1875 Stuart resigned from the secretaryship and became the university's first professor of Mechanism and Applied Mechanics, a post he held until 1889. The mechanical workshops, engineering department and a tripos in applied mechanics were established. Stuart was a member of the London County Council, 1889–1907, chairman of the board of directors of the *Star* newspaper company, 1890–8, and Liberal MP for Hackney, 1884–5; Hoxton, 1885–1900; Sunderland, 1906–10. Hon. LL.D St Andrews, 1875; Lord Rector of St Andrews, 1898–1901. See his *A Letter on University Extension* (1871); *Reminiscences* (1912), and Draper, W.H., *University Extension. A Survey of Fifty Years, 1873–1923* (1923); Welch, E., *The Peripatetic University* (1973).

Symonds, Sir Aubrey Vere (1874–1931). Civil servant. Educated Bedford School and University College, Oxford, first class classical moderations, 1895, third class *literae humaniores*, 1897. Entered the Local Government Board as second class clerk, 1897. Assistant Secretary, 1913–19. Second Secretary, Ministry of Health, 1919–25. Permanent Secretary, Board of Education, 1925–31, succeeding **Selby-Bigge**. Proved to be ineffectual in supporting the President of the Board, **Lord Eustace Percy**, against Conservative demands for more economies in education. Knight, 1919.

Taunton, see **Labouchere**.

Tawney, Richard Henry (1880–1962). Historian. Born Calcutta. Educated at Rugby and Balliol College, Oxford. BA second class, 1903; fellow, 1918–21. Lived for a while at Toynbee Hall. In 1905 Tawney joined the executive committee of the Workers' Educational Association (WEA) formed two years earlier. 1906–8 lectured at Glasgow University; 1908–14, WEA class tutor. Settled in Manchester and his first classes were held in Lancashire and in the Potteries. Tawney was a member of the WEA executive committee for 42 years; vice-president from 1920 and president, 1928–44. Unsuccessful attempts to enter Parliament as an Independent Labour candidate in 1918, 1922 and 1924. Nevertheless he exercised considerable influence on post-war education by his reports *Secondary Education for All* (1922), and *Education: the Socialist Policy* (1924). Member of the Consultative Committee of the Board of Education 1912–31 and strongly supported the Hadow Report of 1926. Between 1917 and 1949 was chiefly associated with the London School of Economics, reader in economic history from 1923 and professor from 1931. Member of the University Grants Committee, 1943–8. Tawney was essentially a Christian Socialist, an opponent of pomp and circumstance not least in education, and a believer in democratic education in a democratic society. He was the leading economic historian of his day and reached a large audience with such works as *The Acquisitive Society* (1921) and *Religion and the Rise of Capitalism* (1926). He received honorary fellowships of Balliol and Peterhouse and honorary doctorates from nine universities including Chicago, Melbourne and Paris. See his writings including *The Attack and Other Papers* (1953); *Commonplace Book* (ed. Winter, J.M., and Joslin, D.M., 1972), and Williams, J.R. *et al.*, *R.H. Tawney, A Portrait by Several Hands* (1960); Terrill, R., *R.H. Tawney and His Times* (1974); Reisman, D., *State and Welfare* (1982).

Temple, Frederick (1821–1902). Theologian and schoolteacher. Born Santa Maura, Ionian Islands, son of an army major. Educated

Blundell's School, Tiverton, 1834–9 and Balliol College, Oxford, gaining a double first class honours in classics and mathematics, 1842. Fellow and tutor, Balliol, 1842–8. Ordained deacon, 1846 and priest, 1847. Examiner, Committee of Council on Education, 1848–9 and principal, Kneller Hall, Twickenham, a training college for workhouse teachers, 1849–55. On its closure, Temple became HMI for men's training colleges, 1855–7. Contributed essay on 'National Education' to *Oxford Essays* (1856). Appointed headmaster, Rugby School, 1857. He introduced natural science into the curriculum as well as history, music and art. Temple believed that English language and literature were the basis of a sound education. The school prospered under his charge. Member, Endowed Schools Commission, 1864–8; he was responsible for the chapters dealing with the kinds of secondary education which are desirable (Chapter 2) and the Commissioners' recommendations (Chapter 7). Bishop of Exeter, 1869–85, where he established a 'scholarship' ladder for poor boys to secondary schools. He outlined a plan some 30 years later, to the Bryce Commission on Secondary Education, for a national system of education, linking the elementary and secondary schools. Temple contended that the teaching of religion should form an essential part of national education and that the church should co-operate with the State in providing it. Bishop of London, 1885–97. Archbishop of Canterbury, 1897–1902. Shortly before his death, Temple spoke in favour of the Education Bill of 1902 in the debate on its second reading in the House of Lords. See Sandford, E.G. (ed.), *Memoirs of Archbishop Temple by Seven Friends* (2 vols., 1906).

Temple, William (1881–1944). Theologian and educator. Born at Exeter, his father **Frederick** was also to be Archbishop of Canterbury. Educated at Rugby School and at Balliol College, Oxford. First class in classical moderations, 1902, and *literae humaniores*, 1904, and President of the Union. His social conscience led him to the university settlements in Bethnal Green and Bermondsey. He was a lifelong supporter of the Workers' Educational Association, becoming its president 1908–24, and was a Labour party member, 1918–25. Fellow of Queen's College, Oxford, 1904–10. Ordained deacon, 1908 and priest, 1909. In 1910 toured universities in Australia. Headmaster of Repton School, 1910–14, rector of St James's, Piccadilly, 1914–18, and honorary chaplain to the King, 1915–21. Temple became canon of Westminster, 1919–21, Bishop of Manchester, 1921–9, Archbishop of York, 1929–42 and Archbishop of Canterbury from 1942 until his death. Temple's concern for presenting the Christian gospel to the nation and particularly to its youth, for promoting the unity of Christian churches, and for applying Christian principles to social problems, kept him in the forefront of public life. He was also a regular broadcaster, and chairman of the advisory council of the British Broadcasting Corporation from 1935. He spoke regularly at the conferences of the Student Christian Movement, and was prominent in missions to the universities, notably that to Oxford in 1931. Temple's crowning educational contribution was the part he played in the achievement of the 1944 Education Act. He was awarded honorary doctorates from Cambridge, Oxford, Manchester, Durham, Leeds, Sheffield, Dublin and Princeton. See his voluminous writings, particularly *Repton School Sermons* (1913); *Christian Faith and Life* (1931); *Men Without Work* (1938); *Christianity and Social Order* (1942); *The Church Looks Forward* (1944), and Baker, A.E., *William Temple and his Message* (1946); Iremonger, F.A., *William Temple, his Life and Letters* (1948); Sadler, J.H., 'William Temple, the WEA and the Liberal Tradition', *Journal of Educational Administration and History*, 18 (2), 1986.

Thomson, Sir Godfrey (Hilton) (1881–1955). Psychologist. Born Carlisle. Educated Rutherford College, Newcastle upon Tyne and Durham University. Pupil-teacher, 1897–1900. B.Sc. with distinctions in mathematics and physics, 1903. Pemberton Research Fellow, Durham University, 1903–6, M.Sc., 1906, and experimental work at Strasbourg University, Ph.D., 1906. D.Sc. in psychology, 1913. Lecturer in education, Armstrong College, Newcastle, 1906–20, professor, 1920–5. Joint posts of professor of Education, Edinburgh University and Director of Studies, Moray House, 1925–51. Thomson developed large-scale intelligence surveys in order to make for equality in educational opportunities for children of all classes, especially in higher education. The so-called Northumberland Tests and the Moray House Tests which he developed became very popular. He also carried out the two Scottish Mental Surveys which tested all children of 11 in Scotland. Thomson is also closely associated with work on the factorial analysis of human ability. This brought him into controversy with other psychologists, notably **Burt** and **Spearman**. Knight, 1949. See his *Instinct, Intelligence and Character* (1932) and *The Factorial Analysis of Human Ability* (1936), *History of Psychology in Autobiography* (1952), and Sutherland, J., 'Sir Godfrey Thomson', *British Journal of Educational Psychology*, 23 (2), 1955; Vernon, P.E., 'The Contributions to Education of Sir Godfrey Thomson', *British Journal of Educational Studies*, 10 (2), 1962.

Thring, Edward (1821–87). Headmaster. Born Alford, Somerset. Educated at a private boarding school at Ilminster, at Eton and at King's College, Cambridge. Winner of the Porson prize for Greek verses. Obtained his degree without examination, took holy orders, became a fellow and in 1847 became a curate at St James's Church, Gloucester. Here Thring became fully involved in the work of the local National school. Suffered a breakdown and during his recovery lived at Marlow where he took private pupils and wrote an *English Grammar*. In 1853 was appointed headmaster of Uppingham Grammar School which post he held until his death. He began with only 25 boys but numbers grew to 300 which Thring regarded as a maximum as he wished to know them all personally. He wanted his school to be a family and understood boys in a way in which **Thomas Arnold** did not. Thring's philosophy was that every boy was good at something and that Uppingham should provide facilities to encourage such success. If a boy could not shine at classics, 'Turn him into the carpenter's shop, make him a botanist or a chemist, encourage him to express himself in music, and if he fails all round, here at least he shall learn to read in public his mother tongue and write thoughtfully an English essay.' In 1869 Thring chaired the first Headmasters' Conference, held at Uppingham, a body which opposed the Endowed Schools' Bill. In 1879 some 140 headmasters and assistant masters attended. In 1887 the annual conference of the Association of Headmistresses was held at Uppingham and Thring formed close friendships with **Beale** and **Buss**. In raising Uppingham from an obscure country grammar school Thring became the best known headmaster of the second half of the nineteenth century. See his writings, particularly *Education and School* (1864); *Sermons* (2 vols., 1858, 1886); *Theory and Practice of Teaching* (1883), and Parkin, G.R., *Life and Letters of Edward Thring* (1898); Rawnsley, W.R., *Edward Thring* (1926); Hoyland, G., *The Man who made a School* (1946).

Tinling, Edward Douglas (1815–97). School inspector. Born Bury St Edmunds. Educated Christ Church, Oxford, graduating in 1837. Curate, Huntspill and Nettlecombe, 1839–44, rector, West Worlington, Devon, 1844–7. Appointed HMI, 1847, as a result of **Lord Lansdowne's** patronage as Lord President, serving until 1881. Prebendary, Wells Cathedral, 1863–7, Canon, Gloucester Cathedral, 1867–97. Proctor, Dean and Chapter, Gloucester Cathedral, 1886–97. See his *A Letter to the Rev. N.T. Ellison relating to the public inspection of Schools* (1850).

Tomlinson, George (1890–1952). Politician. Born Rishton, Lancashire, son of a weaver. Educated Rishton Wesleyan School. Aged 12 he became a half-timer in a mill, full time a year later. A Methodist lay preacher for 40 years. President of the Rishton District Weavers' Association aged 22. Conscientious objector in First World War. Local councillor and Chairman of the Part III Authorities Watching Committee. Labour member of Lancashire County Council from 1931, Chairman of its Scholarships Sub-Committee and Vice-Chairman of the Higher Education Sub-Committee. Member of the Association of Education Committees and President, 1939–41. Labour MP for Farnworth, 1938–52. Junior Minister of Labour and National Service, 1941–5. Chairman of the Committee on the Rehabilitation and Resettlement of Disabled Persons, 1941–3 (Tomlinson Reports) which led to the Disabled Persons (Employment) Act, 1944. Minister of Works, 1945–7. Minister of Education, 1947–51. Hon. LL.D Liverpool, 1947. As Minister of Education Tomlinson won the support both of the local authorities and of the teachers in the difficult issues surrounding the raising of the school-leaving age and the expansion of school places. An architects and buildings branch was established which created a new working partnership of experts. See his *Education for Living* (1950), and Blackburn, F., *George Tomlinson* (1954); Dean, D.W., 'Planning for a postwar generation: Ellen Wilkinson and George Tomlinson at the Ministry of Education, 1945–51', *History of Education*, 15 (2), 1986.

Toynbee, Arnold (1852–83). Social philosopher, economist and scholar. Born London, son of Joseph Toynbee, a distinguished aural surgeon. Intended for the army at an early age, educated at preparatory schools at Blackheath and Woolwich and attended lectures at King's College, London; Pembroke College, Oxford, 1873–4 and Balliol College, Oxford, 1875–8, with a degree in *literae humaniores*. Absorbed in thoughts of religion, Toynbee established close friendships with **Jowett, T.H. Green** and **R.L. Nettleship** and a circle of admirers, including Alfred Milner, A.C. Bradley and **T.H. Warren**. Lecturer in political economy, Balliol, 1875, and later responsible for Indian Civil Service probationers from 1878. Like Green, a fellow idealist, Toynbee demonstrated that individuals should devote themselves to the service of humanity. After studying the philosophy of history, Toynbee investigated the science of economics, in order to improve the condition of the working classes. His unfinished *Lectures on the Industrial Revolution in the Eighteenth Century in England* was published posthumously in 1884. He saw the co-operative movement as a modern day equivalent of the guilds, and he worked out a scheme for workers' education given under the aegis of co-operators in a lecture 'Education for Co-operators'. It would consist of three elements, political education, industrial education and sanitation education. Toynbee suffered from poor health, but nevertheless expended much energy in addressing working-class audiences in many towns on social questions. Toynbee's early death at the age of 30 in 1883, when he was actively engaged in charity organization work, church reform and co-operation, inspired others to continue in his footsteps. Toynbee Hall in Whitechapel, East London, was founded in 1884 in his memory, the first 'university settlement' which brought together those from universities and the working classes. See Milner, A., *Arnold Toynbee: a reminiscence* (1895); Toynbee, G. (ed.), *Reminiscences and Letters of Joseph and Arnold Toynbee* (1910).

Tremenheere, Hugh Seymour (1804–93). School inspector. Born Gloucester, son of an army officer. Educated Winchester and New College, Oxford, BA, 1827, fellow, 1827–56. Barrister, Inner Temple, 1834, and became revising barrister, Western Circuit in 1838. Together with **John Allen**, appointed the first Her Majesty's Inspector of Schools, 1839, with the ancillary job of Assistant Poor Law Commissioner. Tremenheere submitted his final report on 66 British and Foreign Society schools in July 1842. His criticism of the monitorial system roused the Society's hostility. The Lord President, Wharncliffe, unsuccessfully suggested to Tremenheere that the report should be withdrawn. To avoid further conflict with the government, Tremenheere was appointed the first Her Majesty's Inspector of Mines and Collieries in 1843, holding the post until 1871. Member, Royal Commission on Children in Manufactures (1862–7) and on Women and Children in Agriculture (1867–71). CB, 1871. See Edmonds, E.L. and O.P., *I Was There. The Memoirs of H.S. Tremenheere* (1965).

Trevelyan, Sir Charles Edward (1807–86). Administrator. Born Taunton. Educated at the local grammar school, Charterhouse and Haileybury. Entered the East India Company's Bengal civil service in 1826. In 1827 appointed assistant to the governor of Delhi and in 1831 moved to Calcutta as deputy secretary in the political department. He advocated a policy of spreading a knowledge of European literature and science amongst the Indian population. Returned to England and from 1840 acted as Assistant Secretary to the Treasury for some 19 years. KCB in 1848 in recognition of his work in helping to relieve famine in Ireland. In 1853 he investigated the means of improving recruitment to the civil service. This resulted in the Northcote–Trevelyan Report on *The Organization of the Permanent Civil Service*, which marked a major step in the change from recruitment by patronage to recruitment according to ability. Governor of Madras, 1859–60; finance minister in India, 1862–5. In later life was associated with other reform movements including the abolition of commission purchase in the army. Trevelyan's reforms aroused much opposition both at home and in India. See his *On the Education of the People of India* (1838); *The Purchase System in the British Army* (1867); *Christianity and Hinduism contrasted* (1882), and Trevelyan, H., *The India we left* (1972).

Trevelyan, Sir Charles Philips, 3rd Bt. (1870–1958). Politician. Born in London, son of Sir George Otto Trevelyan, 2nd baronet,

Trimmer

MP, a former Liberal Chief Secretary, Ireland, and Secretary of State, Scotland. Educated at Harrow, 1884–9 and Trinity College, Cambridge, 1889–92, where he gained second class in the historical tripos. 1892–3, secretary to **Lord Crewe**, Liberal Lord-Lieutenant in Ireland. Two years later, he unsuccessfully contested North Lambeth, but elected Liberal MP, Elland division, Yorkshire, 1899–1918, unsuccessfully contested this seat as an Independent, 1918 and Labour MP, Newcastle upon Tyne Central, 1922–31. Member, London School Board, 1896–7. He was appointed Parliamentary Secretary, Board of Education, 1908–14, resigning from the government and advocating 'peace by negotiation'. After joining the Labour Party in 1919, he became their leading spokesman on education. Appointed first Labour President of the Board of Education, January–November 1924, when he immediately withdrew Circular 1190 which restricted expenditure on education. He became an effective Opposition front bench speaker, attacking the Conservatives for their parsimonious attitude on education matters. Succeeded to the baronetcy, 1928. In the second Labour government, 1929–31, he was once again President of the Board of Education. Trevelyan introduced an Education Bill which provided for raising the school-leaving age to 15 and for grants for low income families. He at first resisted giving development grants to Church schools, but finally agreed. The Bill was rejected by the Lords in February 1931 and Trevelyan resigned from the government and the Cabinet the following month. He was an admirer of Soviet Communism, but was never a member of the Communist Party. See his *The Cause of the Children* (3rd edn., 1897), and Morris, A.J.A., *C.P. Trevelyan – Portrait of a Radical* (1977).

Trimmer, Sarah (1741–1810). Educationist. Born Ipswich, the only daughter of Sarah and John Kirby a landscape artist. Educated at Mrs Justinier's school at Ipswich. In 1755 moved with her parents to London, where she knew Dr Johnson, Gainsborough and Hogarth. In 1762 married James Trimmer. Educated their 12 children herself and in 1782 published an *Easy Introduction to the Knowledge of Nature*. This work proved very popular and was followed between 1782 and 1784 by the six-volume *Sacred History . . . adapted to the Comprehension of Young Persons*, and *New and Comprehensive Lessons* (1814). In 1793 Trimmer began to write for the Society for Promoting Christian Knowledge; her books and pamphlets remained on their lists for some 70 years. She also herself edited the *Family Magazine*, 1788–9, and the *Guardian of Education*, 1802–6.

She was instrumental in founding Sunday schools in Brentford in 1786 and in the same year, after a two-hour interview with Queen Charlotte, published *The Economy of Charity* about the promotion and management of Sunday schools. In 1787 she established a girls' school of industry at Brentford. Her *Comparative View of the new Plan of Education* (1805) contributed to the rivalry between **Bell** and **Lancaster**. Trimmer was a pious woman, interested in the education and moral improvement of children of all classes. See her several writings and *The Life and Writings of Mrs Trimmer* (2 vols., 1814), Elwood, A.K., *Memoirs of the Literary Ladies of England* (1843); Balfour, C.L., *A Sketch of Mrs Trimmer* (1854).

Tufnell, Edward Carleton (1806–86). Inspector of Poor Law Schools. Assistant commissioner appointed under the Poor Law Amendment Act of 1834, a post he held for twelve years. In 1837 he prepared a plan for the education of pauper children in good workhouse schools. He wanted large district schools to which children from several workhouses would be sent. In 1840 together with **Kay-Shuttleworth** Tufnell established Battersea Normal College for the training of teachers for pauper children. Experiments were made with the use of pupil teachers, but the privately-financed college was handed over to the National Society in 1843. From 1847 to 1874 Tufnell served as inspector of poor law schools. He was in charge of the metropolitan district. Gave evidence to the Newcastle Commission, and to the Select Committee on Destitute Children, 1861. Tufnell was a supporter of government-financed aid for a wide range of elementary schools, for half-time education, for the physical fitness of children, for infant schools and for good teachers. See Phillips, R.J., 'E.C. Tufnell: Inspector of Poor Law Schools, 1847–1874', *History of Education*, 5 (3), 1976.

Turnbull, William Peveril (1841–1917). School inspector. Born Hackness, North Yorkshire, son of a land agent. Educated at St Peter's School, York and Trinity College, Cambridge, 1860–4. 2nd wrangler in mathematical tripos. Fellow, Trinity College, 1865, where published a treatise in analytical geometry, 1867. Appointed HMI, Manchester, 1871 and fellow, St Catherine's College, Cambridge, 1872. Moved to Wolverhampton, 1873 and Chief Inspector, north-east division, 1894–1906. A keen promoter of mathematics in school, published *The Teaching of Arithmetic* (2 vols., 1903). See Turnbull, H.W., *Some Memories of William Peveril Turnbull* (1919).

Valentine

Valentine, Charles Wilfrid (1879–1964). Psychologist. Born Runcorn, Cheshire, son of a Methodist minister. Educated Nottingham High School, Preston Grammar School. Taught before entering University College, Aberystwyth, graduating BA, London University. Following a further spell of teaching, foundation scholar, Downing College, Cambridge, first class moral science tripos, 1908 and 1909. Studied experimental methods at the psychological laboratory at Würzburg University, Germany. Demonstrator, Myers' laboratory, Cambridge University, leading to his first book, *An Introduction to the Experimental Psychology of Beauty* (1913). Lecturer in psychology, St Andrews University, professor of Education, Queen's University, Belfast and professor of Education, Birmingham University, 1919–46. Aesthetic appreciation, both visually and aurally, was for Valentine the object of a lifetime's study. He also explored a wide range of topics, including transfer of training, the reliability of examinations, discipline, mental testing and the educational value of Latin and Greek. One of his most widely read and influential books was *Psychology and its Bearing on Education* (1950). First editor, *British Journal of Educational Psychology*, 1931–55. See his *The Psychology of Early Childhood* (3rd edn., 1946), *The Difficult Child and the Problem of Discipline* (4th edn., 1947) and *The Normal Child and some of his Abnormalities* (1956); and Burt, C., 'Charles Wilfrid Valentine', *British Journal of Educational Psychology*, 24 (3), 1964.

Vaughan, Charles John (1816–97). Headmaster and cleric. Born Leicester. Educated at Rugby School under **Thomas Arnold**, and Trinity College, Cambridge. BA, 1838; MA, 1841; DD, 1845. Fellow of Trinity, 1839–42; vicar of St Martin's, Leicester, 1841–4. Headmaster of Harrow School, 1844–59. Under his headmastership the school was transformed from an establishment of some 60 boys to one of the leading public schools. He gathered around him a distinguished band of scholars, and like Arnold used the chapel sermon to exert his authority over the school. In 1859 Vaughan was made to resign over a homosexual scandal and the threat of exposure forced him to refuse high office in the Church. Vicar of Doncaster, 1860–9; master of the Temple, 1869–94; Dean of Llandaff, 1879–97; chaplain in ordinary to the Queen, 1851–79. Vaughan took a leading part in founding the university college at Cardiff (1883–4), whose president he became in 1894. Vaughan published more than 60 works including *Memorials of Harrow*

THE RELIABILITY
OF EXAMINATIONS

AN ENQUIRY

With Special Reference to the Entrance Examinations
to Secondary Schools, the School Certificate Examination, and the award of Scholarships at Universities

BY

C. W. VALENTINE, M.A., D.Phil.

(Professor of Education in the University of Birmingham)

With the collaboration of
W. G. EMMETT, M.A., F.I.C.

UNIVERSITY OF LONDON PRESS LTD.
10 & 11 WARWICK LANE, LONDON, E.C.4
1932

Sundays (1859) and *The Young Life equipping itself for God's Service* (1872).

Vaughan, Henry Halford (1811–85). Academic. Born London. Educated at Rugby School and Christ Church, Oxford. BA, 1833; MA, 1839; fellow of Oriel, 1835–42. First class in *literae humaniores* and winner of the Chancellor's prize with an essay on the 'Effects of a national taste for general and diffusive reading.' Called to the bar at Lincoln's Inn, 1840. In 1841 appointed clerk of assize on the South Wales circuit and in 1843 an assistant to the Poor Law Commission inquiring into the employment of women and children in agriculture. Professor of Modern History at Oxford, 1848–58. Gave evidence to the Oxford University Commission of 1850 and served on the Public Schools' Commission (Clarendon) from 1861. He had a high reputation as a teacher and like **Pattison** favoured the development of scholarship, research and the professoriate. See his *Oxford Reform and Oxford Professors* (1854), and Bill, E.G.W., *University reform in nineteenth-century Oxford. A study of Henry Halford Vaughan* (1973).

Wallas, Graham (1858–1932). Educationist. Born at Monkwearmouth, Sunderland. Educated at Shrewsbury School and Corpus Christi College, Oxford, where he obtained second classes in classical moderations, 1879, *literae humaniores*, 1881. Taught in schools, 1881–90 and became a university extension lecturer in that year. Was a member of the Fabian Society, 1886–1904 and contributed to *Fabian Essays on Socialism* (1889). In 1894 he became a member of the London School Board and chaired its School Management Committee from 1897 to 1904. Member of the Technical Education Board of the LCC, 1898–1904. From 1904 after the demise of the School Board he served on the London County Council until 1907. Member of the Education Committee of the LCC, 1908–10. Wallas was one of the founders of the London School of Economics and Political Science. In 1895 he became a lecturer there and held the chair of Political Science, 1914–23. He served on the Royal Commission on the Civil Service, 1912–15, was well known as a lecturer in the USA, and received honorary doctorates from Manchester and Oxford. Wallas, through his books, teaching and conversation exercised considerable influence. He argued for the humanizing of modern life, for closer attention to be paid to human beings rather than to institutions, and for a closer connection between psychological and political studies. See his

Human Nature in Politics (1908); *The Great Society* (1914); *Our Social Heritage* (1921); *The Art of Thought* (1926), and Wallas, M. (ed.), *Men and Ideas* (1940); Wiener, M.J., *Between two Worlds: the political thought of Graham Wallas* (1971); Qualter, T.H., *Graham Wallas and 'The great society'* (1980).

Walsh, Edward (1805–1850). Poet and schoolmaster. Born Derry, Ireland, educated in a hedge school, became a teacher at Millstreet, County Cork. Was imprisoned for his part in a tithe war. Sub-editor of the *Dublin Monitor* and also contributed to the *Dublin Penny Journal* and *Nation*. Also taught in County Waterford, at the convict establishment on Spike Island in Cork Harbour, and at the Cork union workhouse. His publications included *Reliques of Irish Jacobite Poetry* (1844) and *Irish Popular Songs* (1847).

Walsh, William John (1841–1921). Cleric. Born Dublin. Educated at the Catholic university there during the time of **J.H. Newman** and at Maynooth College. In 1867 Walsh became professor of Theology at Maynooth, vice-president in 1878 and president in 1881. Archbishop of Dublin from 1885. Commissioner of education and first Chancellor of the National University of Ireland. Walsh played a leading part in public affairs and strongly supported the republican leaders. Wrote widely on education, theology, music and economics. See Walsh, P.J., *William J. Walsh, Archbishop of Dublin* (1928).

Ward, Herbert (1866–1938). School inspector. Born Bradford, attended elementary school winning scholarships to Bradford Grammar School and Corpus Christi College, Oxford, second class in classical moderations and first class in *literae humaniores*, 1889. Master, Bradford Grammar School, 1890–1, Instructor, Borough Road Training College, 1892–5. HMI, 1895–1912, Divisional Inspector, 1918–26 and Chief Inspector, Teacher Training, 1918–26. Honorary lecturer in Education, King's College, London, 1926–38. CBE, 1923. Author of *The Educational System of England and Wales and its Recent History* (1935).

Ward, Mary Augusta (Mrs Humphry) (1851–1920). Novelist and social reformer. Born Hobart, Tasmania, granddaughter of **Thomas Arnold** and niece of **Matthew Arnold**. Her father Thomas Arnold was at the time an inspector of schools in Tasmania. In 1856 the family returned to England. Mary, previously educated in

private boarding schools, settled in 1867 in the family home at Oxford and immersed herself in private studies and the intellectual and social life of the university. In 1872 she married Thomas Humphry Ward, fellow and tutor of Brasenose College, Oxford. She supported the movement for the higher education of women and in 1879 became secretary to Somerville College. In 1881 Mary and her husband moved to London, and in 1890 she founded a settlement at University Hall in Gordon Square. This became a centre for social work, and Bible teaching. Ward also instituted the 'children's play hours' scheme which led to the establishment of recreational centres for London children. The settlement was transferred in 1897 to Tavistock Square and renamed the Passmore Edwards Settlement. In the following year Ward there began the scheme for the education of crippled children which contributed to the general recognition of the need for special educational facilities for the handicapped. Her many writings included 25 novels, three plays and nine non-fiction works, together with numerous newspaper articles and reviews. Though active politically she opposed female suffrage. See her most famous novel, *Robert Elsmere* (1883); *A Writer's Recollections* (1918), and Trevelyan, J.P., *The Life of Mrs Humphry Ward* (1923), Jones, E.H., *Mrs Humphry Ward* (1973); Smith, E.M.G., *Mrs Humphry Ward* (1980).

Warre, Edmond (1837–1920). Schoolmaster. Son of a Lloyd's underwriter. Born Blindon, Somerset and educated at Revd Edward Wickham's School, Hammersmith, 1845–6, Eton, 1846–54 and scholar, Balliol College, Oxford, 1855–9. Gained first class in classical moderations, 1856 and first class in *literae humaniores*, 1859, MA, 1861, DD, 1884. An excellent oarsman, he was a member of the successful crew in the 1857 Boat Race. He, together with the **5th Earl Spencer**, founded the National Rifle Association in 1859. Fellow, All Souls College, Oxford, 1859–62. Assistant master, Eton, 1860–84, where he stressed the importance of the classics as well as athleticism. He introduced a School of Practical

Mechanics in 1879, which included a smithy forge and a carpenter's shop, though it was ahead of its time and proved to be a failure. Ordained, 1867. Headmaster, 1884–1905, during which time the fame of Eton grew. Retired in 1905, but was recalled and served as Provost, 1909–18. See his *Letters from the Peninsula* (1909) and a *Grammar of Boating* (1910); a translation of Selwyn's *Diary of Boating Years at Eton, 1829–30* (1903) (original in Greek); and also Fletcher, C.L.R., *Edmond Warre* (1922).

Warren, Sir Thomas Herbert (1853–1930). Scholar and educational reformer. Born Cotham, Bristol, son of a leading businessman. Educated at Clifton, 1868–72, and Balliol College, Oxford, 1872–6, where he gained first class honours in classical moderations and *literae humaniores* as well as two scholarships. Fellow, Magdalen College, Oxford, 1877, classical tutor, 1878–85, and at the age of 32, became President of Magdalen, remaining in office until 1928. During these 43 years, Magdalen became one of the leading Oxford colleges for scholarship. Inspired by **Arnold Toynbee**, Warren devoted himself to the ideal of service to the community. He taught literature to Extension classes and in 1892, signed a joint letter with **H.J. Mackinder** to **A.H.D. Acland**, Vice-President of the Privy Council on Education, calling for the creation of local education authorities for secondary education. Vice-Chancellor, Oxford, 1906–10 and professor of Poetry, 1911–16. Member, Consultative Committee of Board of Education until 1906. Knight, 1914. See his translation of *Plato* (1888); *Education and Equality* (1895); *By Severn Sea and other Poems* (1897); *Tennyson's Poems* (1910); *Virgil and Rome* (1921), and Magnus, L., *Herbert Warren of Magdalen* (1932).

Watson, Foster (1860–1929). Educational historian. Born Lincoln and educated at Owens College, Manchester, 1878–9, first class honours in English. MA, 1881. Taught in preparatory school and second master, Central Foundation School, London, 1885–91. Supported the Teachers' Guild, which encouraged members of the profession to study education in a more systematic manner. Watson also advocated the award of higher degrees in education and teachers' registration. Lecturer and Head of Training Department, Aberystwyth University College, 1894–5, Professor, 1895–1913. He established education as part of the university degree course in 1905 and at honours level in 1911. Responsible for the early introduction of a system of teacher training which consisted of a three-year undergraduate course followed by a one year teaching course. Author of two important books in the history of education, *The English Grammar Schools to 1660: Their Curriculum and Practice* (1908, repr. Cass, 1968) and *The Beginnings of the Teaching of Modern Subjects in England* (1909) and translated the works of the 16th century Spanish educationist, Juan Luis Vives, in three books, *Tudor School-Boy Life* (1908, repr. Cass, 1968), *Vives and the Renaissance Education of Women* (1912) and *On Education* (1913). Wrote more than 150 articles in Monroe's *Cyclopaedia of Education* (1911–13) and editor of *The Encyclopaedia and Dictionary of Education* (4 vols., 1921, 1922). Retired at the age of 53 in 1913 to devote himself to writing. Professor of Rhetoric, Gresham's College, London. See Armytage, W.H.G., 'Foster Watson', *British Journal of Educational Studies*, 10 (3), 1961.

Webb, Beatrice (1858–1943). Social reformer. Born near Gloucester, the eighth of nine daughters of Richard and Laurencina Potter. Educated at home by governesses and by continental travel, though in 1875 she spent one term in a boarding school at Bournemouth. Interest in social problems was stimulated by her friendship with **Herbert Spencer**. In 1882 after her mother's death she became a business associate of her father, a wealthy industrial and railway magnate. Rent collecting made her aware of conditions in London's East End. In 1892 married **Sidney Webb**, and subsequently much of their work was undertaken in partnership. This included the foundation of the London School of Economics in 1895. Other London interests included the Technical Education Board (of which Sidney was chairman), the reorganization of London University, and the establishment in 1902 of the London Day Training College. The Fabian pamphlet *The Education Muddle and the Way Out* (1901) proposed the abolition of School Boards and the creation of new local education authorities, a reform achieved by the Education Act of 1902. Their nine volume history of *English*

Local Government was published between 1906 and 1929 (11 vols., repr. Cass 1963). From 1906 Beatrice served on the Royal Commission on the Poor Law and relief of distress, and in 1909 produced the famous minority report. From 1912 the Webbs committed themselves to the new Labour Party, and in the following year founded the *New Statesman* as an independent weekly. They became disillusioned with capitalism, turned to Russia, and in 1935 published *Soviet Communism: A New Civilization?* Beatrice was elected FBA in 1931, and received honorary degrees from the universities of Edinburgh, Manchester and Munich. The Webbs exercised a considerable influence over the social and political thought and practice of the early twentieth century. See her *Diaries: My Apprenticeship* (1926); *Our Partnership* (1948), and Cole, M.I., *Beatrice Webb* (1945); Muggeridge, K., and Adam, R., *Beatrice Webb. A Life* (1967); Nord, D.E., *The Apprenticeship of Beatrice Webb* (1985).

Webb, Sidney James, Baron Passfield (1859–1947). Social reformer. Son of an accountant, born in London. Educated in Switzerland, Birkbeck Institute and City of London College. Clerk, City firm of brokers, 1875–8, second division clerk, War Office, clerk, Surveyor of Taxes Office and first division clerk, Colonial Office, 1878–81. Barrister, Gray's Inn, 1885. LL.B, London University, third class honours, 1886. **George Bernard Shaw** introduced Webb to the Fabian Society which he joined in 1885, playing a leading part in its activities. His book *Fabian Essays in Socialism* (1889) was an impressive statement of political philosophy. Resigned from Civil Service, 1891, elected Progressive member, London County Council, Deptford, 1892, representing the constituency until 1910. He married Beatrice Potter in 1892 and began a series of social research projects which were models for future investigations – *History of Trade Unionism* (1894), *Industrial Democracy* (1897), *The State and the Doctor* (1910), *The Consumers' Co-operative Movement* (1921) and *English Poor Law History* (3 vols., 1927, 1929). Educational reform had been one of Webb's interests since 1889. He was concerned to see even the poorest children obtaining the best education of which they were capable. Webb was elected chairman of the London Technical Education Board in 1892 and instituted an inquiry into the state and needs of technical education in London, which was carried out by **H. Llewellyn Smith**. One recommendation was immediately put into effect: to erect a 'ladder of ability', involving the award of 'junior county scholarships' which entitled the recipients to free education at any higher grade or approved secondary school. The scholarships were for children under 13 who had attended public elementary schools. This scheme provided a boost to secondary education in the capital as well as for individual pupils. Webb's achievements also encompassed an expansion of polytechnics, the founding of the London School of Economics in 1895, the establishment of the Imperial College of Science and Technology in 1907, and the London Day Training College (later the University of London Institute of Education) in 1902. The chaotic state of the national administration of education was attacked in a masterly fashion by Webb in a document *The Education Muddle and the Way Out* (1901). **A.J. Balfour,** the author of the 1902 Education Act, had been a visitor to the Webbs' house; he was impressed by Webb's views expressed in the document, which were reflected in the Act itself. Unsuccessfully contested London University for Parliament, 1918. Elected Labour MP, Seaham division, Durham, 1922–9. President of Board of Trade, 1929, Secretary of State for the Colonies, 1929–31 and for the Dominions, 1929–30. Order of Merit, 1944. See Cole, M.I. (ed), *The Webbs and their Work* (1949) and Brennan, E.J.T. (ed.), *Education for National Efficiency: the Contribution of Sidney and Beatrice Webb* (1975).

Welldon, James Edward Cowell (1854–1937). Schoolmaster and cleric. Born Tonbridge, Kent, son of second master at Tonbridge School. Educated at Eton and scholar, King's College, Cambridge. Senior Classic, 1877. Fellow, 1878. Master, Dulwich College, 1880 and ordained as a priest five years later. During his time there, 1880–5, Welldon did much to restore the reputation of the school to its former position. Headmaster, Harrow School, 1885–98. Appointed, at the age of 44, in 1898, Bishop of Calcutta, resigning through ill-health and disagreement with Lord Curzon, the Viceroy, in 1902. Canon, Westminster Abbey, 1902–6, Dean of Manchester, 1906–18. Dean of Durham, 1918–33. Welldon translated and published Aristotle's *Politics* (1883), *Rhetoric* (1886) and *Ethics* (1892). His theological writings include *The Hope of Immortality* (1898) and *The English Church* (1926). See also his two volumes of autobiography *Recollections and Reflections* (1915) and *Forty Years On* (1935).

Whately, Richard (1787–1863). Scholar and divine. Born London. Educated at a private school near Bristol and Oriel College,

258

Oxford. BA, 1808; MA, 1812; BD and DD, 1825. Fellow of Oriel from 1811. A friend of Copleston, Keble and **Thomas Arnold**. Wrote articles on a wide range of subjects. In 1822 became vicar of Halesworth, Suffolk, and in the same year delivered the Bampton lectures which with others of his university sermons were subsequently published. In 1825 became principal of St Alban Hall, Oxford. His works on *Logic* (1826) and *Rhetoric* (1828) became best-sellers. In 1829 Whately succeeded Senior as Drummond professor of Political Economy. In 1831 was appointed Archbishop of Dublin, and as *ex officio* visitor of Trinity College founded there a chair of Political Economy in 1832. Sat in the House of Lords from 1833. He strongly supported the system of national education in Ireland and with Daniel Murray the Roman Catholic Archbishop of Dublin compiled a course of 'Scripture extracts'. He also wrote some textbooks for use in the schools. In 1852 Murray was succeeded by **Paul Cullen** and in 1853 Whately withdrew from the National Board. See his writings including the *Easy Lessons* and *Introductory Lessons* series for children, and Fitzpatrick, W.J., *Memoirs of R. Whately* (2 vols., 1864); Whately, E.J., *Life and Correspondence of Richard Whately* (2 vols., 1866).

Whewell, William (1794–1866). Scholar. Born Lancaster. Educated at the Blue School, Lancaster, and at the grammar schools at Lancaster and Heversham, where he also did some teaching. Trinity College, Cambridge, BA, 1816; president of the Union Society, 1817; fellow of Trinity, 1817–41; assistant tutor, 1818; tutor, 1823–38. Ordained a deacon, 1820, and priest, 1821. Whewell, son of a carpenter, was second wrangler and second Smith's prizeman in 1816; MA, 1819; BD, 1838; DD, 1844; FRS, 1819, and gold medallist, 1837. Professor of Mineralogy at Cambridge, 1828–32, and of Moral Philosophy, 1838–55. Master of Trinity College from 1841 until his death, and Vice-Chancellor of Cambridge, 1842–3 and 1855–6. Whewell was one of a group of able men who raised the standard of Cambridge education. His interests covered mathematics, mechanics, mineralogy, theology and philosophy. He conducted many scientific experiments. He played a leading role in the British Association and presided in 1841. He established the moral sciences and natural sciences triposes in 1848. Whewell, however, opposed many of the proposals of the Royal Commission appointed to inquire into the university in 1850. Marriages and the income of his office made Whewell a wealthy man and he gave money both for new buildings and to endow a chair and scholarships in international law. See his several writings and Todhunter, I., *William Whewell: an account of his writings* (2 vols., 1876); Douglas, J.M., *Life and Selections from the Correspondence of William Whewell* (1882); Garland, M.M., *Cambridge before Darwin* (1980).

Whitehead, Alfred North (1861–1947). Philosopher and mathematician. Born Ramsgate, son of a vicar and private school headmaster. Educated at Sherborne and Trinity College, Cambridge, 1880–3, 4th wrangler in mathematics tripos. Fellow and assistant lecturer, Trinity College, 1884. Senior lecturer, 1903–11. His first major work was *A Treatise on Universal Algebra with Applications* (1898) which led to his election as FRS, 1903. One of Whitehead's most brilliant students, **Bertrand Russell**, attended a congress in Paris in 1900 with him on mathematics and logic. Following this, they concluded that mathematics was a part of logic and wrote the three volumes of *Principia Mathematica* (1910–13): the work constitutes one of the most important contributions to logic for many centuries. Whitehead now turned his attention to formulating a general philosophy of nature. He left Cambridge and worked at University College, London, 1911–14 and as professor of Applied Mathematics, Imperial College of Science and Technology, 1914–24. The discovery of the theory of relativity in 1904 led to two books, *An Enquiry Concerning the Principles of Natural Knowledge* (1919) and *The Concept of Nature* (1920), followed by *The Principle of Relativity* (1922). Professor of Philosophy, Harvard University, 1924–37. Whitehead was interested in educational theory and gathered a series of addresses delivered between 1912 and 1928 in a book *Aims of Education* (1929). He rejected the notion that education merely fostered growth and like Dewey and **Nunn** praised intellectual excellence. Whitehead believed that there was no dichotomy between liberal and vocational education, as schooling should be concerned with the techniques as well as the intellectual aspects of the curriculum. FBA, 1931, Order of Merit, 1945. See Lowe, V., *Alfred North Whitehead. The Man and His Work. Vol 1 1861–1910* (1985).

Whitworth, Sir Joseph (1803–87). Mechanical engineer and philanthropist. Born Stockport, son of a schoolmaster. Attended his father's school and in 1815, attended an academy at Idle, near Leeds, leaving at the age of 14. Worked as a cotton-spinner in Derbyshire before moving to a machinists where his exceptional talents were realized. In 1833, returned to Manchester, where he set up as tool-maker. He was a notable inventor, particularly of the measuring machine, the Whitworth rifle and field-guns; he also perfected a system of standard measures and gauges. President, Institute of Mechanical Engineers, 1856; FRS, 1857. Whitworth's extensive factory was located in Manchester and he donated large sums to the advancement of education in that area, especially to technical schools and Owens College, later the University of Manchester. He endowed the Whitworth Scholarships, some 30 in number, which were supervised by the Science and Art Department and for which he donated £100,000 in 1868.

Wilderspin, Samuel (1791–1866). Educationist. Born Hornsey, Middlesex. Educated at home and at private schools. Apprenticed in 1805 as a calendrer. Followed the Swedenborgian doctrine. In 1807 began to teach in a Sunday school. Met **James Buchanan** and in 1820 took charge of the new Quaker Street Infant School in Spitalfields. His early difficulties in managing the children are recounted in *Early Discipline* (1832). Thereafter his life was devoted to spreading the idea of infant schools, first as travelling agent for the Infant School Society, 1826–8, and then as a free-lance educationist until 1836. Between 1828 and 1830 he was instrumental in founding infant schools in Scotland. In 1836 he was employed by the Corporation of Liverpool to organize infant departments in its schools. Superintendent of the Infant Model School in Dublin, 1838–9. In spite of some patronage and lecture fees, his financial difficulties were not eased until a civil list pension of £100 p.a. was granted in 1846, and a testimonial of nearly £2,000 raised in 1847. Wilderspin was the leading advocate of an enlightened system of infant education. See his writings, especially *On the importance of educating the infant poor* (1824); *A system of education for the young* (1840); *The infant system* (1852), and McCann, P., and Young, F.A., *Samuel Wilderspin and the Infant School Movement* (1982).

Wilkinson, Ellen Cicely (1891–1947). Politician and trade unionist. Born Chorlton upon Medlock, Manchester. Educated in Manchester at Ardwick Higher Elementary School. Became a pupil teacher and won the Jones History Scholarship to Manchester University where she achieved a second class in history in 1913. In 1946 the university awarded her an honorary LL.D. Wilkinson's early career was as a national organizer for the Union of Cooperative Employees. She joined the Independent Labour Party in her student days and the Communist Party in 1920, though resigning in 1924. Member of Manchester City Council, 1923–6. Labour Member of Parliament for Middlesbrough East, 1924–31; Jarrow, 1935–47. She supported the causes of working people in Britain, by fund-raising for the general strike of 1926 and leading the Jarrow march in 1936, and in such countries as Russia, India and Spain. She supported the coalition government of 1940 and was appointed successively parliamentary secretary to the Ministry of Pensions, 1940, and to the Ministry of Home Security, 1940–5. In 1945 she was appointed Minister of Education where she strove to implement the 1944 Education Act. Her aims were 'to improve the lot of under-privileged children and to make secondary education much more than elementary education with frills'. Her first public pledge as Minister was to raise the school-leaving age. Wilkinson was a person of great energy and commitment. See her writings especially *Clash* (1929); *Why Fascism?* (with Edward Conze, 1934); *The Town that was Murdered* (1939), and Lockett, T.A., *Three Lives* (1968); Vernon, B., *Ellen Wilkinson* (1982); Dean, D.W., 'Planning for a postwar generation: Ellen Wilkinson and George Tomlinson at the Ministry of Education, 1945–51', *History of Education*, 15 (2), 1986.

Williams, William (1788–1865). Politician. Born Tredarren, Carmarthen. Educated at the local parish school. By 1820 established himself as a cotton and linen dealer and soon created a great fortune. He travelled widely in promoting his business and had a good command of languages. Was a leading radical member of the House of Commons for many years, MP for Coventry, 1835–47, and for Lambeth from 1850 until his death. In 1846 he moved for an inquiry into Welsh education. The report published in 1847 was condemned in Wales as the 'treachery of the blue books'. Williams wrote two pamphlets on education in 1848. In 1863 he presided at the meeting held in London to further university education in Wales and promised a £1,000 donation, fulfilled in his will. See Evans, D., *The Life and Work of William Williams* (1939).

Wilson, John Dover (1881–1969). Scholar and educationist. Born Mortlake, Surrey, son of an illustrator. Educated Lancing College and Gonville and Caius College, Cambridge, historical tripos. Taught at Whitgift Grammar School, Croydon, 1905–6 and in Helsinki, 1906–9. Lecturer in English literature, Goldsmiths' College, London, 1909–12. HMI, 1912–24, during which time he advocated the continuation school in English education, (see his *Humanism in the Continuation School* (1921)). Member,

Prime Minister's Committee on the Teaching of English under **Sir Henry Newbolt** in 1919, writing part of the report. Professor of Education, King's College, London, 1924–33. Wilson was a notable Shakespearean scholar. An early popular work, *Life in Shakespeare's England* (1911) was followed by editions of Shakespeare's works, published as the New Cambridge Shakespeare; this task occupied 45 years of his life, 1921–66. Regius professor of Rhetoric and English Literature, Edinburgh University, 1933–45. FBA, 1931 and Companion of Honour, 1936. See also his *Milestones on the Dover Road* (1969).

Withers, Harry Livingston (1864–1902). Educationist. Born Liverpool, educated King's College School, London and Balliol College, Oxford, 1883–7, first class honours in classical moderations and *literae humaniores*. Assistant master, Wesleyan Elementary Day School, Oxford, City of London School, Manchester Grammar School and Clifton College. Principal, Borough Road Training College, Isleworth, 1893–9. Professor of Education, Owens College, Manchester from 1899 until his death in 1902. Endowed by Mrs Sarah Fielden of Todmorden, the chair gave recognition to the day training college which had been established there in 1890. His ability and experience were displayed with great purpose in the short period he was at Manchester. Chairman, Teachers' Registration Council, 1902. See his *The Teaching of History in England during the Nineteenth Century and other Papers* (1904) (with biographical introduction and a selection of letters), ed. Fowler, J.H.

Wolfenden, Sir John Frederick, Baron (1906–85). Educationist and chairman of public inquiries. Born Halifax, son of chief clerk in the local education office. Educated Wakefield Grammar School and Queen's College, Oxford, awarded first in classical moderations and *literae humaniores*, 1924–7. Philosophy tutor, Magdalen College, Oxford, 1929. Appointed headmaster, Uppingham School, 1933, at the age of 27 and Shrewsbury, 1944. Vice-Chancellor, University of Reading, 1950–63. He was acknowledged as being one of the most capable committee chairmen in England and his services were constantly in demand. Between 1954 and 1957, he chaired the Committee on Prostitution and on Homosexuals. The Wolfenden Report, which recommended a review of the existing law on these topics, brought his name before the general public. He subsequently campaigned for the implementation of the Report's findings. He served as chairman of the Secondary School

Examinations Council, 1961–7. Chairman, University Grants Committee, 1963–8, at a times when the Robbins proposals for higher education were being implemented. Director, British Museum, 1969–73. Knight, 1956. Life peer, 1974. See *The Approach to Philosophy* (1932); *The Public School Today* (1948); and his autobiography, *Turning Points* (1976).

Wollstonecraft, Mary (1759–97). Writer. Born Epping. Educated at a day school in Yorkshire. Worked as a companion in Bath, 1778–80, and subsequently set up a school at Newington Green with her sister Eliza and a childhood friend, Fanny Blood. The school closed in 1786 but Wollstonecraft's educational theories were outlined in *Thoughts on the Education of Daughters* (1785). Visited Portugal and became a governess in Ireland. Her first novel *Mary. A Fiction* was published in 1787, and she subsequently followed a literary career. *Vindication of the Rights of Men* (1790) and *Vindication of the Rights of Women* (1792) expressed her radicalism, and in this latter year she moved to France. There Wollstonecraft met English supporters of the Revolution, including Tom Paine, and *An Historical and Moral View of the French Revolution* was published in 1793. In 1797 she married the philosopher William Godwin. Their daughter, Mary, the future author of *Frankenstein* and wife of the poet Shelley, was born in August but Wollstonecraft died shortly afterwards. Her later writings, notably the unfinished *The Wrongs of Women, or Maria* (1798) exposed the double standard in political, economic and sexual matters. See Sunstein, E.W., *A Different Face. The Life of Mary Wollstonecraft* (1975); Tomalin, C., *The Life and Death of Mary Wollstonecraft* (1977).

Wood, Edward Frederick Lindley, 1st Earl of Halifax (1881–1959). Politician. Born Powderham Castle, Devon, youngest son of Charles Lindley Wood, later 2nd Viscount Halifax. Educated at Eton and Christ Church, Oxford. Gained first class in history, and fellow, All Souls, Oxford, 1903. Elected Conservative MP, Ripon, 1910–25. Under-Secretary for the Colonies, 1921–2, President, Board of Education, 1922–4 and 1932–5, Minister, Agriculture and Fisheries, 1924–5 and Viceroy of India, 1925–31. Created Baron Irwin, 1925; KG, 1931. Succeeded as 3rd Viscount Halifax, 1934. Created Earl, 1944. Secretary of State for War, 1935 and Lord Privy Seal, 1935–7. Lord President, 1937–8, Foreign Secretary, 1938–40, Leader of the House of Lords, 1935–8 and 1940. Ambassador, Washington, USA, 1941–6. Chancellor, Oxford University, 1933–

59 and Sheffield University, 1948–59. Halifax accepted the post of Education Minister in both spells of office with some reluctance: it is significant that his autobiography *Fullness of Days* (1957) is almost entirely silent on his time at the Board. He was, however, largely responsible in June 1935 for the final withdrawal of the unpopular Circular 1413 issued in September 1931 which introduced severe cuts in the education service. See his *Thirty Years of Educational Progress* (1935).

Woodard, Nathaniel (1811–91). Founder of schools. Born Basildon, Essex. Educated privately and at Magdalen Hall, Oxford. BA, 1840; MA, 1866. Ordained deacon, 1841; priest, 1842. Curacies at Bethnal Green, Clapton and New Shoreham. Here in Sussex he established a small day school in 1847 and became impressed with the shortage of good Anglican schools for children of the middle classes. In 1850 he resigned his curacy and devoted himself to this work. St Nicholas College was founded in 1848 and later moved to Lancing. Woodard was its provost until his death. Hurstpierpoint was opened in 1853, and Ardingly in 1870. Thus there were in Sussex three schools for the southern division, for the upper, middle, and lower ranks of the middle classes. Woodard proposed to establish a similar pattern in the east, west, north and midlands of England. For example there were foundations at Denstone, Ellesmere, Worksop and Taunton for boys and at Bromley and Bangor for girls. In 1870 Woodard's work was recognized by his appointment as a canon of Manchester, and by the conferral of the degree of DCL by the University of Oxford. See his *A Plea for the Middle Classes* (1848); *Public Schools for the Middle Classes* (1852), and Otter, J., *Nathaniel Woodard* (1925); Heeney, B., *Mission to the Middle Classes* (1969).

Wyse, Sir Thomas (1791–1862). Author, politician and diplomat. Born in County Waterford, educated at Stonyhurst and Trinity College, Dublin. Graduated BA, 1812. Winner of the Chancellor's prize. Studied at Lincoln's Inn, but was never called to the bar. Travelled widely, in Europe, Asia and North Africa, studying art and classical literature. In 1821 married Letitia, daughter of Lucien Bonaparte, Prince of Canino. Prominent in the campaign for Catholic Emancipation. MP for the County of Tipperary 1830–2, and for the City of Waterford, 1835–47. Lord of the Treasury in the Melbourne government, 1839–41 and one of the secretaries of the Board of Control, 1846–9. Appointed British minister to Athens in 1849, a post he held until his death. KCB, 1857. Wyse promoted national education in three ways. He was a founding member and chairman of the Central Society for Education, wrote several of the contributions to its publications and attended numerous meetings. In 1830 he drew up a plan for Irish education and in 1831 introduced a bill which was dropped when **Lord Stanley** announced a scheme of national education for Ireland based on the same principles. Similarly Wyse's advocacy of government control, school inspection and the training of teachers for England found expression in the Whig government's scheme of 1839. His scheme for provincial colleges in Ireland led to the Queen's Colleges established by Peel's government in 1845. Wyse was an accomplished linguist, writer and orator. See his *Education Reform* (1836), and Wyse, W.M. (ed.), *Notes on Education Reform in Ireland . . . compiled from speeches, letters, etc . . . of Sir T. Wyse . . .* (1901); Auchmuty, J.J., *Sir Thomas Wyse* (1939).

Young, Robert Fitzgibbon (1879–1960). Civil servant. Born Ulster. Educated at Belfast and Trinity College, Oxford. Second class in classical moderations, 1900 and first class *literae humaniores*, 1902. After further studies at Jena and Berlin he taught at Manchester Grammar School and at Leeds University. Through his cousin **James Bryce**, Young secured an entry in 1907 into the office of the Board of Education. He served as secretary to the Board's Consultative Committee and contributed introductory chapters to several important reports including those of **Hadow** and **Spens**. He retired in 1939. Young had a wide knowledge of European history and philosophy and was a particular expert on Czechoslovakia. See his several writings including *Comenius in England* (1932).

Yoxall, Sir James Henry (1857–1925). Teachers' union leader. Born Redditch, Worcestershire, son of fishing-tackle manufacturer. Educated at Wesleyan Elementary School, Redditch, leaving school before the age of 14 to become a pupil teacher at Bridgehouses Wesleyan School, Sheffield. Attended Westminster Training College, 1876–8. Taught in Sheffield, becoming head of Sharrow Lane Board School, 1887–95. Yoxall was active in teacher politics. He was elected to the Executive of the National Union of Teachers in 1889, President in 1891 and General Secretary, 1892–1924. He also became editor of *The Schoolmaster* in 1909. Unsuccessfully stood, as a Liberal, for Bassetlaw, Nottinghamshire, in 1892 but was elected in 1905, retaining the seat until retirement in

1918. Yoxall was able to advance the cause of the Union through his influence as a politician, drawing attention of Ministers and the Commons to educational issues affecting teachers. Member, Bryce Commission on Secondary Education, 1894–5; member, Prime Minister's Committee on the Study of Modern Languages, 1916. When the Burnham Committee was set up in 1919, Yoxall was the teachers' leader on the joint standing committee. Knight, 1911, possibly the first certificated teacher to receive this honour. See his *Secondary Education* (1896) and book of essays, *The Wonder Years* (1909).

Zimmern, Sir Alfred Eckhard (1879–1957). Educationist and authority on international relations. Son of a merchant. Educated at Winchester and New College, Oxford, obtaining first class in classical moderations, 1900 and in *literae humaniores*, 1902. Lecturer in ancient history and fellow and tutor, New College, 1904–9. Zimmern was a supporter of the movement for higher education for working people. He was one of the seven members of his university who met with seven 'representatives of Labour' nominated by the Workers' Educational Association (WEA) to discuss this problem. Their report, *Oxford and Working-Class Education* (1908) recommended an extension of educational opportunities. He was also an active worker for the WEA cause. His book *The Greek Commonwealth* (1911) was widely acclaimed. HMI, 1912–15, and later joined the political intelligence department, Foreign Office, 1918–19. A founder member of the Royal Institute of International Affairs at Chatham House, London. Wilson professor of International Politics, Aberystwyth, 1919–21. Zimmern devoted much time to League of Nations affairs. First Montagu Burton professor of International Relations, Oxford University, 1939–44, and briefly after the war, executive director of Unesco. Knight, 1936.

FURTHER READING

Bibliographical references for the entries in this work have been confined to selected books and articles. This section indicates other possible sources of information.

1. ARCHIVE AND MANUSCRIPT SOURCES

Manuscript holdings are to be found in the great public collections, for example the British Library, Great Russell Street, London, WC1, and the Public Record Office, Ruskin Avenue, Kew, Richmond, Surrey. Others have been deposited in County Record Offices, Public Libraries, the libraries of Educational Institutions and Societies. Others still remain in private hands. The starting point for the location of manuscripts, archives and records of all kinds outside the public records is the National Register of Archives, Quality Court, London, WC2.

2. THESES AND DISSERTATIONS

Many biographies of educationists exist in unpublished thesis or dissertation form. Three important guides to such material are V.F. Gilbert and C. Holmes, *Theses and Dissertations on the History of Education presented at British and Irish Universities between 1900 and 1976* (Leicester, 1979), P.M. Jacobs, *History Theses 1901–70. Historical Research for higher degrees in the universities of the United Kingdom* (London, 1976), and J.M. Horn, *History Theses, 1971–80* (London, 1984). These guides are kept up to date by regular supplements. See also the annual *Index to theses accepted for higher degrees by the universities of Great Britain and Ireland and the Council for National Academic Awards* (London, Aslib).

3. BIBLIOGRAPHICAL GUIDES TO BIOGRAPHY AND EDUCATION

The British Library, with its right of copyright deposit, is the principal library in the United Kingdom. Its General Catalogue is the latest in a series which began in 1787 and includes books and periodicals published up to 1975. The Current Catalogue, which is in microfiche form, contains material dated 1976 or later. Both catalogues are currently housed in the Reading Room of the British Museum. The *British Library Catalogue of Printed Books to 1975*, together with a supplement to 1982, is being published in 410 volumes. *Bio-base* (Detroit) is a periodic, cumulative master index on microfiche to sketches found in current and historical biographical dictionaries. P.M. Riches, *An analytical bibliography of universal collected biography* (Detroit, 1980, a reprint of the 1934 edition) includes works published in the United Kingdom. R.B. Slocum, *Biographical dictionaries and related works: an international bibliography* (Detroit, 1967) has been updated by several supplements. *Biography index* (New York, 1946–) is a cumulative index to biographical material in books and magazines. See also A.M. Hyamson, *A Dictionary of Universal Biography* (London, 2nd edition, 1951), T.R. Thomson, *A Catalogue of British Family Histories* (London, 3rd edition with addenda, 1980) and the Library Association research publication No. 5, *Select biographical sources: the Library Association manuscripts survey* (London, 1971). C.W.J. Higson, *Sources for the History of Education* (London, 2 vols., 1967, 1976) is the general guide to educational works, and the *British Education Index*, published quarterly, lists articles in educational journals. See also A. Christophers, *An Index to Nineteenth-Century British Educational Biography* (London, 1965).

4. GENERAL BIOGRAPHICAL DICTIONARIES

The major biographical dictionary remains the *Dictionary of National Biography* (London) which first appeared in 1885 and is currently published in ten-year supplements. This vast work, with its several supplements and concise edition, may be supplemented for the second half of the nineteenth century by F. Boase, *Modern English Biography* (6 vols., 1891–1921, reprinted Cass, London, 1965), and for the twentieth century by *Who was Who* (London, 7 vols., covering the years 1897–1980). The annual *Who's Who* (London) was first published in 1849. Obituaries constitute another important source of information. Those in *The Times* can be located through the quarterly indexes, but major notices for the years 1951–75, together with a list of all entries for those years, have been collected in three volumes. *Chambers Biographical Dictionary* (Edinburgh, 1974 edition) is the leading single volume compilation with 15,000 entries. All previous British biographical works, however, are currently being eclipsed by the new *British Biographical Archive* to be published in microfiche form by Klaus Saur, London and Munich. This, when completed, will include 300,000 entries, the equivalent of a 600-volume library.

5. SPECIALIST BIOGRAPHICAL DICTIONARIES

Irish collections include A. Webb, *A Compendium of Irish Biography* (Dublin, 1878), J.S. Crone, *A Concise Dictionary of Irish Biography* (Dublin, 1937), and H. Boylan, *A Dictionary of Irish Biography* (Dublin, 1978). R. Chambers, *A Biographical Dictionary of Eminent Scotsmen* (edited by Thomas Thomson, 3 vols., 1870, reprinted Hildesheim, 1971) may be supplemented by G. Donaldson and R.S. Morpeth, *Who's Who in Scottish History* (Oxford, 1973) and D. Daiches (ed.), *A Companion to Scottish Culture* (London, 1981). The standard volume for Wales is the *Dictionary of Welsh Biography down to 1940* (London, 1959) published under the auspices of the Honourable Society of Cymmrodorion. Women in general and female and male members of the working classes in particular have often been under-represented in biographical dictionaries. This imbalance is now being corrected by such recent publications as the *Macmillan Dictionary of Women's Biography* (London, 1982) edited by J.S. Uglow, the *Europa Biographical Dictionary of British Women* (London, 1983) edited by A. Crawford *et al.*, and the first volume of the *Biographical Dictionary of British Feminists* (Brighton, 1985), edited by O. Banks. See also the *Dictionary of Labour Biography* (London, 7 vols., 1972–84) edited by J. Bellamy and J. Saville, and the *Biographical Dictionary of Modern British Radicals* (Brighton, 2 vols., 1984) edited by J. Baylen and N. Gossman.

Occupational biographical dictionaries are too numerous to be listed here in their entirety. Recent examples include T. Williams (ed.), *A Biographical Dictionary of Scientists* (London, 3rd edition, 1982), D. Abbott (ed.), *The Biographical Dictionary of Scientists: Engineers and Inventors* (London, 1985), and the *Dictionary of Business Biography* (London, 5 vols., 1984–6) edited by D.J. Jeremy, which covers those active in business in Britain during the period 1860–1980.

6. EDUCATIONAL BIOGRAPHIES

University registers are often simply restricted to the names of students, but J. Foster, *Alumni Oxonienses, 1715–1886* (4 vols.,

1887–8, reprinted Nendeln, Liechtenstein, 2 vols., 1968), together with the much fuller J.A. Venn, *Alumni Cantabrigienses. Part II, 1752–1900* (Cambridge, 6 vols., 1940–7) also contain brief biographical details. Important college registers include those of Balliol, Oxford, edited by Sir Ivo Elliott (Oxford, 2 vols., 1934, 1953) which cover the period 1833–1950, and the *Newnham College Register, 1871–1950* (Cambridge, 2 vols., 1965). Similarly the several editions of the *Eton College Register* (Eton), *Harrow School Register* (London), *Merchant Taylors' School Register* (London), and *Rugby School Register* (Rugby) include details of school and subsequent careers.

Two earlier publications in the field of educational biography are the *Dictionary of Educationists* (London, 1914), compiled by the Revd J.E. Roscoe, and the *Encyclopaedia and Dictionary of Education* (London, 4 vols., 1921–2) edited by Foster Watson. Though the latter has some particularly useful British biographies, both works are international in their perspectives and include entries from the ancient times through to the twentieth century. Brief obituary notices can be found in the 89 volumes of the *Journal of Education* which covers the years 1879–1958 and in *The Times Educational Supplement* (London, 1910–) and *The Times Higher Educational Supplement* (London, 1971–).

Modern works include R. Bradfield (ed.), *Who's Who in Education* (London, 1974), E. Kay (ed.), *The World's Who's Who of Women in Education* (Cambridge, 1978), E. Kay (ed.), *International Who's Who in Education* (Cambridge, 2nd edition, 1981), and J.E. Thomas and B. Elsey (eds.), *International Biography of Adult Education* (Nottingham, 1985).

Brief biographical details of particular groups of educationists are to be found in such specialist studies at T. Gautrey, *'Lux Mihi Laus': School Board Memories* (London, 1937) – chapter 3 is entitled 'Sixty-Five Notable Members' – and in J.E. Dunford, 'Biographical Details of Her Majesty's Inspectors of Schools appointed before 1870', *History of Education Society Bulletin*, 28, 1981. Biographical articles occur in several educational journals, for example *History of Education* and *Vocational Aspects of Secondary and Further Education*. The *British Journal of Educational Studies* under the editorship of A.C.F. Beales devoted considerable space to the history of education, and Volume X, 1961–2, includes articles on a number of nineteenth- and twentieth-century educationists. Similarly the History of Education Society occasional publication No. 5 entitled *Biography and Education: Some Eighteenth- and*

Further Reading

Nineteenth-Century Studies (Leicester, 1980), edited by R. Lowe, includes useful material in article form.

272